D1496148

DUBCON

DUBCON

Fanfiction, Power, and Sexual Consent

MILENA POPOVA

The MIT Press
Cambridge, Massachusetts
London, England

The MIT Press would like to thank the anonymous peer reviewers who provided comments on drafts of this book. The generous work of academic experts is essential for establishing the authority and quality of our publications. We acknowledge with gratitude the contributions of these otherwise uncredited readers.

This book was set in Adobe Garamond and Berthold Akzidenz Grotesk by Jen Jackowitz. Printed and bound in the United States of America.

Library of Congress Cataloging-in-Publication Data

Names: Popova, Milena, author.
Title: Dubcon : fanfiction, power, and sexual consent / Milena Popova.
Description: Cambridge, Massachusetts : The MIT Press, [2021] | Includes
    bibliographical references and index.
Identifiers: LCCN 2020041672 | ISBN 9780262045964 (hardcover)
Subjects: LCSH: Fan fiction—History and criticism. | Fan fiction—Social
    aspects. | Erotic literature—History and criticism. | Sexual consent in
    literature.
Classification: LCC PN3377.5.F33 P67 2021 | DDC 809.3/85—dc23
LC record available at https://lccn.loc.gov/2020041672

10 9 8 7 6 5 4 3 2 1

To my queer found family. <3

Contents

1 INTRODUCTION

Content note: This chapter discusses rape culture and rape apologism and includes some references to and descriptions of sexual violence.

You know what the magic word, the only thing that matters in American sexual mores today is? One thing. You can do anything the left will promote, and understand, and tolerate anything—as long as there is one element. Do you know what it is? Consent. If there is consent on both or all three or all four, however many are involved in the sex act, it's perfectly fine, whatever it is. But if the left ever senses and smells that there's no consent in part of the equation, then here come the rape police. But consent is the magic key to the left.

—RUSH LIMBAUGH, OCTOBER 2016[1]

This is a steep price to pay for 20 minutes of action out of his 20 plus years of life. The fact that he now has to register as a sexual offender for the rest of his life forever alters where he can live, visit, work, and how he will be able to interact with people and organizations.

—DAN A. TURNER, JUNE 2016[2]

I am here today not because I want to be. I am terrified. I am here because I believe it is my civic duty to tell you what happened to me while Brett Kavanaugh and I were in high school.

—DR. CHRISTINE BLASEY FORD, SEPTEMBER 2018[3]

American talk radio host Rush Limbaugh defends US presidential candidate Donald Trump for boasting about how he can "grab [women] by the pussy," casting the idea of sexual consent as a strange, outlandish, immoral invention of "the left."[4] The father of Brock Turner, a college student convicted of three counts of felony sexual assault of an unconscious woman after a campus party and sentenced to six months in prison, bemoans the harsh sentence for what he calls "20 minutes of action." A woman relives her sexual assault on national television in the hope of stopping her assailant's confirmation to the United States Supreme Court. She fails. (And she is not the first to do so.)

This is rape culture. The #MeToo movement has brought the endemic nature of sexual violence into the public eye. In the United Kingdom alone, over 200 women are raped every single day.[5] At the same time, those in power—from members of Parliament to judges to talk-show hosts—routinely dismiss rape allegations. Even in the most egregious cases, like that of Brock Turner, they find ways of blaming the victims and protecting the accused and guilty. And while feminist campaigners have been pushing against rape culture and for better education about consent, it is clear that sexual consent is—at best—a contested topic in contemporary Western societies and cultures. Comments and cases such as these have gained public attention and prominence in the media partly because they are relatively clear-cut: two men witnessed and stopped Brock Turner, and their testimony was crucial in securing his conviction.[6] But focusing solely on these cases means we obscure experiences of sexual violence and consent violations that are less clear-cut: experiences that fall in a problematic liminal space, a gray area between "yes" and "no," for a variety of reasons.

2017
Then something happened that was not ok
    Everything wobbled.
    "That is unacceptable to me."
    How does she voice that and feel safe.
    Not knowing the rules.

The one condom two women situation.

She was confronted by her inability to ask for what she needed, to know what it was she needed and then ask for it. She is shocked at not being able to say no in the moment—she didn't trust her own sense of that's not ok. Why was she so worried about how that would look in the peer group? There was an incipient fear that she would be ostracized; become an even more peripheral participant than she was feeling.[7]

This is an extract from a paper presented by two colleagues of mine at a conference. In it, they reflect, among other things, on how their conception of who they are as individuals has shaped their sexual experiences. Here, Davina, at her first sex party, is struggling to communicate her needs and boundaries for fear of being made to feel like she does not belong in this space.

2017

But rather: it's clear in retrospect that between the ages of, like, 15 and 22, *I Was Not In A Position To Assent To Sex*. . . . and that's about culture & sex education & ace-invisibility & how we talk about desire. It happened bc I lacked the necessary awareness. When I think about my sexual history, such as it is, it feels like being raped by no one in particular.[8]

In a Twitter thread, writer Alex Gabriel talks about how the erasure of asexuality from the UK's Sex and Relationships Education curriculum left Alex, as an asexual person, poorly equipped to meaningfully consent to sex for a long time. Being unable to distinguish between sexual and other types of attraction put Alex in a position where sex that was consensual on the surface nonetheless felt like a violation.

2018

"He said something along the lines of, 'How about you hop up and take a seat?'" Within moments, he was kissing her. "In a second, his hand was on my breast." Then he was undressing her, then he undressed himself. She remembers feeling uncomfortable at how quickly things escalated.[9]

A young woman describes a date with comedian Aziz Ansari that seemed to follow a script—dinner, kissing, undressing—that made her feel deeply uncomfortable. Even in a post-#MeToo environment, many doubt whether the behavior described constitutes sexual misconduct on Ansari's part. What these three accounts have in common is that the sexual experiences they describe would, by both law and "common sense," be regarded as consensual. And yet, upon reflection, those who experienced them now characterize them as consent violations. If the words of Rush Limbaugh and Dan Turner and the way the Kavanaugh allegations were simply brushed away paint a picture of consent as contested, the latter three testimonies would suggest that it is more complex still than even those of us Limbaugh calls "the left" would imagine. And although there is still plenty of work to be done in both research and activism with regard to the arguably less complex cases (i.e., those perceived as consent violations at the time they occurred), we desperately need a better understanding of the other ones: those cases in which the ways that we are taught to think about what "normal" sex is, about what constitutes a date or a romantic relationship, or about the kind of sex we have and what it says about us as people make it more difficult for us to meaningfully consent to sex.

Feminist academic approaches to sexual violence and consent are diverse and multidisciplinary. Scholars from fields such as psychology, feminist legal theory, and cultural studies have made important contributions. But even within feminist academia, consent in its own right is significantly undertheorized,[10] and scholars struggle to account for the vast gray areas revealed by stories like those of Davina, Alex, and the anonymous woman who went on a date with Aziz Ansari.[11] The psychologist Nicola Gavey argues that we, as a society, have a particular way of conceptualizing what "normal" (hetero)sex looks like. It is a combination of many, sometimes conflicting ideas, but it generally involves exactly one cisgender man and one cisgender woman; it starts with kissing and touching, progresses through undressing, and culminates in penile-vaginal intercourse, which ends when the man ejaculates. (This, of course, sounds remarkably like that script Aziz Ansari was following in his interaction with the young woman.) We also have dominant cultural ideas about what exactly requires consent, and when and how consent can be withheld or withdrawn (not, for instance, due to the "one condom two women situation"). We even have an idea that all people experience sexual attraction and want to have sex, and that if someone doesn't, something must be wrong with them (hence Alex's sense of "being raped by no one in particular"). It is these dominant ideas that make it difficult to name such experiences as violations, and Gavey calls them the "cultural scaffolding of rape."[12] There is, however, another community—not academic, not overtly activist—that has developed a word for this. Readers and writers of erotic fanfiction would call these three examples "dubcon": dubious consent.

EROTIC FANFICTION AND CONSENT

This book started its life as a PhD thesis, with a title taken from a tag on the fanfiction website Archive of Our Own (AO3): "slight dub-con but they both wanted it hardcore." Tags on AO3—an online archive owned and operated by fans that hosts nearly 7.4 million fanworks as of March 2021—are pieces of metadata, intended to facilitate the organization and searchability of such fanworks. Yet their usage in the fanfiction community makes them so much more than that. And those eight words, "slight dub-con but they both wanted it hardcore," perfectly encapsulate one of the remarkable things about this community, not only in its tags but also in large sections of its creative output and day-to-day interactions and practices: its nuanced engagement with issues of sexual consent, which I found in fanfiction circles long before I started researching it, that is at the same time delightfully playful and deadly serious.

Fanfiction is amateur-produced fiction based on existing, generally proprietary media such as TV shows, books, movies, and video games. Fans—mostly women and nonbinary people, and mostly members of gender, sexual, or romantic minorities[13]—take the settings, plots, and characters from these "properties" and make them our own. We rewrite endings. We resurrect the dead. We give life to minor and marginalized characters. We imagine ourselves in the magical worlds we are passionate about. And in slash—the subgenre of fanfiction that focuses on same-gender relationships—we put queerness and sex back into texts they have been meticulously scrubbed out of. Of course Mr. Spock has been banging Captain

Kirk, Sherlock has been sucking Watson's cock, Cho Chang and Pansy Parkinson have been researching innovative uses for wands at Hogwarts, and Link, the pointy-eared protagonist of the Legend of Zelda video game franchise, is a trans woman! Have you not been paying attention? And considering that over 2.2 million of AO3's 5 million fanworks are rated as mature or explicit, and that its community consists predominantly of women and nonbinary people, meaning that it is disproportionately affected by sexual violence,[14] it would be more shocking if the community *didn't* think about issues of sexual consent.

Fandom—the community of readers and writers of fanfiction—is where I first encountered the concept of "dubcon": the idea that sometimes, for whatever reasons, consent is not clear-cut, not a matter of "yes" or "no." I have been a part of this community for so long that I have no conscious memory of when I first came across the word. Fanlore, the fandom wiki, traces early usages of it to sometime in 2003,[15] but fanfiction's engagement with the gray areas of consent predates this usage by decades. Wedged awkwardly between the academic books in my bookcase, there is a collection of slim, US letter–sized, perfect-bound volumes older than me. Among them are Barbara Wenk's *One Way Mirror* and Jean Lorrah's *The Night of the Twin Moons*.[16] In one of the origin stories of fanfiction I tell my undergraduate students, Lorrah and Wenk would be considered some of the foremothers of today's fanfiction community. Decades before fandom found its way onto the internet, they wrote stories about the characters of *Star Trek*, typed them out, mimeographed them, had them bound into fanzines, and sold them at conventions or through the mail. Wenk's novel-length story explores, among other themes, material and social dependency within an intimate relationship. The first volume of Lorrah's series focuses on the relationship between Spock's parents, and particularly the emotional impact of *pon farr*, the Vulcan "fuck or die" mating drive. It is ultimately stories like these, where consent is a vast gray area between "yes" and "no," mired in power relations and inequalities, that give us the most nuanced and productive engagements with questions of consent, and that are the focus of this book. It is those stories that are epitomized by those eight words: *slight dub-con but they both wanted it hardcore.*

In eight words, the author who tagged the story this way draws a distinction between consent and the "wantedness" of sex. This is something that feminist researchers of consent from disciplines ranging from psychology to law have struggled with for decades. Sometimes, we may very much want to fuck someone silly, but other factors, such as the power imbalance between them and us, may impact whether we can genuinely and meaningfully give consent. Other times, we may feel little or no desire, and yet we may consent to sex for other reasons. Power still plays a role in these cases: sex consented to for relationship maintenance when we are materially, financially, or socially dependent on our partner may still fall in the gray area of dubcon. These are things I should perhaps have been given the opportunity to learn at school in sex and relationships education, or from my parents, or maybe even by cultural osmosis from media representations of sex and relationships. But I wasn't, and ultimately I learned them from fanfiction, and from a handful of other feminist spaces I found myself in over the years. Was I alone in this? Did everyone else know these things already, and I had somehow missed them? Or were the discussions I was seeing in the fanfiction community around sexuality and consent part of a wider landscape of feminist activism, a space where women and nonbinary people got together to work these things out because no one had told us—maybe even because no one else knew to begin with? These are some of the questions we will explore in this book.

THE POTENTIAL OF FANFICTION

Feminist understanding of sexual consent—in law, psychology, and culture—has evolved significantly over the last five decades, as we will see in the next chapter. And yet, there are still gaps, at least in part because the dominant ideas in our society of gender, sexuality, sex, and consent are so ubiquitous and resistance to change is so great that dismantling them is the task of generations.[17] Feminist scholars and activists see popular culture, including pornography and romance novels, as a key source of our dominant ideas about sex and consent. Popular culture is where we learn that pulling pigtails is a sign of affection, and that rejection is an invitation to keep making bigger and bigger romantic gestures. However, even though culture can reinforce many of the harmful ideas that feminists have identified as contributing toward sexual violence and rape culture, it also has the potential to drive change. Audiences, after all, aren't passive and don't always read popular culture in exactly the same way; we bring our own ideas and experiences to it, and we interpret it and shape it as much as it shapes us. So, what do audiences *do* with media and culture that tell us that potentially coercive sexual situations are normal, romantic, or, in Nicola Gavey's words, "just sex"?

Scholars of fandom and fanfiction have long seen fans as a particularly active type of audience. In his groundbreaking 1991 ethnography of fandom, Henry Jenkins calls them "textual poachers."[18] Fans, he argues, take bits of popular culture and repurpose them for their own ends. And those ends are generally subversive, counter to the dominant meanings and ideas of our society and the raw material we use. So, can such active audiences mount a meaningful resistance to dominant ideas of sex and consent? The fanfiction community consists predominantly of women and nonbinary people, a majority of whom identify as members of gender, sexual, or romantic minorities. This community produces a significant amount of work focused on sexual and romantic relationships, much of which is sexually explicit.[19] It would certainly be a likely suspect for the kind of active audience that critically engages with dominant ideas of sexuality and consent, that challenges those ideas and creates alternatives, and that is able to resist the idea that coerced, forced, or unwanted sex is normal or "just sex." With that in mind, the rest of this book explores two key questions: How do erotic fanfiction and the communities around it engage with issues of sexual consent? And can this engagement be meaningfully viewed as a form of cultural activism?

OVERVIEW

To answer these questions, I immersed myself in fanfiction communities for three years—or rather, I started paying scholarly attention to communities I had been part of for decades. I started analyzing stories, tropes, events, and practices to understand precisely how I myself had come to learn about concepts like dubcon—how these communities were examining consent issues, creating new knowledges, and spreading them to new members or even potentially beyond their boundaries. In this book, I will take you on a tour of fanfiction stories and tropes, community discussions and practices, and the views that fanfiction readers and writers at a convention shared in conversations with me.

To start, however, we will take a small detour into theory. In the next chapter, I explore in depth two sets of ideas. First, I look at the evolution of feminist scholars' and activists' engagements with sexual violence, rape culture, and consent. In line with the opening of this book, rather than focusing on some of the more clear-cut cases of sexual violence, I pay particular attention to what we do (and do not) know about the gray areas of consent—about dubcon. An understanding of how those gray areas come to be then leads to the question of how the way we are taught to think about certain things—like gender, sex, sexuality, or consent—shapes the world around us, which in turn leads to the question of whether (and how) it is possible to create *new* ways of thinking. I explore these questions by turning to the theories of French philosopher Michel Foucault on how power operates through "discourse." Foucault's view of power is arguably somewhat bleak: it is difficult to see how we can resist dominant ways of thinking because sometimes alternatives are simply unimaginable. To find a way past this, I look at the role of culture and bring in approaches from the margins: postcolonial, civil rights, queer, and feminist traditions of resistance, which I term *discursive resistance*.

Before I dive into the specific case studies of fanfiction communities and consent, I offer a short interlude—a very brief introduction to key parts of fanfiction scholarship and research that will help you understand how fanfiction *works*: how readers and writers as a community make meanings from the bits of popular culture we poach in a kind of *communal textuality*.

In chapter 3, we dive straight into the deep end of the pool and take a look at the Omegaverse: a science-fictional alternate universe collectively created by fanfiction readers and writers, where human gender and sexuality look rather different from what we are used to. In the Omega-verse (also known as alpha/beta/omega or A/B/O stories), humans have six possible genders determined to varying degrees by biology and social roles. If terms like "alpha" and "beta" sound remarkably similar to the pre-vailing cultural idea of how wolf packs work, that is because they are.[20] The Omegaverse has its origins in part in bestiality fiction, and features estrus cycles (or heat), penises with knots, and scent marking, as well as more fic-tional elements such as self-lubricating anuses and male pregnancy. A/B/O stories are deeply controversial in fanfiction communities, and have been dubbed by some as "dogfuck rapeworld." So, what can dogfuck rapeworld tell us about consent? The weird and wonderful Omegaverse provides a less familiar lens through we which we can examine ideas about gender, sex, sexuality, and consent in our own society. Like all good speculative fiction, A/B/O stories show us something alien to prompt us to look for similarities and differences with our own world and to question how *we* do gender and sex. At the same time, the squelchy, messy, erotic nature of the stories provokes strong affective reactions in readers, compelling us to engage with the consent issues inherent in the A/B/O setting on affective, emotional, and intellectual levels.

We stay with fanfiction stories and tropes in chapter 4, where I look at arranged-marriage fanfiction. Arranged marriage is a popular trope in fan-fiction stories and borrows heavily from the marriage-of-convenience trope in Regency romance novels, which are set in the early nineteenth century. Both romance novels and fanfiction stories using the arranged-marriage trope focus on relationships characterized by social and material inequality: characters from different social backgrounds are thrust together with no way out, and frequently one character is dependent on the other finan-cially, socially, or in other ways. Fanfiction readers and writers use some of the genre conventions of the romance novel while carefully rewriting oth-ers, thereby creating meaning through both similarities and differences to the romance novel genre. One important aspect of the romance novel that fanfiction stories rewrite is the marriage consummation scene. In romance novels—and in our culture more generally—marriage consummation as a practice tends to go unquestioned. To be legally valid, a marriage between a man and a woman must be consummated, and that is all there is to it. There is, however, something bizarre about the fact that (these days, and in most Western jurisdictions, at least) we recognize marital rape as a crime, yet we also force this one state-mandated instance of intercourse on those who wish to be married. By focusing on the marriage consummation scene in arranged-marriage stories, fanfiction readers and writers highlight this paradox and recast the practice and legal institution of consummation from normal and always consensual to at least *potentially* coercive. Having cast that doubt on the consensual nature of consummation, fanfiction communities then make small changes to the genre conventions of romance novels to explore the conditions under which inequalities in sexual and romantic relationships can be leveled to make sexual consent between unequal partners truly meaningful.

The case studies in chapters 3 and 4 show how fanfiction readers and writers engage with issues of consent in the presence of power differentials in their creative output. Such tropes as the Omegaverse and arranged marriage allow fanfiction communities to take a fresh look at things we take for granted: gender roles, attitudes toward sex, and institutions such as marriage. Through these stories, fanfiction readers and writers get to ask questions like: What if the way we see these things shapes how we act? What if the dominant ways we think about gender, sex, marriage, and other related concepts are, in fact, ways in which power operates on us, limiting our freedom and choices when it comes to how we do sex? And what if we imagined these things differently? The Black American philosopher and activist Cornel West calls these questions the demystification and demythologization of dominant ways of thinking.[21] In chapter 5, we shift focus away from fanfiction stories and begin to look at how fanfiction communities apply such demythologization and demystification to their experiences in the real world. I do this by looking at the fanfiction space where the fictional and the real interact most obviously: real person(a) fiction or RPF, a type of fanfiction based on real-life celebrities. What happens, as one fan asked, "when the RP gets in the way of the F"? Specifically, what happened when Patrick Kane, an American ice hockey star and central fan object in the Hockey RPF fandom, was accused of rape?

The controversy around the Kane rape allegations (and the subsequent unsatisfactory closure of the case) revealed deep conflicts within both individuals and fanfiction communities. Driven by a desire to live by feminist values, community members found themselves reexamining their fandom, their past fiction, and their future involvement with a now problematic fan object. More importantly, though, the Kane controversy provided a vehicle for fanfiction readers and writers to grapple with the role of the law and the criminal justice system in rape culture. Community members used the same techniques they normally employ to make a celebrity such as Kane more human and relatable to examine and give an inner life to other key individuals in the case, most notably Kane's accuser and the district attorney in charge of the case. This in turn allowed them to humanize the law as an institution, and thereby highlight its many flaws. Although a minority of community members accepted the law's version of events, a majority of the group either found ways of bracketing the law: accepting some of its premises in specific contexts while acknowledging its failings in sexual violence cases and challenging its universal applicability. Others rejected the law outright and highlighted its biases and key role in perpetuating rape culture.

In chapters 6 and 7, I draw out more of the links between fanfiction stories, community practices, and the real world when it comes to sexual consent. These two chapters are based largely on conversations I had with fanfiction readers and writers at a fan convention in London. In chapter 6, I look at the epistemology of consent: How do we know what consent looks like, and whom do we consider a qualified knower of this? Psychology, philosophy, and the law offer only limited answers to these questions and frequently disqualify individuals' own experiences as a valid source of knowledge of consent. At the same time, our experiences *are* shaped by our environment and the dominant ways we are taught to think about sex, gender, sexuality, and consent, and that is also difficult to account for. Fanfiction is helping its readers and writers not only to redefine and better understand consent based on lived experience and emotion—both theirs and those of their characters—but also to grapple with the role social power structures play in their interpretations of such experiences. Fanfiction communities create knowledges about consent that are fundamentally epistemologically different to those generated in academia or by the law.

Chapter 7 takes us full circle back to fanfiction texts, the paratexts that surround them, and how these do real work in the real world. Fanfiction readers and writers have an at times paradoxical relationship with ideas of authorship. On the one hand, we claim for ourselves the right to reinterpret and rewrite any work in any way we see fit. We tend to think of the author of the originary work as well and truly dead: their intent does not matter to our reading. At the same time, the fanfiction readers and writers I interviewed repeatedly talked about how much it mattered to their enjoyment of fanfiction that there were ways of knowing whether the author intended to explore problematic aspects of consent, or wrote something "rapey" by accident. This suggests that fanfiction communities recognize the work that fiction, art, and culture do in the real world by either entrenching dominant ways of thinking or enabling us to imagine alternatives. Out of that recognition arise a number of community practices, norms, and infrastructures that seek to facilitate fanfiction's ability to let us imagine things differently. These practices also enable survivors of sexual violence to make informed choices about what kinds of content to engage with, thus allowing them to exercise autonomy and informed consent. In these ways, fanfiction readers and writers enact the knowledges and feminist values they develop in their creative output and interactions with each other, making them manifest in the real world: a *praxis of consent*.

Finally, in chapter 8, I speculate about the future of fanfiction by examining both its failures and its potential as an activist space. I look at how consent-related cultural activism is not evenly distributed in fanfiction communities, and how existing discourses and practices marginalize and harm fans of color in particular. In light of the #MeToo movement and an increasing mainstreaming and commercialization of fanfiction, I also speculate about where cultural activism on sexual consent may head in the future. Here, an increasing focus both in fanfiction communities and among more casual audiences on the impact that fiction, culture, and art have on the real world points toward potential avenues to leveraging fan communities' knowledges in a wider context.

Ultimately, this book argues that fanfiction is among the forms and spaces in popular culture that have the potential to make significant contributions to conversations around gender, sex, sexuality, and consent; and that the fanfiction community's engagements with issues of sexual consent can be viewed as a distinct form of cultural activism: the use of culture to challenge dominant ways of thinking, and to imagine and even enact alternatives. The production, circulation, and discussion of fanfiction (a kind of communal textuality) allows the community to enact a discursive resistance to dominant ways of thinking by forming powerful alternative imaginaries of sexuality and consent. Fanfiction communities also establish a praxis of consent through practices that encourage active engagement with consent issues and center the wellbeing of survivors of sexual violence, thus enacting within community spaces what a world free of sexual violence might look like. The knowledges generated in these ways challenge, demystify, and demythologize dominant discursive constructions of gender, power, sexuality, and consent, as well as the institutions that support these constructions. They are then applied to community members' own day-to-day lives and engagements with sexuality, consent, and rape culture. Yet fanfiction communities are far from perfect and are undergoing rapid changes. Our challenge is to recognize the knowledges they create and their limitations, and to find ways to mitigate the latter while disseminating the former to a wider audience.

2 THINKING THE UNTHINKABLE

About a week into the UK's 2020 COVID-19 pandemic quarantine, I found myself explaining to a stranger on Facebook that they didn't actually have to have sex with their partner, with whom they were currently in lockdown.[1] This person, after complaints from their partner that they weren't having enough sex, had constructed an elaborate tracker in their bullet journal: When were they having sex? How often? What kind of sex? Who had initiated it? "Do I," they asked, "show this tracker to my partner so they see that, actually, I initiate sex just as often?" What I tried to get this person (and later, my Twitter followers) to understand is that it didn't matter how often they had sex, or who initiated it; that it would, in fact, be OK if they never had sex with their partner again.

I am honestly not sure if they believed me. Do you believe me? What was your first reaction when you read that? *But they're my partner, of course I have to have sex with them sometimes! But they want it! But they need it! But if we're not having sex, then we're obviously just friends (with no benefits)! But they'll leave me! But they won't do the washing-up! But I want it! But I need it! But if they never want to have sex with me again, I'll leave them!*

Here's something else that might be hard to process: for sex to be truly consensual, never having sex again has to be a meaningful, available option. In the rest of this chapter, we will explore why these ideas are so hard to articulate and so hard to believe, and why it is vital that we do.

CONSENT/NONCONSENT

Issues of sexual violence became a core part of feminist thought and campaigning in the 1970s and 1980s. Second-wave radical feminists were particularly concerned with power structures such as the law and dominant ideas in our culture, and how these shaped consent. Andrea Dworkin, for instance, showed how marriage law in many Western countries at the time completely invalidated women's nonconsent: legally, a married woman could not be raped by her husband because her perpetual consent to sex with him was effectively assumed by the law.[2] In fact, marital rape was not outlawed in England and Wales until 1991, and in Germany not until 1997.[3] Radical feminists also identified more subtle power structures with similar negative effects on consent. Catharine MacKinnon argued that the way women and girls are socialized in a patriarchal society means they think of their own bodies as "for sexual use by men"—and if that is the case, it becomes difficult to distinguish between consensual sex and rape.[4] Questions of power, then, were central to radical feminists' understanding of sexual violence and consent, and their campaigns for legal reform were eventually at least partially successful. But beyond the legal realm, the radical feminist approach offers a rather bleak outlook for positive social change.

As the influence of radical feminism waned in the 1980s and 1990s, feminist theory and activism shifted focus toward questions of individual agency and interpersonal consent negotiation. There was a growing awareness of issues such as acquaintance rape and date rape. That led scholars and activists to examine how women in particular refuse sex, and how men hear such refusals. Initiatives teaching women to say "no" more forcefully and campaigns telling men that "no means no" aimed to address what many assumed was simply a miscommunication.[5] At the same time, legal reform campaigns used "no means no" as a slogan to demand a more consent-centric definition of rape in jurisdictions where, legally, "no" was or is not enough to recognize an act as rape—a problem that sadly still persists in many countries today.[6] Yet while the idea that a clear refusal or withdrawal of consent should be respected is important, "no means no" does not address a range of situations and circumstances where consent is commonly assumed. Lois Pineau, for instance, shows that in Western culture we tend to read women's unrelated actions, such as wearing a short skirt or accepting a drink, as a commitment to having sex (more specifically, penile-vaginal intercourse). She calls this the contractual model of consent. This implicit contract both makes it more difficult for us to say "no," and is used by defense lawyers in rape trials to argue that sex was consensual even when "no" was in fact said.[7]

With increasing recognition of the flaws of a "no means no" approach, emphasis in feminist activism and theory shifted again in the 1990s, this time toward "enthusiastic consent" or "yes means yes": the idea that the mere absence of a "no" was not enough and only clearly, verbally, and enthusiastically expressed consent was valid.[8] But both the "no means no" and "yes means yes" models are based on the assumption that sexual violence results from interpersonal miscommunication, and that this is a problem that can be resolved at a level of individual agency: if only women communicated more clearly; if only men listened better, or looked for different expressions of consent. Suggestions for improving interpersonal consent negotiation emerging from these models assume that communication and negotiation happen on equal terms: that all partners are free to know and express their own desires and limits without any external pressures or power structures. And so both approaches fail to account for power imbalances and how they map onto intimate relationships.

We can see that negotiation doesn't generally happen on equal terms if we think about how we define "sex," and what that means for consent negotiation. There is a dominant view in our society that the only act that "counts" as sex is penile-vaginal intercourse. This is so pervasive that even feminist researchers and activists working on consent negotiation define intercourse as the only act that requires consent. They conceptualize actions such as kissing, touching, and undressing as expressions of consent instead.[9] In fact the idea that intimate actions other than intercourse might require consent in their own right is something that opponents of feminist movements often use as a hook to show how "ridiculous" and "outrageous" feminists' demands are. In 1991, for instance, Antioch College implemented an "affirmative consent" policy in order to reduce the frequency of date and acquaintance rape on campus. US mainstream media almost universally ridiculed the suggestion that we should ask for consent before we kiss or touch someone. Such attitudes make it more difficult for us to say "no" to things like touching and kissing. In turn, the idea that kissing, touching, and undressing automatically lead to intercourse makes it harder to say "no" to intercourse. Negotiation here is not taking place on an even playing field at all, because it is shaped by how we define what we are even negotiating.

Our definition of sex is just one of many complex external factors that affect whether and how we are able to negotiate consent. Approaches to consent that focus on individual agency and negotiation frequently conflate consent with "wantedness" of sex: negotiation models and research tend to imply that sex is either wanted and therefore consented to, or not wanted and therefore not consented to. But there is also mounting evidence of "unwanted sex"—sex that is, according to a strict legal definition at least, consensual, but that for a range of reasons may not actually be wanted. In casual situations, research suggests, young women agree to or even initiate unwanted sex because they feel they should act as sexually liberated, they should please their partners, or because they have previously agreed to a particular act and feel that consent to that same act is now assumed.[10] Women in long-term relationships tend to think of the unwanted sex they engage in as "relationship maintenance."[11] Most existing research tends to frame unwanted sex as predominantly affecting women, and no research exists specifically on nonbinary people and unwanted sex. But more recent work and anecdotal evidence suggests that men, too, experience unwanted sex.[12]

This prevalence of unwanted sex that is nonetheless (in some sense) consented to raises significant questions about the meaning of "consent" beyond strict legal definitions. It suggests that we live in a society where saying "no" may be harder than saying "yes," and may be even harder for particular kinds of people. In the late 1980s, the feminist psychologist Wendy Hollway started looking at how ideas of femininity, masculinity, and what sex or a romantic relationship should look like all influence how we approach sex in our own lives. She identified three dominant ideas (or, using a term coined by French philosopher Michel Foucault, discourses[13]) of heterosex. The male sexual drive discourse is the idea that men have a stronger "sexual drive" than women and are less able to control their "urges" as sex is a biological necessity for them. The have/hold discourse is the idea, named after a popular phrasing of Christian marriage vows, that women exchange sex for romantic relationships and should therefore act as gatekeepers to sex if they want to hold on to "their" man. Finally, the more recently emerged permissive discourse is the idea that sex is natural for everyone and we all have a right to sexual expression.[14] It is important to understand that none of these discourses has a basis in science or actual human experience of sexuality; rather, they are how we collectively think gender roles and sex (should) work. But because we are all steeped in them, they ultimately shape our ideas, behavior, and experiences, as we can see from the examples of unwanted sex presented here. Young women's aspiration to be seen as sexually liberated reflects the permissive discourse; women who engage in unwanted sex as relationship maintenance are strongly influenced by the have/hold discourse; and men who engage in unwanted sex do so in part because the male sexual drive discourse suggests that not doing it would be a failure of masculinity.

Consent, then, is not a straightforward matter of negotiation, because our negotiating positions are shaped by the society we live in. As a result of this realization, feminist theory and activism have more recently returned to the role of power in consent and sexual violence. Sexualities theorist Lisa Downing has coined the term "sex-critical" to describe this new approach.[15] Like radical feminism, sex-critical approaches pay attention to the operations of power in consent negotiation, but they also offer a more nuanced and complex understanding of how power works. In her groundbreaking sex-critical work *Just Sex? The Cultural Scaffolding of Rape*, Nicola Gavey looks at the social power imbalances and prevalent ideas in our culture that make sexual violence possible. She places rape on a continuum of sexual violence and argues that many forms of sexual assault and even rape are often subsumed in our understanding of "just sex" or normal sex: the dominant ways we think about sex, gender, and relationships combine into a version of "normal" (hetero)sex that is broad enough to encompass many kinds of what is actually forced, unwanted, or nonconsensual sex.[16] The very dominance of these ideas in our society exerts pressure on us in ways that lead us to consent to, or sometimes even initiate, sex we do not want. An unwanted sex approach simply says, "Huh, people seem to be consenting to sex they do not want." Sex-critical approaches like Gavey's and Downing's, on the other hand, fundamentally question the validity of that consent. They challenge key assumptions of interpersonal negotiation, and highlight the need to consider social and cultural forces in our understanding of "normal" sexuality. After all, if we think that having unwanted "relationship maintenance" sex is normal, it can't possibly be nonconsensual or coerced, right?

We are all steeped in these dominant ideas of what normal sex looks like. They are the reason why Alex Gabriel, quoted in the previous chapter, felt "raped by no one in particular." They are why, in the moment, it is difficult to ask a partner to change a condom, but at the same time almost impossible to name that experience as a violation. They are why we see a famous, charming man follow a familiar script with a woman who is clearly uncomfortable, and still don't think he has done anything wrong. All of these things are, after all, "just sex." If we don't have the words to name our experiences as violations, how do we even begin to resist and challenge those dominant ideas?

POWER/RESISTANCE

Sex-critical approaches to sexual violence and consent, then, suggest that the ways we are taught to think about sex shape how we *do* sex. The dominant ideas we have in our society of what sex should look like limit what we as individuals even see as possible. If it doesn't count as sex if a penis doesn't go into a vagina, and we want to be having sex, then the penis has to go into the vagina even if, in reality, everyone involved would rather do something else. Sex-critical approaches highlight such dominant ideas and show how they have a direct impact on what we think we can and can't do—how they limit our ability to meaningfully give consent.

These approaches build on a complex and nuanced understanding of how power works, rooted in the ideas of French philosopher Michel Foucault. One of Foucault's main interests lay in how power is exercised in modern Western societies. For the most part, he argued, we are no longer told by someone at the top what we can or can't do. Rather, power is dispersed and multidirectional: we exercise it over each other through something Foucault calls a discourse. Discourses are dominant ideas and practices in society that allow us to say some things on a topic while making other ways of thinking about it unthinkable or unintelligible. Discourses don't describe social phenomena; they *produce* them.[17]

Let's look at an example. Historically, we have tended to think of romantic and sexual attraction—and therefore romantic and sexual relationships—as the same: a relationship that is romantic has to be sexual; one that is sexual has to be romantic.[18] We also have some pretty definite ideas of the other components of romantic/sexual relationships: dating, holding hands, kissing, sharing living space and finances, marriage, children. If you stop to think about it, these are all fairly distinct activities that we could do completely independently of each other. We could hold hands with or kiss our friends. We could have sex with people we are not in a romantic relationship with. We could be married but not live together or have children. We could have and raise children with people we are not in a romantic relationship with. We could be in a romantic relationship with someone and not be having sex with them.

As you went through that list, I suspect some of those ideas felt more "natural" than others. Having sexual relationships with people we are not romantically involved with (whether one-night stands or friends-with-benefits arrangements) has become increasingly normalized. But just holding hands with or kissing a friend feels a bit weird. Divorced couples raise children together, but despite how common divorce is nowadays, we still tend to think of it as a failure rather than something normal. And if we are not having sex with our romantic partner, most of us would tend to feel that something is wrong with the relationship: we have managed to normalize nonromantic sexual relationships, but romantic relationships still have to also be sexual. The neat discursive package of "romantic relationship" gives us an idea of how things *should* be, and any deviation from that at best needs explanation ("I have kids with my ex") or intervention ("We haven't had sex in six months—let's get counseling"), and at worst is completely unimaginable ("I am sharing finances and cuddles with my friend, and neither of us is sexually or romantically attracted to the other").

In our society, then, we have a very clear idea of what a romantic relationship should look like, coupled with an idea that a romantic relationship is something we should all be aspiring to. At best, this strongly discourages us from exploring some less "normal"-feeling relationship arrangements that might actually be right for us; at worst, it can trap us in dangerous situations. This is what we mean when we say that discourse is not descriptive but rather productive: "romantic relationship" doesn't simply describe an arrangement between people—it actively shapes what we do with our lives. The operation of power through discourse in this way constructs what can and cannot be true, to the extent that such constructions appear normal and natural and alternatives become absurd or unthinkable.

The same is true of our ideas of sex and consent. There are dominant ideas in our society about what "counts" as sex (a penis going in a vagina), how sex happens (you start with kissing and touching and end with ejaculation), how much sex you should be having (lots if you're a man, probably less but also lots if you're a sexually liberated young woman, some and regularly if you're in a long-term relationship so you and your partner can "keep the spark alive"). We also have ideas—though these are more contested—about what kinds of things count as consent. They range from wearing a short skirt and accepting a drink to not saying no to outright saying yes. One utterly uncontested indicator of consent, though, is if we initiate sex. If we start it, we must both want it and consent to it, right? Anything else would be unthinkable, unimaginable. Hopefully by now we have already begun to see the cracks in that story. Because we *should* be having a certain amount of sex (so society tells us). And we *should* be having sex in a particular way. So, what if we don't want to, but we should, and so we initiate it anyway? Is that consent? This is such as normal experience for many of us that it is really hard to imagine it as anything but consent, and it is almost impossible to label it as coercive, let alone rape.

Recall Alex Gabriel's Twitter thread from chapter 1. Who, after all, would be the rapist here?

We are so steeped in our society's dominant ideas of what normal sex is, that trying to think through some of these contradictions feels like wading through molasses. We unthinkingly reproduce and reinforce ideas of what is normal to the point where questioning them is almost impossible. This is what Foucault calls a "regime of truth": a set of ways of thinking and talking about something that solidifies some ideas while making others unintelligible. And this is also why for him power and knowledge are inextricably linked to the point of becoming "power/knowledge." What we can know about something is a way of exercising power; and exercising power shapes and limits what is knowable.[19]

Feminist theorists have found Foucault's ideas about power/knowledge, discourses, and regimes of truth both immensely useful and deeply frustrating. They are useful in showing us how what we think of as normal and natural (such as the idea that sex involves a penis going in a vagina, or the idea that a romantic relationship must also necessarily be sexual) is actually socially constructed—just a set of dominant ideas we keep reproducing rather than a given of the universe. And feminist theorists have done substantial work in showing the material impact of dominant discourses. Cultural philosopher Susan Bordo, for instance, has shown us how dominant ideas of femininity act directly on women's bodies through diet culture: women monitor what they eat and how much they exercise in order to conform to society's ideas of what a woman should look like, and women who do not do this are punished for it.[20] Here, ideas of how things *should* be have a direct, material, and distinctly gendered impact on bodies.

But this view of power as operating on us from all sides, in all directions, without a meaningful "outside" to this system is also frustrating because it leaves little room for resistance. If we are all steeped in these ideas and unthinkingly reproduce them, how do we even begin to meaningfully challenge them?[21] We are looking for approaches that will let us identify and challenge concepts that seem "natural" but are actually socially constructed; that will allow us to see how the way others talk about us shapes what we can do; that will let us tell our own story even when it contradicts dominant ideas; and that will enable us to think and say things that under the dominant regime of truth are unthinkable and unsayable. To find such meaningful and effective approaches for resistance from within, we can turn to those most affected by oppression: scholars, theorists, thinkers and activists from marginalized backgrounds have a long history of grappling with questions of meaningful resistance in the face of all-encompassing power and oppression. Feminist and Black American intellectual traditions in particular have engaged with postmodern understandings of power such as Foucault's and offered useful insights. Key themes in these traditions are questions of how we know things about ourselves and the world, and how representation, self-representation, and cultural expression can help us reimagine ourselves and what is possible.

In order to start spotting concepts that seem "natural" and begin to challenge them, we first have to understand how they work. The Black feminist theorist Patricia Hill Collins argues that one way in which oppression works is by giving us a set of limited choices of what we can be. She calls these "controlling images." We see and reproduce such images in media and popular culture but also through institutions such as government agencies and the education system. Collins shows how such images are applied to Black women in the United States and the impact they have: "[p]ortraying African-American women as stereotypical mammies, matriarchs, welfare recipients, and hot mommas has been essential to the political economy of domination fostering Black women's oppression."[22] How we think of ourselves, and how we are thought of by others, has a direct material impact on us: controlling images have negative associations that are in turn used to justify the oppression of Black women. And as with dominant ideas of what sex is and how it should work, the problem with controlling images for those steeped in them is that it is very hard to imagine being something else. In fact, Collins finds that Black women in the United States react to controlling images in a range of complex and sometimes contradictory ways. Some internalize them and come to identify with them. Others may try to escape them through drugs or alcohol, or find ways of setting themselves apart while not resisting the overall message of the images—"I'm not like *those* women." But Collins also argues that some Black women do manage to resist controlling images by finding their own voice and telling their own stories.

In this, Collins draws on another Black feminist scholar and activist, bell hooks, who argues for the importance of marginalized people and communities finding their "critical voice." Such a critical voice allows us to tell our own stories without reproducing the dominant ideas used to oppress us. This means that in telling our stories we have to pay attention not just to our own experiences but to those of others, and to the power structures that have shaped those experiences. A critical voice is not individual; it is developed in and by communities. Art, culture, self-expression, and self-representation can play a crucial role in finding it, and hooks gives the emergence of rap and hip-hop as art forms as an example of poor or working class young Black people coming together to develop such a critical voice.[23] Collins, too, shows us some of the spaces and communities where Black women are able to reject controlling images and find their own critical voices. Cultural traditions such as Black women's blues and writing, as well as Black women's supportive relationships with one another are where they are able to collectively articulate their experiences and come to a positive self-definition that challenges and rejects controlling images.

Still, doing all of this is not easy, either for Black women or for other marginalized people, even when we find supportive environments to do it in. Controlling images of Black women as mammies, welfare queens, hot mommas, and matriarchs still abound in US culture—and slightly different but equally harmful images of other marginalized groups are pervasive in both US and other cultures. What we create when we try to resist dominant ideas and controlling images are what both Foucault and Collins call "subjugated knowledges." Foucault uses this term to show how attempts to counteract dominant ideas are frequently dismissed as naive, inadequate, or illegitimate. Think of the debate around gun ownership in the United States, where gun proponents' first response to those seeking tighter controls is that they know nothing about guns, or of the way concerns about the effects of capitalism on people and the environment are routinely dismissed with the assertion that there is no alternative. Alternatives exist—they are just kept out of the debate by making them seem impractical, inadequate, or downright foolish. Those alternatives, then, are subjugated knowledges. Collins borrows this term from Foucault, but uses it a little differently. She emphasizes that these knowledges are not naive; they are simply being "made to appear so by those controlling knowledge validation procedures."[24] Some people and institutions elevate themselves to being the arbiter of what counts as knowledge on a particular topic, and that in turn gives them the right to dismiss other ways of knowing things. So White people, White culture, and the White-dominated institutions of the state are the arbiters of truth about Black people. This is what gives them the power to (re)produce and use controlling images of Black women in the way Collins describes. That does not make the knowledges created by Black people, and especially by Black women, about their own experiences in a racist world any less valid—it just means that those in power are able to dismiss them as invalid. The good news is that, through the creation of subjugated knowledges, Black women have moved beyond the point where any positive expression of Blackness and Black womanhood is unthinkable and unsayable.

Black feminist thought, then, gives us some useful ways of thinking about how dominant ideas have a material impact on our lives, and how—through finding a critical voice and creating subjugated knowledges—we may begin to counteract those ideas. These techniques are just as applicable to our understanding of power, sex, and consent as they are to other types of oppression and marginalization. Another Black American scholar and activist, Cornel West, breaks down into four categories the kinds of things we may want to focus our knowledge-making efforts on: destruction, deconstruction, demythologization, and demystification.[25] *Destruction* is the process of challenging the grand theories and ideas of Western/White philosophical thought and showing that rather than universal, they are a product of a particular time, place, and set of power structures. It is, for instance, tempting to think that Hollway's three dominant discourses of (hetero)sex have always operated in this way, and when we think and write about the past, we tend to map those discourses onto it. But social historians know that even something as entrenched as the male sexual drive discourse is only a relatively recent invention (as well as specific to White, Christian-dominated cultures), and in medieval Europe it was women who were seen as sexually insatiable.[26] *Deconstruction* is challenging the binary opposites in which so much of Western/White philosophical traditions operate: black/white, good/bad, man/woman, consent/nonconsent. Deconstruction allows us to see and challenge the implicit hierarchies in those binaries but also to open up spaces for things to exist between the ostensibly complete and opposite terms: concepts like "gray," "morally ambiguous," "nonbinary genders," and, as we will see over the course of this book, "dubcon." *Demythologization* refers to paying attention to and continually highlighting how the dominant ideas, stereotypes, and metaphors in our society are socially constructed rather than natural, and how they are linked to politics and the operation of power. The "male sexual drive" is not any more or less natural than a "female sexual drive"—but our acceptance of it as fact is a key enabler of rape culture. "He couldn't help himself," after all. Finally, *demystification* examines the operations of power in our world in an attempt to find alternative ways of thinking about and doing things. What would a world free of rape culture look like? What would a *consent culture* look like, and how do we get there?

CULTURE/ACTIVISM

Finding a critical voice, creating subjugated knowledges, and challenging and offering alternatives to problematic ideas that have become normalized are all ways of resisting the all-encompassing, multidirectional, productive operation of power that Foucault draws our attention to. I call these approaches *discursive resistance*: leveraging the power of discourse to resist . . . the power of discourse. Discursive resistance is about making the unthinkable thinkable, the unnameable nameable, the unsayable sayable. Only when we can do those things can we actually meaningfully act and fight for material change in the world. It is not until we can intelligibly articulate that for "yes" to be meaningful, "no" has to be an equally available option, that we can identify those spaces where that might not be the case—and start doing something about them.

In the last fifteen to twenty years, the relatively White-dominated field of cultural studies in Europe and, to a lesser extent, the United States has started looking at instances of "cultural activism." Research in this area has tended to focus on highly visible public stunts, frequently targeted as political events—for example, the activities of the Clandestine Insurgent Rebel Clown Army during the 2005 G8 meeting in Scotland; citizen projects protesting the selection of the Finnish city of Turku as European Capital of Culture; and the London-based Reclaim the Streets network, which advocates for community ownership of public spaces by, among other things, digging up roads to plant flowers.[27] In all of these cases, the activities labeled as cultural activism are performed by a relatively small, existing activist group and directed outward at the general public.

Cultural activism scholars Michael Buser and Jane Arthurs define cultural activism as "a set of activities which: a) challenge the dominant interpretations and constructions of the world while b) presenting alternative socio-political and spatial imaginaries c) in ways which challenge relationships between art, politics, participation and spectatorship."[28] And Christian Scholl identifies four features of the kind of public "disruptive art interventions" that cultural activism scholars study: they are bubbles of extraordinariness within our everyday lives; they are participatory, do-it-yourself initiatives outside of capitalist production and consumption; they use dominant cultural codes and ideas in strange and new ways, thereby subverting them and prompting us to see them in a new light; and they are exemplary gestures, showing us how a different world might work. Both of these definitions overlap significantly with the kind of discursive resistance coming out of Black, feminist, and other marginalized groups and schools of thought. They are concerned with identifying and challenging dominant ideas and controlling images, showing us alternatives, and doing so in ways and spaces outside the control of dominant systems of power such as capitalism.

But cultural activism as it is currently conceptualized—carried out by a vanguard few, aimed at the many—has limits. For all its protestations about participatory culture and blurring the lines between the creators and the beholders of art, there is a cultural hierarchy at its core: the vanguard few who are activists/the many who are invited to participate. More importantly, though, it leaves one big question unanswered: how do the vanguard few get to a point where they are able to see and challenge the dominant ideas we are all steeped in? Many of these ideas, after all, are so pervasive and so powerful that we think of them as natural. For most of us, Collins's controlling images of Black women and the ideas we have about what "normal" (hetero)sex looks like—Gavey's "just sex"—fall under this category. Therefore, activism directed outward with respect to these issues is impossible without first naming the problem, without finding a way to see that what we have been taught is "natural" or "common sense" is anything but: without discursive resistance.

So, how do we discover for ourselves the kinds of dominant ideas about sex that we have been steeped in our whole lives? How do we begin to see that there is nothing natural about them? And how do we start to imagine alternatives? How do we begin to believe that it would be OK if we never wanted to have sex again, and that if that's not OK, then consent isn't meaningful? In the rest of this book, we will see how the fanfiction community does these things, and what we can learn from them.

INTERLUDE: WHAT WE TALK ABOUT WHEN WE TALK ABOUT FANFICTION

Fanfiction does not exactly have a reputation as a respectable art form. When not actively bombarded with cease-and-desist letters by rightsholders, fanfiction writers are, at best, dismissed by mainstream media and opinion as "derivative" and "unoriginal."[1] Occasionally, someone might grudgingly admit that it might be a good way for kids to improve their writing. Of course, the idea of originality as valuable in art and fiction is itself relatively new. Before the early eighteenth century (when the idea of copyright became enshrined in law), fiction was commonly built on top of other fiction, using the same settings or characters, making tweaks, and coming up with new plots, much like modern fanfiction does. This is true of some "classic" works of the Western literary canon, going as far back as the ancient Greeks. Homer's *Iliad* and *Odyssey* fall somewhere between fanfiction about Greek gods and what we might call RPF, or real person(a) fiction. Virgil, in the *Aeneid*, plucked a minor character from the *Odyssey*, gave him a love interest and a plot of his own, and scored some political points by tying the whole thing into the founding mythology of the Roman empire. Dante writes Virgil and Homer RPF, but also writes himself into it—a choice that would get him dismissed as a Mary Sue by modern fanfiction authors. Then, there are the myriad retellings of the Arthurian legend, which picks up from the *Aeneid* and puts Aeneas's descendants in Britain, conveniently providing a link between medieval Britain and ancient Greece. A significant chunk of medieval literature is, in fact, either King Arthur or Bible fanfiction, and that's before we get to Shakespeare, whose entire oeuvre has all of two original plots, and everyone who subsequently wrote Shakespeare fanfic.[2] So, fanfiction is only as derivative as some of these prominent works of the Western literary canon, and "derivative" isn't necessarily synonymous with "bad." In fact, once we start looking closely at what is possible after being relieved of the obligation of originality, things get quite interesting.

Fan studies scholars tend to approach fanfiction in one of two ways: either as text or as a community practice.[3] But I would argue that these are the two sides of the same coin. The fancy academic word for what makes fanfiction work the way it does as text is "intertextuality." Fanfiction texts constantly reference other works. Most obviously, those are the works that the fanfiction stories are "based on"—or what fanfiction scholar Abigail De Kosnik calls the "originary" work.[4] It is not impossible to read a fanfiction story without knowing the originary work, but it is certainly harder, and it is likely to make less sense. Fanfiction writers, after all, have a ready-made setting and characters to play with, and they rarely spend time rehashing them. They simply (and generally correctly) assume that readers know the characters, the setting, and the plot of the originary work, and that leaves them free to play with those things in new and exciting ways. This is the community practice part of things: if you know your target audience well and there are established community norms for how to read fanfiction, that shapes what you can and can't do with the text, thus shaping the text itself.

A lot of the way readers and writers make meaning from fanfiction is through similarities and differences with the originary work. The differences can range from imagining the entire cast of our favorite TV show as the staff and regulars of a coffee shop to changing the gender of a main character or imagining them as transgender. (Or, if you prefer your fanfiction published, you can recast *Pride and Prejudice*'s Lizzie Bennet as a somewhat neurotic mid-1990s singleton or add some zombies, or retell the plot of *Gone with the Wind* from a Black character's point of view, as Alice Randall does in *The Wind Done Gone*.[5]) The reason all these new stories about familiar characters make sense is that when we read them, we are reading them *side by side* with the originary text. We are looking for similarities and differences. What elements of the originary work did the author choose to retain, and what did they change? What effect do those changes have on the characters, the setting, or the plot? And sometimes, those little differences will cause us to reevaluate the entirety of the originary work. They can make us ask, for instance, what it feels like for a cross-dressed Link to wander around the streets of Gerudo Town in *Breath of the Wild*, and compare that to what we think it might feel like for a Link who is actually a transgender woman to explore her gender for the first time. They can make us wonder about the choices the creators of the game made in how cross-dressed Link is treated, and about why Link *isn't* a trans woman in the originary work. Or, again, if you prefer the published version, they can make us wonder what on earth is so special about Scarlett O'Hara that she deserves her own story when none of the Black characters around her do. *The Wind Done Gone* is only one story to be read side by side with its originary work. Fanfiction communities write thousands and we read them all side by side with each other and the originary work. Writing and reading lots of very similar stories about the same characters, making small tweaks each time (repetition with a difference), lets us layer lots of different meanings, explore different aspects of a character or situation, and ask interesting questions about the originary work.[6] In this way, fanfiction is both text and community practice: without the specific community of readers and writers, these texts simply don't work in the same way. Fanfiction is a *communal textuality*.

But the originary work is not the only thing we draw on when we read and write fanfiction. Rather, fanfiction stories are in dialogue with each other, with tropes and genre conventions from popular culture, with other works of art and culture, and even with our own lived experiences and real life. Faced with thousands of stories of male characters from TV shows in relationships with each other, early fan studies scholars built an entire academic field around the foundational question: "Why do straight women enjoy reading and writing about men banging?"[7] Since then, it has turned out that the fanfiction community is a lot queerer than fan studies scholars originally thought, and that there are many and complex answers to that question. But one of the early answers that still resonates with many fans and scholars is that by writing about two men, fanfiction writers were trying to imagine what a truly equal relationship might look like—the kind that they may not have been able to have in their own lives because the structural inequalities of gender got in the way. So, in some cases, the similarities and differences we seek out to make sense of stories are similarities and differences to our own lives.[8] And if a piece of fanfiction can cause us to reevaluate the originary work through intertextual reading, then maybe it can cause us to reevaluate our own experiences, too.

This is what we talk about when we talk about fanfiction: a literature created by and for a community, together; writing based on other works in ways that that expand, challenge, rewrite, and fill in the gaps in those works; stories that are constantly in dialogue not only with the originary work but also with each other, and with culture more generally. And, like all stories, when we read fanfiction, we bring our own experiences and interpretations to it—and sometimes we walk away changed.

3 "DOGFUCK RAPEWORLD": SEXUAL SCRIPTS AND CONSENT IN THE OMEGAVERSE

Content note: This chapter discusses the graphic depiction of rape in a fanfiction story in some detail.

One of the foundational questions of fan studies can be phrased (a little flippantly, perhaps) as: "Why do straight women enjoy reading and writing about men banging?"[1] There are many answers to this, and over time we have begun to realize that the question itself is perhaps rather flawed: fanfiction communities are much more obviously queer spaces now than they were when it was first asked.[2]

One early answer to this question, however, that appears over and over even in more recent literature is this: by focusing on sexual and romantic relationships between two men, fanfiction readers and writers are trying to level the gendered power imbalance inherent in relationships between men and women. They imagine, instead, what love and romance between true equals could look like. It is a tempting answer, particularly if we think of fanfiction readers and writers as straight women struggling to negotiate relationships with men in their day-to-day lives. It is an answer that is almost certainly true for some types of slash, and for some slash readers and writers. But it is far from a complete answer. There are many subgenres of slash where, gender aside, equal is the last word we would use to describe the relationship dynamic. Rather, they foreground inequality—both interpersonal and social—in the relationships they explore, with examples including the romance staple of arranged marriage, alternate universes in which everyone is designated either dominant or submissive, and, perhaps most extremely and most controversially, the Omegaverse. And these subgenres are not confined to one single fandom or originary work—they spread across fandoms, taking on a life of their own.

These are the spaces that first drew my attention to fanfiction's potential for exploring issues of sexual consent in more depth and in different ways to those that legal, psychological, or philosophical approaches could offer. These are the stories that seemed to me to be asking such questions as: What does it *feel* like to negotiate power dynamics in a relationship? Where do power dynamics come from? How can individuals challenge them? And what happens if they don't do that? What does it take, in a sexual and romantic relationship, to negate or at least minimize those power dynamics to the point where individual agency—and individual consent—can be considered meaningful? And the slash subgenre that asked these questions most impactfully and most viscerally, and provoked the strongest reactions, was the Omegaverse.

The Omegaverse, also known as alpha/beta/omega dynamics or A/B/O, is a science-fictional shared alternate universe jointly created by fanfiction writers across many fandoms. It is characterized by the reuse and repeated combination of several common tropes. There is now a growing body of academic work about A/B/O,[3] but fans themselves were the first to produce a large amount of so-called meta: histories of the genre's emergence, guides to its common features, and other commentary.[4] Fan writer and historian netweight traces the origins of the A/B/O genre to the fandom of the horror-fantasy TV series *Supernatural* and, in particular, real person(a) fiction (RPF)—that is, fanfiction about the actors in the series rather than the characters they play. The first stories recognized as A/B/O emerged in mid-2010, and what began as another trope has evolved into a fanfiction genre in its own right and has since gained popularity across a number of large fandoms, including *Supernatural*, *Teen Wolf*, and *Sherlock*. As of March 2021, nearly 90,000 works can be found in the "Alpha/Beta/Omega Dynamics" tag on AO3. This accounts for around 1.2 percent of AO3 works—a number comparable to popular tropes such as the coffee shop setting.

A/B/O is an amalgamation of several common tropes, and the exact interpretation and configuration varies by author and story, so it can be difficult to pinpoint exactly what makes an A/B/O story. At its most basic, though, as well as being male or female, characters in the Omegaverse have a "secondary gender." This may be alpha, beta, or omega. Betas are effectively "normal everyday humans as you know them."[5] Alphas are socially and, in some interpretations, biologically dominant, whereas omegas are submissive. Combining the primary genders (male/female) and secondary genders (alpha/beta/omega) means that in the A/B/O universe there are effectively six genders: male alphas, betas, and omegas, and female alphas, betas, and omegas. Other common elements in Omegaverse stories include human anatomy, sexuality, and social behavior altered to resemble that of dogs or wolves (including a heightened sense of smell, mating cycles or heat, and male alpha characters having a penis similar to a canine's); male pregnancy; and a potentially lifelong psychic bond with a partner.[6] The vast majority of stories in the setting focus on male/male relationships,[7] and particularly on the male alpha/male omega configuration.

Some fans and fan studies scholars have argued that this gender configuration and focus on one particular type of pairing shows that A/B/O fans have an essentialist approach to gender; that is, they think of gender as purely biologically determined.[8] But a closer look at Omegaverse stories shows that writers and readers interpret the extent to which the six genders are anchored in biology as opposed to socially constructed very differently to one another. Unsettling and moving away from a biological view of gender is, in fact, a key theme of many A/B/O stories, and one of the aspects of the subgenre that allow it to examine issues of consent in complex and interesting ways.

Omegaverse stories can be found across a number of different fandoms: the genre has an appeal of its own, beyond the particular fandom and originary work where it began. Variations of the Omegaverse are especially popular in some fandoms, such as more pronounced dog or wolf characteristics in stories set in the *Teen Wolf* fandom, or social structures that emphasize sexual dominance and submissiveness in Hockey RPF. But readers and writers also follow Omegaverse stories across fandoms: they are fans of the Omegaverse as much as they are of the originary material. This means that they are familiar with the broad range of genre conventions that commonly feature in A/B/O fiction. They read the variations on the particular elements adopted or foregrounded in any given story against this background knowledge of the Omegaverse as a whole. A/B/O readers and writers use both differences and similarities between stories to further flesh out the universe and to explore the issues the setting raises. Reader comments on stories often highlight especially innovative elements or compare how the author has handled an aspect of the setting to its treatment by other authors. A lot of the meanings that readers and writers make from A/B/O stories are also made in intertextual readings with the wider Omegaverse. Different interpretations are read side by side with each other, and readers pay attention to similarities and differences between interpretations. Rather than a collection of individual stories, the Omegaverse is a growing, collectively created body of work.[9]

Although the Omegaverse is extremely popular and continues to expand to new fandoms, it is also highly controversial in fanfiction communities. Many readers and writers object to its roots in bestiality fiction or to the extremely gendered power imbalances at the core of the setting. Some fan communities have even dubbed the Omegaverse "dogfuck rapeworld," showing a concern with issues of sexual violence and consent in the setting.[10]

Readers and writers who enjoy A/B/O stories also freely admit, in author's notes, tags, and comment discussions, that many of the stories they enjoy contain at the very least dubcon—dubious consent—if not outright representations of rape. These representations are also highly eroticized and fans read and write these stories at least in part because they are hot—that is, as pornography. This, too, is reflected in the paratexts around the works: as of March 2021, 70 percent of stories tagged as A/B/O on AO3 are rated "mature" or "explicit." This eroticized representation of sexual violence is at the core of the Omegaverse controversy in fanfiction communities. Yet, as we will see in the rest of this chapter, readers and writers who enjoy and embrace the genre are highly conscious of the consent issues involved, and actively use the features of the Omegaverse setting—including its purported gender essentialism and resulting power imbalances—to explore them.

SEXUAL SCRIPTS

When reading A/B/O stories for the first time, we almost can't help but compare the science-fictional elements of the setting to our own world. In Western society, we commonly recognize two genders and associate them with particular biological characteristics. (This is, of course, a cultural construct, and there is increasing recognition that gender is, in fact, much more complex than that.) In the Omegaverse, there are six commonly recognized genders, also associated with biological characteristics. In Western society, we predominantly think of sex as happening between one cisgender man and one cisgender woman, and we have a pretty good idea in our heads—a script, if you will—as to how such sexual encounters start, develop, and end. Penises go in vaginas. The scripts in the Omegaverse are more varied than that and are more fleshed out for some gender combinations than others, but they do exist. Alphas are dominant and possessive. Omegas are needy and submissive. Penises with knots go into self-lubricating anuses or sometimes vaginas. No one is quite sure what female alphas do, but most sexual interactions in the Omegaverse are just as scripted as they are in our own world. The idea of a sexual script, in fact, is a really good way of conceptualizing the differences between the Omegaverse and our own culture, and of understanding what exactly A/B/O readers and writers are doing when they play around in their fictional sandbox.

Sexual script theory was first proposed by sociologists John H. Gagnon and William Simon in 1973.[11] They were looking to move beyond purely biological understandings of sex and explore its social aspects instead. They suggested that without a kind of a script—a high-level idea of how a sexual encounter *should* proceed—we would not associate elements such as privacy, the presence of a person we might be attracted to, or even nudity with arousal and sex. Sexuality is a social and cultural construct, and that is what gives some body parts, situations, and actions a sexual meaning in certain contexts. Without a script that tells us what behaviors are part of sex, who gets to do them, and in what order, there would be a lot less sex in the world.

Sexual scripts exist at three different levels. At the cultural level, scripts tend to be quite abstract and generic, with little detail. The next level down are interpersonal scripts. They are based on the cultural scripts, but we (along with our partners) also modify and rewrite them to fill in the gaps. Intrapsychic scripts are the ones we rehearse in our heads, and where we reconcile some of the complexities and ambiguities of the cultural scripts. As a result, we can sometimes find that our interpersonal and intrapsychic scripts no longer match the cultural ones. The interactions and conflicts between the three levels are how, over time, the scripts we have as a society change and evolve.

In Western societies, the dominant sexual scripts are highly gendered and heteronormative. This means sex is generally seen as happening between one cisgender man and one cisgender woman, and who gets to do what is determined in part by the person's gender. We tend to view men as active in sex: they initiate it, they actively move through the steps of the script. Women, on the other hand, are passive gatekeepers: they get to say "yes" or "no" to men's advances, but the dominant sexual script allows them little agency beyond that.[12] We are exposed to these cultural scripts through conversations with our peers, through some kinds of sex and relationships education, and, crucially, through popular culture.[13]

Sexual script theory, then, suggests that how we as a society and as individuals think and talk about sex materially shapes how we *do* sex. This in turn sounds not entirely unlike the discourse-analytical and sex-critical approaches to sexuality we discussed in chapter 2. The dominant Western sexual scripts are rooted in the male sexual drive discourse, the have/hold discourse, and, to a lesser extent, the permissive discourse.[14] We can also think of the conflicts between the different levels of sexual scripts as conflicts between different discursive constructions of sexuality and our own lived experience. We realize, perhaps, that we want to have sex with people of genders different to the one the script prescribes. We realize that our assigned roles as initiators or gatekeepers don't fit us very well. We may even realize that there are other fun ways of having sex than penises going in vaginas. We, as individuals, have started thinking about sex differently, and therefore we start doing it differently.

In practice, however, making these mental shifts can be quite difficult. Dominant sexual scripts are so pervasive that even imagining doing things differently can be nearly impossible for some. When we find that our desires (or our interpersonal and intrapsychic scripts) diverge from how our culture tells us sex *should* work, how do we cope? Researchers have found that we tend to employ one of three strategies. Some of us conform: we fully accept and internalize the dominant cultural scripts and implement them in our sexual and romantic relationships. If we are men, we initiate sex (sometimes even when we don't actually want it), and we awkwardly offer flowers on Valentine's Day in hopes that the gatekeeper won't reject our advances. If we are women, we carefully monitor how much sex we accept and how much we reject, striving to find a balance between meeting our partners' needs so they stay with us and not appearing too keen, lest they think us a slut. These are some of the extremes that conforming can result in, but there are a variety of ways it can manifest. Another strategy for reconciling the disjunctures between the cultural scripts and our own desires is exception-finding: we tell ourselves that we, either as individuals or as partners in a relationship, are somehow different to everyone else. A husband who cooks and cleans, a wife who is the main earner in the family, or a same-gender couple can all use exception-finding to effectively say to themselves and others, "We know this is not how it normally works, but we are different." Finally, some of us choose to outright challenge and seek to transform cultural scripts for sex and relationships. We can find supportive communities such as queer, feminist, and BDSM spaces where we can collectively acknowledge that something is wrong—not with us for being different but with the cultural scripts as a whole.[15]

In chapter 2, we saw that different waves of feminist consent theorists have struggled to reconcile the role of individual agency in interpersonal consent negotiation with the power of society and culture to tell us how to think and behave.[16] A model of sexual scripts existing at different levels, as well as an understanding of how we deal with conflicts between those levels, might help us better understand how we as individuals may still have some agency in matters such as consent negotiation, even when there are very clear cultural scripts (i.e., dominant ideas about what sex should look like) to follow. It might also help us map out both the extent and the limits of that agency.

An alternate universe where gender and sexual scripts work radically differently to ours, such as the Omegaverse, is the perfect tool to explore the effect of scripts and dominant ways of thinking on our actions and our ability to meaningfully negotiate consent. A/B/O stories feature themes of power, desire, pleasure, intimacy, romance, control, and consent. Readers and writers playing in this shared universe can examine gender roles as either socially constructed or driven by the strange biology of the Omegaverse, or a mixture of both. The distance created by the unfamiliar setting allows us to use A/B/O stories to ask questions about the power structures and inequalities around gender, and how they map onto intimate relationships. Looking at such stories through the lens of sexual script theory, in turn, allows us to understand both the similarities and differences they present to our own world and what those might say about sexual consent. The Omegaverse's supposed biological or social construction of different genders and sexualities leads to sometimes radically different, and sometimes strikingly similar, dominant sexual scripts in the societies depicted in A/B/O fanfiction. It is how such stories explore and manipulate these scripts, and how their characters negotiate the disjunctures between the dominant scripts and their desires, that makes them interesting.

THREE STORIES REPRESENTING THE OMEGAVERSE

Omegaverse stories are rarely stand-alone, unconnected works, even when we set aside the fact that they are pieces of fanfiction. Rather, they are in dialogue with each other: by choosing which elements and tropes of the A/B/O setting to incorporate in their particular story, writers create their own unique interpretation that simultaneously functions as a response to others' versions of the Omegaverse. Readers, too, are skilled at picking up on the similarities and differences between stories, so a lot of the meaning of any given story is derived from its relationship to the rest of the

Omegaverse. This makes it really hard to analyze a single A/B/O story on its own, especially without in-depth knowledge of the wider subgenre.

To understand what readers and writers of the Omegaverse do with issues of consent . . . I read a lot of A/B/O stories. The academic term for this is deep ethnographic immersion.[17] In this process, I found three key trends in Omegaverse fanfiction. The first is a "straight-up" take on the collection of tropes that make up the setting—what my fan studies colleague Mafalda Stasi calls the "You? Omega. Me? Alpha. . . . I can't help it, that's basic biology" approach.[18] The second is a trend to subvert or invert some of the tropes, particularly those around gender and sexuality: What if two alphas fell in love with each other? Can alphas and omegas ever be friends? Finally, some Omegaverse stories take the science-fictional premise of the setting, and especially its biological essentialism, to their extreme conclusion: "What if we were so ruled by our sexual roles in society that we had no meaningful agency at all?"

There are tens of thousands of Omegaverse stories on AO3. To keep things manageable, and to explore the roots of A/B/O fanfiction, I decided to focus on the fandom that gave birth to it: the *Supernatural* RPF fandom, which focuses on the actors starring in the TV series *Supernatural*. The cast of the show has expanded over the years, but in early seasons the main focus was on Sam and Dean Winchester (played by Jared Padalecki and Jensen Ackles, respectively), two brothers who hunt demons and other supernatural creatures. And so early *Supernatural* fans who wanted to write sexy stories about the two hot guys had to choose their moral high ground between writing about the fictional characters (and thus writing incest), and writing about the actors (a practice still frowned on in some corners of fandom). As a result, many stories in both of these branches of the fandom were published online anonymously on LiveJournal "kinkmemes"—online forums that allowed fans to anonymously prompt a particular type of story and respond to (or "fill," in fandom parlance) such prompts. This gave both prompters and authors some protection from backlash and shaming from other fans. Fan commentators and historians such as netweight[19] have remarked that if any fandom was going to give birth to something as weird and wonderful as the Omegaverse, it was always going to be one of the branches of the *Supernatural* fandom: if you are already dabbling in either incest or RPF, and largely anonymous, why not add a dash of bestiality to it and see where it goes?

I am not a *Supernatural* fan, and so while looking for stories to analyze I also had to come to grips with the fandom itself—although I must admit, even to this day I have to look up which one is Jensen and which one is Jared. Doing this, however, allowed me to follow the process that any fan new to fandom likely would: read primers and other meta (fanspeak for "commentary"), look for rec (recommendation) lists, find the Big Name Fans and the popular, impactful stories, before branching out further. What I was after were stories that represented each of the three trends I had identified, and that had been popular and impactful in the fandom. Fannish histories and rec lists pointed me in the right direction, and I selected three very early Omegaverse stories from the *Supernatural* RPF fandom.

"Heat: Between You and Me" by Miss Lv is one of the earliest stories to feature most of the tropes commonly recognized as constituting the Omegaverse.[20] Interestingly, it contains several elements of trope subversion and inversion, even as it works to establish said tropes. "Slick" by tryfanstone is the third most popular A/B/O story for the Jared/Jensen pairing on AO3. It is another relatively early A/B/O story, and is an example of the tropes that make up the setting being taken to the most extreme possible conclusion. "Sure to Lure Someone Bad" by mistyzeo and obstinatrix is a relatively straightforward early take on the A/B/O subgenre, and has been featured on multiple rec lists.[21]

In all three stories, Jared is the alpha and Jensen is the omega. In real life, Jared Padalecki is taller than Jensen Ackles, and this physical difference may have something to do with writers' artistic choices. An important part of the premise of each story is also that Jensen has either never had sex or a relationship with a male alpha, or has stopped doing so some time ago. All three stories are written in very close third person from Jensen's point of view, and two are written in the present tense. This is a common style in contemporary fanfiction: it allows the reader an insight into a character's thoughts and feelings and creates a sense of immediacy, but also leaves more distance between writer, reader, and character than a first-person narrative would.

"Heat: Between You and Me" is widely acknowledged by the fandom community as one of the early stories that established the A/B/O genre. It was originally published in late 2010 in response to a request on the *Supernatural* kinkmeme. In this story, Jared (alpha) and Jensen (omega) have been sharing a house and secretly harboring romantic feelings for each other. When Jared announces his engagement to Genevieve Cortese, Jensen—who up to this point has never had sex or a relationship with a male alpha—decides to get over his feelings for his friend by having a one-night stand with another alpha. This plan goes awry when Jared returns early from a trip away. Jared and Jensen have heat-fueled sex followed by a serious discussion about their mutual feelings, and agree to begin a romantic relationship. What is striking about this story is that even in this early version of A/B/O, there are clear attempts at exploring and challenging the power structures at the core of the setting. The story contains several elements that subvert what would effectively later become the common Omegaverse tropes, most notably the fact that Jared and Jensen are open about their gender and share a house together as friends. This may be partly due to the fact that "Heat: Between You and Me" is a very early A/B/O story, from a time before the setting had truly taken shape and solidified, but such subversion of the core Omegaverse tropes continues to be a staple of the genre today. "Sure to Lure Someone Bad" is a relatively straightforward example of the A/B/O genre. In this story, Jared and Jensen are not colleagues and actors. Rather, they meet on the subway as omega Jensen is making his way home in the early stages of his heat, and alpha Jared makes a move. Again, the two characters have sex, initially positioned as a one-night stand, but by the end of the story they agree to see each other again. "Slick" takes the biological imperative ideas behind parts of the Omegaverse to their extreme. In this story, Jared, a manipulative alpha, tricks omega Jensen into heat, and proceeds to repeatedly rape him, probably impregnate him, and trap him in an abusive long-term relationship. The story is sexually explicit, and both the author and readers talk about it as a blend of horror and pornography.

SEXUAL SCRIPTS IN THE OMEGAVERSE: THE QUESTION OF GENDER

Writers of Omegaverse fanfiction have a well-developed shared setting and collection of tropes to draw on. But because each story offers a slightly different interpretation of the A/B/O setting, a certain amount of world-building is necessary to let readers know what this particular version of the Omegaverse looks like: which of the tropes has the writer adopted for this story, and what are their precise effects on the society the characters live in? This kind of worldbuilding anchors the story within the wider body of A/B/O works, showing the reader the similarities and differences between the specific story, the standard A/B/O template, and our own world. As we saw in the interlude preceding this chapter, it is these kinds of similarities and differences that allow fanfiction readers and writers to make complex meanings from relatively short pieces, as the stories are read "side by side" with each other, with the originary works, and sometimes even with the reader's own lived experience. In the Omegaverse, even PWP—shorthand for "porn without plot"—stories contain subtle elements of world-building. The world building in "Slick," "Sure to Lure Something Bad," and "Heat: Between You and Me" shows us the different gendered social power structures and resulting sexual scripts that operate in these three versions of the Omegaverse.

In both "Slick" and "Heat: Between You and Me," alphas are clearly the dominant and privileged social group, and all three stories at least hint at omegas being oppressed or marginalized in some way. "Sure to Lure Someone Bad," by contrast, shows us a society dominated by betas, in which both alphas and omegas are relatively rare. But even in this society, alphas are seen as domineering and omegas as submissive, and that submissiveness is viewed negatively:

> Some people got domineering, type-A personalities to go with their thick cocks, and some people got an urge to submit and the ability to self-lubricate. Jensen's done a solid job busting the stereotypes about Omegas . . . ("Sure to Lure Someone Bad")

There are a few things to untangle here. The writer plays with ideas of biology and the social construction of gender. Jensen explicitly makes connections between sexual characteristics and personality traits: "type-A personalities" are linked with "thick cocks," and submissiveness is linked with self-lubrication. A possible equivalent in our society would be something like "women are naturally caring." In the very next sentence, however, Jensen already throws doubt on those links: he himself does not fit within this framework and has actively worked to counter omega stereotypes. He is, as we might say in our world, "not like other girls." At the same time, Jensen never quite challenges the idea that submissiveness is less good than being domineering.

This is a good example of how the way we think and talk about things shapes both those things and how we act, and of how difficult it can be to question and challenge those dominant thought patterns. Continuing with the real-world analogy, we tend to associate "women" with "caring," which in turn frequently translates to "better suited to being homemakers or to caring professions such as nursing." (In cultural studies, we call such linkings of concepts "articulations."[22]) At the same time, caring activities both inside and outside the home are undervalued: housework is largely unpaid, and nurses get paid less than doctors. So, the idea that women are "naturally" more caring takes about three articulations to translate to the economic oppression of women. There are several possible ways to resist this. We could—and this is roughly the strategy Jensen adopts in "Sure to Lure Someone Bad"—say "women might be naturally more caring, but this particular individual woman is an exception and should therefore be allowed to be a doctor rather than a homemaker or a nurse." We could question why qualities associated with femininity, such as caring, are systemically undervalued—feminists have a long history of campaigning for wages for housework, for instance.[23] Or we could question the whole idea of biology determining gender or personal characteristics. The latter two approaches, especially when used together, are much more likely to lead to long-term social change. But they are also much more difficult to implement, especially because we are all deeply immersed in dominant ideas of gender.

In "Sure to Lure Someone Bad," just as in our world, ideas of what the natural characteristics of a particular gender are also translate into ideas about how people of those genders should engage in sex. In the story, alphas are sexually dominant, whereas omegas are sexually submissive. In our world, as we saw in chapter 2, we have dominant ideas such as the "male sexual drive" and the "have/hold" discourse, and both of those are built on the assumption that certain expressions of sexuality are "natural" for people of particular genders. Men are "naturally" more interested in sex and therefore initiate it, and women are "naturally" less interested in sex and more interested in stable relationships, therefore acting as gatekeepers to sex.[24] In "Sure to Lure Someone Bad," ideas about gender and corresponding sexual scripts are so pervasive and all-encompassing that Jensen has clearly internalized them. Challenging them is a struggle for him both personally and socially. Reading this story side by side with our own lived experiences might highlight the kinds of dominant ideas about gender and sex that we ourselves have internalized.

The opening paragraphs of "Heat: Between You and Me" reveal another society with significant power imbalances between alphas, betas, and omegas, but also introduce more complexity. In this world there have been "equality movements" leading to changes in legislation and an improvement in the situation of omegas. At the same time, however, negative stereotypes about omegas still persist, and there are significant geographical and cultural differences in how strictly gender roles are enforced. Jensen's internal monologue early on shows this: "Going from Texas where the stereotypes were encouraged, expected even, to the free-minded LA had been liberating for [Jensen]." "Heat: Between You and Me," then, parallels the successes and failures of feminist movements in Western countries: some gendered restrictions on omegas have been changed or lifted in some locations, some of the time, much as some of the oppression women experience in Western societies has changed, evolved, and been redressed to some extent.

"Slick" presents the most overt and significant power imbalance between alphas and omegas. So strictly are omegas controlled in this setting that Jensen has had to hide his gender in order to be able to work as an actor and live independently. Omegas in this story do not have the legal status of independent persons, and are instead owned by alphas. The revelation of Jensen's gender has dire consequences: "His career's shafted, contracts void, fuck, he's gonna lose the house without an Alpha co-sign—." As an omega, Jensen does not have the legal ability to sign employment contracts, rent a home, or own property. Were he not hiding his gender, he would be completely socially, legally, and financially dependent on an alpha partner.

The extent of the social inequality between alphas and omegas varies significantly between the three stories, but it is there in all three. These variations between authors' interpretations of the setting are key for how readers familiar with the Omegaverse interpret the stories. But A/B/O fans don't just look for similarities and differences between individual stories: much like I did in the last few paragraphs, they compare the Omegaverse to our own world. So, let's see how the inequalities between alphas and omegas might map onto dominant ideas of gender and sexuality, and sexual scripts in Western cultures.

Thinking back to the male sexual drive discourse so prevalent in our culture, we can see that writers of A/B/O stories apply much of it to alphas in the setting. Alphas are to varying degrees written as incapable of resisting omegas in heat. They are socially and sexually dominant and controlling, while at the same time they can lose control—and thus avoid responsibility—when it comes to sex with omegas. The male sexual drive discourse in our world is leveraged in very similar ways: men are seen as active initiators of sex but, especially once aroused, we also see them as out of control and unable to help themselves. This idea is so pervasive that judges and juries in rape trials are frequently swayed by it.[25] But some stories also suggest that alpha dominance and avoidance of sexual responsibility is not universal. The society described in "Sure to Lure Someone Bad" is dominated by betas, and in "Heat: Between You and Me," we are told that there have been equality movements and that these have challenged some of the gender and sexual stereotypes of alphas and omegas. "Slick," on the other hand, presents a view of the Omegaverse where alpha power and the alpha sexual drive are not only unchallenged but actively enshrined in the formal legal structures of the society. As far as we can tell, alphas in this setting have free rein to do as they please with omegas, especially ones they are married to.

The social power imbalances in the Omegaverse also shape the sexual scripts of the societies depicted in the stories. The Omegaverse has six genders, and so we might expect sexual scripts to be considerably more complex and varied. But the focus on the male alpha/male omega pairing predominant in most A/B/O fanfiction effectively reduces the complexity back down to two genders. The resulting dominant sexual scripts feel remarkably familiar to Western audiences, with a few key differences. Much as the male sexual drive discourse applies to alphas in the Omegaverse, the cultural sexual script for men in Western societies does, too: alphas penetrate their partners, and their orgasm determines when sex ends. The omega script is, in turn, in some ways similar to the script for women: omegas are relatively passive, and they are the receptive partner during sex.

But there are also some very important differences. In Western sexual scripts, the default sexual act—the one thing that *counts* as sex, if you will—is penile-vaginal intercourse.[26] In the male alpha/male omega pairing, however, that default act is anal penetration of the omega by the alpha. "Knotting"—the swelling of the alpha's penis to keep it anchored in the omega's rectum for up to an hour (an idea borrowed from canine physiology)—is also a key part of the dominant Omegaverse sexual script. In many interpretations, it has connotations of romantic or emotional bonding, or of ownership. Things get more complicated and start to diverge from the sexual scripts we are familiar with when it comes to who initiates sex and how. Omegas have a mating cycle and periodically go into "heat." Depending on the specific interpretation, this varies from making them slightly more horny than normal to a full-on "fuck or die" scenario. As a result, sex in the Omegaverse is frequently initiated by omegas in heat—though not always voluntarily or through their own agency. And, in parallel with the Western male sexual script, alphas become powerless to resist omegas in heat once aroused, losing all responsibility for their actions. Different interpretations of the setting treat this either as a biological inevitability or as a social construct, which allows readers and writers of A/B/O stories to explore questions about the effects of each. And regardless of whether they are treated as biological or social, these scripts further highlight the social and sexual inequality between alphas and omegas.

With its six genders, the science-fictional Omegaverse holds up a mirror to our own world. Gender, both in A/B/O stories and in the real world, profoundly shapes how we think of and have sex. Readers and writers of the Omegaverse use the strangeness of the setting's gender system to ask questions about how we do gender and, as a result, how we do sex in our own lives. The similarities and differences between A/B/O gender roles and sexual scripts and our own work to make us question the things about gender and sex that we take for granted in our own world—the things we have been told are "natural."

NEGOTIATING DISJUNCTURES IN SEXUAL SCRIPTS

We have seen how the way gender works in the Omegaverse has a knock-on effect on how sex works—on the dominant sexual scripts in the setting. But we also know from sexual script theory that we don't all follow the cultural scripts—and neither do characters in A/B/O fanfiction. In fact, how individual alphas and omegas negotiate their interpersonal relationships and reconcile their own desires with societal expectations are central themes of the genre.

Research on how we do sexual scripts in real life tells us that whenever our interpersonal and intrapsychic scripts don't match the cultural ones, we have three options: we can just go along with the cultural script, we can tell ourselves that we are an exception, or we can find supportive communities that can help us try to transform the cultural script.[27] These kinds of disjunctures between sexual scripts at different levels are also a useful model for how we can start questioning some of the things we have been taught to think of as natural and take for granted when it comes to sex—the kinds of "just sex" that might actually be coerced, or abusive, or outright rape if we stopped to think about them for a moment. With that in mind, we can look at how the characters in our three A/B/O stories deal with what society expects of them and what they as individuals want in their relationships.

We have already seen that in all three stories, Jensen (who is always in the omega role) has either never had or has stopped having sex or relationships with alpha partners. His motivation for this is fairly similar across all three stories: he wants to avoid discrimination and does not want to conform to omega stereotypes of being "lesser" or "under" someone. This choice of (lack of) partner is then Jensen's first way of negotiating social expectations, sexual scripts, and how he personally wants to live his own life.

> What was really annoying was that Jensen had lived his life vehemently opposed to being under anyone, much less an alpha. Being an omega was no cakewalk, while equality movements had changed the laws in the last century, discrimination was still present. Old way thinking and stereotypes still surfaced from time to time and it was hard when someone would off handedly suggest Jensen belonged under someone, under an alpha, even a beta, just under. ("Heat: Between You and Me")

The author of "Heat: Between You and Me" does several things with this passage. First, she gives us an idea of what the dominant ideas of gender and sexuality are in her interpretation of the Omegaverse: there is a social hierarchy that places omegas firmly at the bottom, subordinate to both alphas and betas. At the same time, there have been attempts to resist and reform this social order. There has been legal and social change, but it has not been as extensive and effective as Jensen would like, and stereotypes and prejudice against omegas are still common. We also get Jensen's view of his own position in this society: he feels oppressed and marginalized and has had to actively resist this through choices he makes about how he lives his life. We find out fairly early on in the story that one such choice is Jensen's decision not to engage in sex or relationships with male alphas. Jensen sees himself as not fitting the template of how omegas should behave sexually and in relationships—he tells himself he is an exception from the normal cultural scripts.

The idea of the abstinent omega is central to Jensen's character in all three of our stories. Readers familiar with the history of different Western feminist movements—as many fanfiction readers and writers are—might spot a parallel here with the "political lesbianism" of some feminists in the 1970s. This was the idea that women, regardless of their actual sexual orientation and attractions, should not engage in sex or relationships with men, as men were so culturally, socially, and sexually dominant as to make meaningful consent all but impossible.[28] But, in addition to parallels, our stories also show some key differences between political lesbianism and how Jensen tries to keep control of his life. His abstinence or choice of non-alpha partners is an individualized kind of resistance to the oppression of omegas: it is something he does on his own, not as part of a wider, organized movement. Even in "Heat: Between You and Me," where the author tells us equality movements exist, Jensen is not formally part of one as far as we can tell. Looking at this through a sexual script lens, Jensen is either exception-finding or in some stories possibly even trying to transform the scripts by completely removing himself from them. In stories where he is not completely celibate but chooses non-alpha partners, there may even be more scope for Jensen and his partner to explore and make up alternative scripts.

"Sure to Lure Someone Bad" gives us another reason for Jensen's abstinence:

> Something about Jared makes him yearn to be that idiot again. God, it's not like he doesn't remember all the reasons he decided it was a bad idea, the dangers that accompany surrendering himself like that. Alphas fuck hard, relentless, and Jensen in heat is too pumped up on pheromones and need to recognise when things are getting out of hand. ("Sure to Lure Someone Bad")

There is a contrast here between Jensen's past experience of sex with alphas, his abstinence, and his yearning "to be that idiot again." There is a tension between him clearly having enjoyed sex with alphas in the past but also having had negative, possibly even coerced experiences. His current solution to this is abstinence, but he is finding that restrictive. What Jensen would like to be able to do is enjoy sex on his own terms, without societal or interpersonal coercion. As the story progresses, Jared is presented as an atypical alpha, giving Jensen a sense of safety. Here, Jensen is again finding exceptions to the cultural scripts by positioning himself and his new partner as different or outside the script, without necessarily trying to transform it. Out of the three stories, "Sure to Lure Someone Bad" is the least subversive interpretation of the Omegaverse—it is very much a straight-up "You? Omega. Me? Alpha" kind of story. But even here, the idea of coercive cultural scripts is presented as a problem, and characters have the opportunity to explore possible solutions within the restrictions of the setting.

Of course, what solutions are possible within those restrictions depends on the exact kinds of restrictions—on the precise interpretation of the Omegaverse an author has chosen. This is most visible in "Slick," which takes the Omegaverse to its most extreme conclusions. In this way, it shows how social power structures can have a very immediate and direct impact on our ability to exercise agency and negotiate consent. In the world of "Slick," omegas are socially and legally subordinate to alphas: they are not able to work independently, own property, or sign contracts. At the same time, the biological essentialism elements of the Omegaverse are exaggerated and fully accepted within the society of this setting. For omegas, heat is close to a "fuck or die" situation; by contrast, alphas get a free pass for anything that happens between them and an omega in heat—regardless of whether the omega consents.

Both Jensen and Jared in this story are hiding their gender. Jensen, an omega, does so in order to be able to live an independent life. Jared's reasons for hiding that he is an alpha are less clear. When Jensen agrees to have sex with Jared during his heat in this story, he is under the impression that Jared is a beta. As soon as Jensen discovers that Jared is an alpha, he attempts to withdraw consent, but Jared is able to both physically overpower him and use Jensen's heat against him in order to get what he wants. Throughout the rest of the story, Jared uses Jensen's heat as leverage against him. Notably, on a superficial level, a verbal consent negotiation is conducted, as Jared repeatedly asks Jensen what he wants and reduces Jensen to begging to be fucked. But this verbal consent is made meaningless by the effects of Jensen's heat on his decision making. Jensen repeatedly thinks that "his head [is] a mess," "his mind running in circles." In effect, his heat incapacitates Jensen and makes him both physically and psychologically vulnerable—he is in no fit state to give consent. But even when he is able to clearly verbally deny or withdraw consent, Jared ignores this. Instead, he points to Jensen's physical arousal and takes it as evidence of consent. This plays on the male sexual drive and permissive discourses, both of which link sexuality to nature and physicality: we tend to think of physical arousal as both natural and an incontrovertible expression of desire and, by extension, consent. But in reality, we may well be physically aroused and still not want to have sex with someone.

"Slick" portrays biological essentialism as fully accepted within society, but, at the same time, it also does a lot of work to destabilize that understanding for the reader. The extreme version of the alpha and omega stereotypes would have us understand omegas in heat as seducers, and alphas as helpless and out of control when confronted with that. Think, again, about the male sexual drive discourse and associated rape myths: "She was wearing a short skirt and I couldn't help myself." But even though "Slick" shows us a society that completely accepts this portrayal of alphas and omegas, it also shows us through the characters' experiences that the reality might be rather different. Jensen here is not depicted as a seducer. He has, in fact, done everything he can to avoid going into heat in the first place. His heat does not put him in control; it makes him vulnerable. And far from helpless and just following his urges, alpha Jared is in complete control of both himself and the situation throughout. By the end of the story, Jensen has no choice but to reluctantly conform to the dominant sexual script. He is legally owned by Jared and probably pregnant, leaving him trapped in an abusive relationship. The legal and social framework around him completely negates any agency he might try to exercise in negotiating consent.

"Sure to Lure Someone Bad" offers us a relatively straightforward take on Omegaverse tropes but still allows for some exploration of conflicts between cultural sexual scripts and individual desires. "Slick" shows how cultural scripts can be so pervasive that they completely invalidate individual agency. "Heat: Between You and Me," by comparison, offers the most complex and nuanced approach to conflicts and disjunctures between different levels of sexual scripts. In this story, Jared and Jensen have been living together as friends. As seen in the other stories, Jensen here has made a conscious choice not to pursue sex or relationships with male alphas.

Unlike the other stories, Jared has been respectful of this choice through-out their friendship, even though he has been in love with Jensen for some time. Even when Jensen goes into heat for the first time while living with Jared, Jared chooses to leave rather than force himself on his friend: he is not ruled by his sexual drive, and he is not the out-of-control alpha that the dominant sexual scripts of his society would have him be. But the author also lets us know that this respect for Jensen's boundaries on Jared's part is unusual for the setting:

> "No offence man, but up until last night," Jensen refused to fucking *blush*. "I would have sworn you were a omega." He expected Jared to grin, flush sheepish or roll his eyes like he always did when Jensen teased his lack of alpha drive. ("Heat: Between You and Me")

This scene is set the morning after the two characters first have sex. Jensen here explicitly says Jared has not been acting like a typical alpha: he has not been following the dominant scripts. A rough equivalent in our world would be a man making sure a drunk woman got home safely rather than sexually assaulting her. That may simply seem like the decent thing to do, but there is still a dominant idea in our society that women's drunkenness equals consent, and that men should follow their "natural" sexual drive and take advantage of it. That is certainly what Brock Turner's father wanted us to think when he referred to his son's rape of an unconscious woman as "20 minutes of action." Similarly, in the setting of "Heat: Between You and Me," it would be "natural" and "alpha-like" for Jared to take advantage of Jensen's heat. Jared and Jensen, then, see themselves as exceptions to the dominant ideas in their society.

But Jared and Jensen's friendship and living situation are more than just exceptions in this story. Segregation of unbonded alphas and ome-gas is typical of the sexual scripts in many A/B/O stories. "Heat: Between You and Me" is one of the very early Omegaverse stories, so it is possible that this simply wasn't an established feature of the shared setting at the time it was written. But reading this story within the wider context of the Omegaverse makes this piece of world-building more important and changes its meaning. Jared and Jensen's cohabitation flouts social norms and expectations in what, for two popular actors, is quite a public way. In this way, they may be acting as role models to others, showing them that deviation from the dominant ideas of society is possible, and helping them transform the dominant sexual scripts in their own lives.

Beginning a sexual and romantic relationship with Jared is also personally transformative for Jensen and how he sees himself. He realizes that even though he is now, to an extent, following the dominant script in being in a relationship with an alpha, that can be a part of himself he enjoys and accepts without it necessarily changing his wider role in society or how he lives his life. He reframes his enjoyment of sex with Jared as a "newly discovered kink":

> Not that he would ever admit that out loud just yet but Jensen was man enough to realize in the safety of his own mind that he had gotten off hard while being dominated, it wasn't just his heat alone. It was something to think about later, and suddenly he felt like an ass for every time he belittled an omega happy under an alpha. ("Heat: Between You and Me")

Importantly, Jensen also extends this insight to other omegas in relationships with alphas: their choice of partner does not make them weak or devalue them, just as it doesn't him. His own transformation of the cultural sexual script, then, applies beyond his relationship with Jared. These realizations help Jensen move to a place where he can enjoy sex on his own terms. He is in a relationship where his consent is respected and he knows that this is something he can have. Where previously his only way out of the dominant cultural scripts was abstinence, a happy relationship on his own terms has now become thinkable and achievable for him. He now has more options than just conform to the dominant cultural script or remove himself from it entirely.

"Heat: Between You and Me" is one of the earliest recognized Omegaverse stories. It sets out a lot of the setting's power dynamics, its dominant sexual scripts and how characters in the Omegaverse think about and therefore have sex. At the same time, its characters work hard to navigate around these power dynamics and make consent in their relationship meaningful—that is the heart of the story and the source of its narrative tension. A/B/O fanfiction is often dismissed by parts of the fanfiction community as pornography that romanticizes and glorifies rape, and there are certainly stories that do that. But "Heat: Between You and Me" and the other early A/B/O stories we have looked at in this chapter show that questions of consent in the face of social power inequalities have been central to the Omegaverse since its very beginning—even in stories that do eroticize rape.

One of the early answers to the foundational question of fan studies—why do straight women like to read and write about men banging?—was that removing gender from the equation allows fanfiction readers and writers to explore what truly equal relationships might feel like. But the Omegaverse does the exact opposite: it sets up a society that is even more unequal than ours. So, if not equality between partners, what *is* the attraction of such stories? I would suggest that they give readers and writers a safe space to explore how to deal with the inequalities and power structures we face in our own day-to-day lives. On the one hand, stories such as "Sure to Lure Someone Bad" and "Heat: Between You and Me" highlight how social inequality can translate into power dynamics in relationships, and they offer potential methods for negotiating a way through those power dynamics. "Slick," on the other hand, shows us the dangers of failing to question the dominant ideas about gender, sex, and relationships in our society, to the point where they become so ingrained that alternatives become unthinkable.

PORN, AFFECT, AND THE OMEGAVERSE

Omegaverse stories play around with sexual scripts and highlight the kinds of things we have come to take for granted about gender, sex, and consent. In doing so, they make us question whether these natural-seeming ideas are truly natural, and what they might be doing to our ability to negotiate consent and sexual scripts in our own lives and relationships (Cornel West's demythologization and demystification). But let's face it: A/B/O stories are also very much pornography. (I am using an inclusive definition of pornography here, meaning any material that is either produced with the intention to arouse or enjoyed because it arouses—and Omegaverse fanfiction definitely falls in both those categories.) And as many fanfiction community members have pointed out, some A/B/O stories very openly eroticize sexual violence. As much as "Slick" is the story of a rape and the beginning of an abusive relationship, it is also hot. Don't take my word for it—almost every single reader comment on the story says as much. So how does that fit with the idea of these stories as tools for exploring issues of consent? Or is it "dogfuck rapeworld" after all?

The comment exchanges between the author of "Slick" and readers shed some light on how a clearly pornographic telling of a rape can help readers work through issues of consent—even while getting off on it all. One of the most striking features of these exchanges is how many readers describe the story as both "hot" and "disturbing." dunsparce, for instance, says:

> I am so happy that I am not the only one who is disturbed by the dynamics of this story and you yourself make such a point of how incredibly fucked up this beginning to a "relationship" is. I nevertheless have to compliment you on your porn. It is exquisite and had me squirming because *how* can this fucked-up dynamic turn me on so much?

Readers have very visceral, affective, and yet conflicted reactions to "Slick": They (we) are turned on just as much as they (we) are disturbed, to the point of feeling physical discomfort and, as dunsparce says, squirming. We clearly recognize the situation depicted in the story as a rape and a powerful violation of the omega character, and that gives rise to the discomfort, sometimes even horror, described in the comments. We feel all of this in our bodies before we get a chance to emotionally or rationally process what is going on. And we struggle to make sense of these contradictory physical sensations.[29]

These conflicting affective reactions give us a deeper access to the story and different ways of making meanings from it. One of these meanings is a powerful empathy with the character of Jensen and a deep understanding of what effect the events in the story have on him. Reader ursaring describes this as "the destruction of his person":

This was wonderful in so many ways. It was wrong and I just wanted to rescue Jensen from the destruction of his person but then he presented his ass so pretty and I wanted it to keep happening.

I love stories that dig deeper into ideas and present the not so pretty injustices.

Here, ursaring's reference to stories that try to unpack complex ideas and wrangle with disturbing scenarios shows us the transition from feeling bodily arousal and discomfort to beginning to process the story at an emotional and intellectual level. And that processing goes back to reading the story side by side with the sexual scripts and ideas of what a healthy romantic relationship should look like in our own world. There is a clear sense that what is happening to Jensen is wrong, and both the author and readers repeatedly refer to the events of the story as being no basis for a healthy romantic relationship. Several comments specifically cite how the premise and tropes of the Omegaverse limit characters' agency and ability to seek, give, or withhold consent.

The author also repeatedly notes that it was her intention to explore the extremes of the A/B/O subgenre and what she calls the "absolute biological determinism" of it. Both she and several readers note how, in the context of the society depicted in the story, what Jared does in "Slick" would not be considered rape. Taking this to its logical conclusion, rape in this version the Omegaverse is impossible: an omega in heat—in fact, possibly any omega—is always assumed to be consenting. In this extreme version of the setting, any alpha/omega sex is, in Nicola Gavey's terms, "just sex." The omega's consent does not enter the picture. This complete destruction of Jensen's, or any omega's, agency gives rise to readers' strong, visceral horror. The story is written from Jensen's point of view. We see that he lives in a world where dominant sexual scripts leave him with no meaningful way of giving, withholding, or withdrawing consent. At the same time, we also see and experience his pain and the harm he suffers as a result of these constraints. This highlights the differences between the A/B/O setting and our own world, but also shows some disturbing similarities. It raises questions in readers' minds about the things we have been taught to think of as "just sex" in our own world and how they relate to our internal, embodied, lived experience of sexuality. Which of our experiences that society tells us are perfectly normal sex might we actually have experienced as violations? And what can we do about them?

Readers' reactions to "Slick" and other similar stories are highly complex, frequently ambiguous or downright contradictory. We feel aroused and viscerally disturbed at the same time. We get off on "dogfuck rapeworld" while physically squirming with the discomfort it gives rise to. Far from simply eroticizing rape, Omegaverse stories like "Slick" use their pornographic elements and readers' embodied reactions to them to make us both think about and *feel* the effects of dominant sexual scripts on our own agency and bodily autonomy. Reading these stories, we can start groping our way toward asking what scripts we have been following just because we didn't know that other options might be available. We can start demystifying ideas about what normal sex looks like. We can maybe even start creating new (subjugated) knowledges about how we break out from the dominant scripts in our own lives and relationships.

But the Omegaverse is only one example of how erotic fanfiction, and slash in particular, engages with issues of power and sexual consent: how fanfiction readers and writers actively construct power imbalances in intimate relationships in order to explore their effects on characters. In the next chapter, we turn to another popular trope: arranged-marriage fanfiction. We will see how such stories play around with and highlight the problems with two fundamental institutions of Western society: marriage and the law.

4 REWRITING THE ROMANCE: EMOTION WORK AND CONSENT IN ARRANGED-MARRIAGE FANFICTION

I really love how you describe the tension that builds up in the same time than their relationship gets closer and they start having all these feelings for each others [*sic*], feelings that are maybe unexpected and also unwanted. Because it's always easier to hate someone than get the risk of being hurt, especially considering how much influence Thor has over Loki's life in this situation. I think you have captured that very well.

—POLIWRATH, AO3 COMMENT ON *XVII*

a: Hmm Thor as Loki's queen . . . yes, I think I can work with this (not the anon but yes)
u: what? really??! another fic omg! but yes I'd like to see Thor as the "queen" for once. Loki's always forced to leave his family and kingdom to be Thor's wife and even tho I like this kind of fic I want to see Thor, still young and naive ruling Jötunheim with Loki.

—AMPHAROS AND UMBREON ON TUMBLR

These two comments were posted by readers of fanfiction stories in which the Marvel Cinematic Universe characters Thor and Loki find themselves in an arranged marriage with each other. In the first comment, poliwrath talks about some of the elements that made the story enjoyable for her. Seeing the characters grow closer over the course of the story is one of the key draws of the romance genre, whether in commercially published romance novels or in fanfiction. But what really stood out for poliwrath were the personal and emotional stakes of the arranged marriage set-up: the control that Thor would be able to exercise over Loki and the power imbalance inherent in the relationship. This power imbalance forces the characters to take emotional risks. Successfully negotiating it is the ultimate payoff of the story for both the protagonists and the reader.

The second set of comments is a conversation between two Tumblr users (ampharos and umbreon) about an idea for another similar story, but one in which the power imbalance is reversed. Here, Loki is the one in control while Thor is "young and naive." Look at the words used to describe the less powerful partner in this ostensibly same-gender arrangement: queen; wife. This conversation highlights not only that marriages tend to be unequal arrangements, but also suggests that inequality in marriage is deeply gendered: Wives are worse off than husbands. The marriages that poliwrath, ampharos, and umbreon are talking about are fictional. In this chapter, however, we will see how fanfiction readers and writers use arranged-marriage stories to explore and comment on the institution of marriage—and its implications for consent—in the real world.

The arranged-marriage trope is popular in slash fiction across different fandoms. It is closely related to the extremely popular marriage-of-convenience subgenre in romance novels. Goodreads, a social networking platform for readers, has multiple user-created recommendation lists of romance novels featuring this trope, split into contemporary and more traditional Regency or other Western historical settings.[1] On the fanfiction side, as of May 2019, there are around 11,000 works on AO3 tagged as "Arranged Marriage."[2] In arranged-marriage stories, characters are forced together by circumstances and have to learn not only to live with each other but also, given that these are ultimately romance stories, to love and trust each other despite all that divides them. In fanfiction, arranged marriage is often (though not exclusively) used as a way of bringing together two characters who may be enemies, rivals, or an otherwise unlikely pairing—a "crack ship," in fandom parlance. The fanfiction stories mirror the plot and structure of marriage-of-convenience romance novels, with the protagonists starting out as reluctant strangers or even enemies and, over time, developing increased intimacy with and love for each other. Readers and writers are drawn to the trope by the journey that brings these sometimes antagonistic, almost always unequal characters together: the risks they take, and the personal development they undergo as a result of growing closer.

The parallels between arranged-marriage fanfiction stories and marriage-of-convenience romance novels are interesting. But even more interesting are the differences. Both start out with characters in unequal social positions. Both result in a happily ever after ending. But, as we will see in the remainder of this chapter, the journey is quite different, even where it does hit the same milestones. By rewriting romance tropes, fanfiction readers and writers challenge some of the more problematic elements of the romance genre and explore the impact of power imbalances on romantic relationships and consent.

ROMANCE, WORK, EMOTION

For many of us, romance novels are a bit like Marmite: we love them or we hate them. The genre is vast and diverse, but the basic definition of what counts as a romance novel is a book that focuses on the development of a romantic relationship between two people and that has a happy ending. Historically, the majority of romance novels have focused on heterosexual couples, and the happily ever after ending has been a monogamous marriage. More recently, we have seen a growth in LGBTQ romances alongside the straight ones, and more open "happy for now" endings.[3] Romance novels are a genre largely written by and for women, and in feminist circles they have historically had a reputation of being problematic, to say the least. The bodice rippers of the 1980s certainly do play fast and loose with consent, and even in more modern romance fiction, we sometimes see abusive and coercive relationships portrayed as romantic. When scholars first started to examine romance novels in more detail back in the 1980s, one key question they asked was, "How do these books influence their readers' relationship with patriarchy?" These early romance scholars were unimpressed with what they found.

Janice Radway, the pioneer of romance research, studied a group of romance readers and some of the books they read. One of the things she found was that romance novels tend to show a loving and caring heroine "taming" an initially cold or ambivalent hero. Not only that, but over the course of the novel, the hero barely changed: rather, the heroine learned to read his cold and gruff behavior as an expression of affection. And because the heroines of their favorite books did this, romance readers learned to reinterpret what was happening in their own day-to-day lives and relationships as well. Tania Modleski, looking at Harlequin romances, found a similar trend: the romance heroine is transformed into someone who can accept and adapt to patriarchy, but the hero remains untouched.[4]

Both Radway and Modleski were working in the 1980s—the heyday of the bodice ripper. Romance novels have evolved significantly since then, and scholars have developed a more nuanced understanding of the genre in addition to recognizing that it is not monolithic. Plus, as Pamela Regis remarks in her 2010 call to reevaluate the romance novel, *A Natural History of the Romance Novel*, readers do not all take away the same messages from these books. They are free to reject what scholars perceive as the core messages and make their own meanings instead.[5] In a more recent work, romance scholar Catherine M. Roach (who writes romance novels under the pseudonym Catherine LaRoche) also points to the positive impact romance novels have on their readers: they are safe spaces for imaginative play where readers can think through the challenges they are faced with in their day-to-day encounters with patriarchy. Because they offer a guaranteed happily ever after (or happy for now), romance novels offer readers pleasure, an escape from reality, and imagined healing. The takeaway message of contemporary romance novels, says Roach, is a simultaneous and contradictory "You can't fight the patriarchy/You must fight the patriarchy."[6]

As a romance writer, Roach also identifies some key elements of the romance narrative. The most notable of these are risk and hard work: the heroine is entitled to happiness with the hero, but that happiness can only be achieved through taking risks and putting in the work to build the relationship. Unfortunately, her analysis often glosses over how exactly this hard work is performed and how risk is taken by characters in romance novels. Here, earlier romance scholars such as Radway and Modleski offer a more in-depth and persuasive account. The hard work is largely done by the heroine, and it mostly transforms her rather than the hero. She gets to know him, learns to read his behaviors, moods, and feelings, and ultimately adapts to them. Roach herself admits that even at the end of the romance novel, the "alpha hero" remains deeply embedded in patriarchy, made only safe for the heroine by his love for her: the changes to his life are limited and private; the changes to hers are fundamental and public.

Feminist theory offers us some useful ways to conceptualize what is going on in a romance novel when the heroine learns to read and reinterpret the hero and transforms herself to build and sustain a relationship. The idea of emotion work, first proposed by sociologist Arlie Russell Hochschild,[7] is particularly relevant here. Emotion work is the work we do to manage our feelings to bring them in line with what society expects of us. Emotional labor, a term that has come up often in recent years, is a similar and related concept: it is labor we do in the workplace to manage our own feelings and those of others. When a salesperson builds rapport by asking you about your day or validating your choice of product ("That one's my favorite!"), that's emotional labor. Emotion work happens in private contexts, in our interactions with our friends and families rather than in the workplace. Both emotion work and emotional labor are feminists' ways of recognizing that dealing with feelings—both our own and those of others—requires effort and is therefore a type of work. Both these types of work are also distinctly gendered: women typically perform more emotion work than men, and work in jobs where more emotional labor is required.[8]

The concept of emotion work has evolved over the years, but there are some key elements. It can be work we can do on ourselves to either inhibit or modulate our own feelings to make them appropriate to a particular situation: suppressing our anger at our mother-in-law for the sake of maintaining peace at a family gathering, or thinking of sad things to make ourselves cry at a funeral. It can also be work we do to make others feel better: comforting a child, listening to someone tell us about their problems and sympathizing. To be able to do these things, we also need to be able to read and interpret others' and our own emotions correctly—this, too, is a type of emotion work.[9]

All of these activities sound remarkably similar to what romance novel scholars are telling us a romance heroine does to build and maintain her relationship with the hero. She interprets the hero's actions—even sometimes his violent and aggressive behavior—as motivated by love. She listens to his problems. Her attention to his needs transforms him (or perhaps just her and the reader's interpretation of him) from gruff, cold, and indifferent to caring and loving.

Pamela Regis also notes that this kind of taming, healing, or transforming trope is very much a feature of marriage-of-convenience romance novels. In Georgette Heyer's *A Civil Contract*, Regis says, "Jenny heals [Adam] through her careful attention to his needs and wants: she manages his households with determined efficiency, she learns the duties of being the lord's wife."[10] I read Regis's analysis of *A Civil Contract* long before I read the book itself. In fact, when I eventually did pick up the novel I didn't immediately make the connection—but as the plot unfolded it began to sound very familiar. In hindsight, Regis rather undersells the extent of the emotion work Jenny does for Adam here. In one memorable scene, Adam returns from a trip of several days, late in the evening, to find that Jenny just so happens to be still up and have his favorite comfort food prepared. What Adam does not know—but the reader finds out—is that Jenny has been staying up late and having the servants make the same meal every single night he has been gone, for just this eventuality. Jenny is not only doing emotion and domestic work to look after Adam's emotional needs here—she is also actively hiding the fact that she is doing it. And although Adam is, to an extent, dependent on Jenny's money to salvage his estate, she, as his pregnant wife, is far more dependent on him for shelter and a place in society. This may make us wonder: Would she be doing this if she had a meaningful choice? Using emotion work as a lens to analyze romance narratives allows us to start asking questions about how such work is divided between the partners, and how it may be affected by power imbalances in the relationship.

Given that we are already wondering if Jenny would be doing all this emotion work for Adam if she were not dependent on him, this raises a second question: Would she be having sex with him if things were different?

Emotion work theory and research in this area let us think through this, too. We know from research that a high degree of emotion work within a relationship leads to partners feeling better about the quality of their relationship.[11] We also know that there is a sexual aspect to emotion work. We tend to think of romantic relationships (including, and perhaps especially, marriages) as necessarily also sexual relationships: we see sex as the key difference between close relationships that are romantic and ones that are not. But not all of us want the same amount of sex in a relationship all the time. We know that women who want less sex than their male partners often try to increase their own desire. This is a kind of emotion work aimed at maintaining the relationship, but women who do it also frequently experience it as a one-sided effort.[12] Here, dominant ideas that we *should* be having sex with our romantic partners, and sometimes ideas about *how much* sex we should be having, shape how we act in our relationship. They nudge some people to agree to, or sometimes even initiate, more sex than they might actually want. So, where and how do we draw a line between emotion work, including sex, that we willingly and happily do for our partners, and emotion work and sex that we perform because the dominant ideas in our society tell us we should? At what point do we move from "this is 'just sex' I'm having with my partner" to "this is actually, in some ways, coerced"? And does that line move if there is a power imbalance in our relationship—for instance, if we are financially or otherwise dependent on our partner?

Marriage-of-convenience romance novels like *A Civil Contract* rarely pursue the full implications of these questions: we never do find out if Jenny would be doing all of the things she does for Adam if she had other options. Our commonsense understanding of marriages and relationships also rarely raises those questions, as we tend to take dominant ideas of how relationships work at face value. But fanfiction readers and writers reuse the tropes and trappings of the marriage-of-convenience genre in their own arranged-marriage fanfiction. And, in doing so, they find clever ways of highlighting and exploring these questions, as we will see over the course of this chapter. In the process, they make us question and challenge a range of social institutions such as marriage and the law and their role in undermining individual consent.

THOR/LOKI ARRANGED MARRIAGE

When you search AO3 for stories tagged as "arranged marriage," one of the most popular pairings of characters for the trope is the Marvel Cinematic Universe's Thor and Loki. In the Marvel movies, the two characters, although not related by blood, are raised as brothers. They also have an adversarial relationship, or at least they do in the early MCU films. So, fanfiction writers who want to write romantic stories about Thor and Loki generally need to make some changes to the setting to make them work as a pairing. The arranged-marriage trope, frequently combined with changes to the originary material to do away with the sibling relationship, then allows fanfiction writers and readers to explore Thor and Loki as a romantic couple.

To better understand what arranged-marriage fanfiction did with Thor and Loki, I followed a similar process to the one I used for selecting Omegaverse stories to analyze. I immersed myself in Thor/Loki fanfiction for a while, and paid particular attention to those tagged "Arranged Marriage." I used popularity metrics such as the kudos count (i.e., the number of readers who "liked" the story) to pick five influential stories and looked for common themes and key differences in those. Finally, I narrowed my selection down to two complementary stories for in-depth readings: "Bride" by themantlingdark and "XVII" by stereobone. Like the Omegaverse stories analyzed in chapter 3, these two stories reflect some of the key thematic trends I found in my wider reading.

Both "Bride" and "XVII" depart from the MCU canon by having Thor and Loki grow up separately rather than be raised as brothers.[13] This is relatively common in Thor/Loki stories: it allows writers to avoid depicting a sexual and romantic relationship between adoptive siblings. (It is also worth noting, however, that a minority of stories do retain the characters' canon relationship as brothers and explore its impact on their romantic relationship.) In both stories, Loki is intersex, as are all Jötnar, and his gender presentation tends toward the masculine but is sometimes ambiguous. This is a common depiction of Loki in fanfiction. It goes significantly beyond MCU canon and leans heavily on elements of Norse mythology (some of which are also present in the Marvel comics). Fanfiction Loki in general has considerably more feminine qualities than MCU Loki, and his use of magic is frequently contrasted with Thor's prowess as a fighter and thus feminized.[14] Loki's gender and gender presentation, then, highlight his otherness. Both stories are told predominantly from Thor's point of view, though in "Bride," the point of view shifts to Loki on a few occasions. It is the structure of the marriage arrangements that makes these two stories a complementary pair for analysis. In "XVII," Loki leaves his home to marry Thor and secure a lasting peace between Jötunheim and Asgard. This is by far the more common premise of Thor/Loki arranged-marriage fanfiction. Conversely, and unusually for this pairing, in "Bride"—the story inspired by the conversation between ampharos and umbreon quoted at the beginning of this chapter—it is Thor who must leave his home to marry Loki. As in many other arranged-marriage fanfiction stories, these marriage arrangements, alongside other factors, mean that there is significant inequality between the partners at the start of each story.

THOR/LOKI AND THE INEQUALITIES OF MARRIAGE

Marriage is one of those social and legal institutions that we tend to take for granted and not think too much about. Little girls are raised to imagine their dream wedding. The standard social scripts for how romantic relationships should work generally culminate in marriage (much like the happily ever after of the romance novel). Most of us go through our early (and increasingly later) life simply assuming that one day we will find the right person and marry them. Marriage is so fundamental in our society that a significant proportion of the effort of LGBTQ+ activists over the last twenty years has (rightly or wrongly) gone into achieving "marriage equality"—ensuring that people of the same gender can marry. Although many of us accept the idea marriage as a societal norm, feminist theorists have long been drawing attention to some of its more problematic aspects as a social institution.

A key part of the feminist argument against marriage is that it constructs and legitimizes gendered social inequalities. The history of marriage law and reform shows us that we have been able to counteract some of these, but others still remain. English common law, for instance, established a doctrine of coverture that was enforced well into the late nineteenth century: upon marriage, a woman lost the right to own property or enter into legal contracts, making her completely dependent on her husband. And many Western countries had de facto or de jure exemptions for marriage in their definition of rape—that is, a wife was always assumed to be consenting to sex with her husband—until the late 1990s.[15] These are particularly egregious examples of how marriage law has historically made women subservient to men, but in many ways, they remain part of the mythology of marriage to this day; there are still plenty of pop culture references to sex as a wifely duty, for instance.[16] Such dominant ideas about what a wife is and how she should act are one of the ways in which gendered inequalities are cemented in marriages. We are all too busy picking out wedding dresses and imagining our happily ever after to see that entering a marriage may actually perpetuate and exacerbate existing gendered inequalities in our relationship.[17]

Some fanfiction readers and writers are clearly aware of the problems with the institution of marriage, and how it can be a tool of oppression. We can see this in the comments quoted at the start of this chapter, where ampharos and umbreon discuss the idea of Thor being the "wife" for once. It is implied that this would be a more vulnerable position to the one he is usually cast in, and their comments indicate a desire to explore the implications of that scenario for the character. So, how *do* arranged-marriage fanfiction stories depict marriage as an institution, and how do they tackle the inequalities it produces, reproduces, and amplifies?

Historically, marriage has been a gendered institution (and even today there are those who would prefer it remain between one cisgender man and one cisgender woman), and that has been a major source of inequality. Marriage both thrives on and reproduces gendered power differentials. But that is not the case in arranged-marriage slash fanfiction stories: there, both partners are men, so if we believe early fan studies scholars, those relationships should be perfectly equal[18]—and yet, they are not. As we saw from the reader comments quoted at the beginning of this chapter, the inequality of arranged marriages is precisely what attracts readers and writers to the trope. There are, however, still gendered elements to how Thor and Loki are written in arranged-marriage stories, and they interact in important ways with other sources of inequality in the relationship. So, let's have a look at what arranged-marriage fanfiction writers do to put the inequality back into the same-gender relationships they explore.

In trying to answer the foundational question of fan studies, early fan studies scholars Patricia Frazer Lamb and Diana L. Veith showed how, in *Star Trek* fanfiction, Kirk and Spock both have feminine and masculine qualities, resulting in much more androgynous characters than they were in canon. Kirk is a leader (masculine) but also emotional (feminine), and Spock is logical (masculine) and virginal (feminine).[19] We see this kind androgynous characterization of both Thor and Loki in many arranged-marriage stories, too. Thor is most obviously feminized in "Bride," where even the title associates him with the feminine role in a heterosexual marriage (i.e., the wife). In this story, Thor is both younger and, in contrast to most fanfiction about this pairing, physically smaller than Loki. Loki is heir to the throne of Jötunheim, but Thor's arranged marriage with Loki will stop Thor from inheriting the throne of Asgard and it will pass to his younger brother instead. Reading this side by side with our knowledge of the real world, there is an analogy here with male-preference primogeniture: if the eldest child is a girl, she can inherit *only* if she has no younger brothers. For the reader, this feminizes Thor further—he is being treated as a woman would be in our world. He is also forced to leave his home and join the family and household of his husband. While getting dressed for the wedding—in a white gown, no less—Thor is explicitly described as feeling "feminine" and "delicate," particularly compared to the frost giants surrounding him. Conversely, Loki in this story has a reputation for coldness and cruelty (typically masculine qualities, especially in the romance genre), and this adds to Thor's apprehension about the marriage.

Janice Radway breaks down the structure of the romance novel into a number of typical elements, the first being the destruction of the heroine's social identity.[20] This is what happens to Thor in "Bride": he has to leave his home and family and make a new life for himself. This casts him in the traditional role of the romance heroine, while Loki's coldness and cruelty mark him out as a romance hero. Fanfiction readers approach arranged-marriage stories with their frequently extensive knowledge of the tropes and genre conventions of marriage-of-convenience romance novels. So, when a writer clearly flags which of the protagonists here is the "hero" and which is the "heroine," that gives readers certain expectations of how the story will go: by the end, Thor will have taken risks and done hard (emotion) work to tame Loki and transform him into a loving and caring husband.

These gendered inequalities within the context of the arranged marriage also highlight the structural inequalities of the marriage itself: Thor leaves behind his own family to formally become part of Loki's, and the settlement of property and titles is a key aspect of the marriage arrangement. Thor becomes both materially and socially dependent on Loki.

But the characterization of Thor as feminine heroine and Loki as masculine hero is complicated in "Bride" in two key ways. First, Loki himself has feminine characteristics as well as masculine ones. He is physically smaller than other Jötnar, and is known for his intelligence, gift for magic, and manipulativeness—all characteristics more frequently associated with femininity. He is described as both beautiful and handsome. Unlike the typical romance novel hero, Loki's body is also not represented as cisgender and male; rather, he is intersex.[21] Second, on several occasions, factors that make Thor feel feminine and vulnerable in the context of his wedding are shown to have gender-neutral or masculine associations in other contexts. So, when Thor objects to wearing the white wedding "dress," his mother, Frigga, explains that Loki will also be wearing a white gown. When Thor balks at the expectation to be nude for part of the wedding ceremony, Frigga again recontextualizes this for him by pointing out that in Asgard Thor is frequently nude—for instance, in the public baths. By complicating characters' gender coding in this way, arranged-marriage fanfiction writers establish the first difference between these stories and the romance novel tropes they are loosely based on. Similarities and differences with the originary material are a key way for fanfiction readers and writers to make meaning. Small tweaks like these begin to highlight some of the more problematic elements of romance tropes and allow fanfiction readers and writers to explore, negotiate, and challenge them.

"Bride" is unusual in Thor/Loki arranged-marriage fanfiction in that it casts Thor as the heroine—the opposite arrangement is much more common. Part of the inspiration behind the story (as we can see in the Tumblr conversation quoted at the start of this chapter) was to explore how the usual dynamic changes when the roles of the protagonists are switched. "XVII," by contrast, is representative of the typical approach to Thor/Loki arranged-marriage stories. In this story, Thor is in the more powerful position in the relationship: he is the heir of Asgard, and Loki has to leave his family and make a life for himself in a realm strange to him. But much the same as in "Bride" and many other Thor/Loki arranged-marriage stories, both Thor and Loki are ambiguously gendered in "XVII." Loki in this story is physically beautiful, intelligent, and manipulative. He is also a magic user. These are feminine-coded qualities that, taken together, might make the reader think of Loki as a witch. On the other hand, Thor is too nervous to eat at their wedding feast (something more typically associated with women), and Loki is a muscular, competent fighter (masculine-coded qualities).

In these ways, the authors of both "Bride" and "XVII" rework their central characters—men in the originary work—into more androgynous versions of themselves. To an extent, this would fit with early fan studies ideas about leveling power imbalances in relationships. But the tropes borrowed from romance novels, the structure of the arranged marriage in each story, and other choices the writers make provide us with new sources of power imbalances and inequality.

A popular way for fanfiction authors to introduce such power imbalances and play around with them is the physical size difference between characters. We see this in both "Bride" and "XVII," where Thor does not meet Loki before the wedding and expects him to be a giant like other Jötnar. This causes him significant anxiety:

> The Frost Giants that Thor sees on his way through the palace leave him shaken.
>
> I'm going to be torn apart, he thinks. ("Bride")

Even in "XVII," where Thor, in many ways, has the upper hand in the marriage arrangement, he is concerned about Loki being a frost giant:

"This is your duty," [Frigga] says. "I know it is hard, my darling, but it is for the good of our realm."

Thor knows that, he does, but it doesn't stop it from being hard. Jötun are not an ugly people by any means, but they are giants. And they are cold. Thor doesn't see how anyone can expect him to marry one. He doesn't say this, but his mother seems to sense it anyway. ("XVII")

In both stories, once he actually meets Loki, Thor is palpably relieved to find him human-sized, and his idea of the power imbalances between them begins to shift. Thor is generally the physically bigger and stronger character in MCU fanfiction, but in both "Bride" and "XVII," Loki is a competent fighter, again balancing the two characters out somewhat. Loki is also a powerful magic user, and often uses his magic and intelligence to manipulate those physically stronger than him and get his way. Differences in age and experience also contribute to inequality in the relationship, especially in "Bride." The author specifies in the author's notes alongside the story that Thor is 18 and Loki is 27 in this setting. We can see this age difference reflected in the characters' behaviors, attitudes, and even physicality throughout the story. Even after he finds out that Loki is not a giant, Thor here continues to be intimidated by his physical size and muscular build. Loki is also more sexually experienced than Thor. The author of "Bride" uses physicality, age, and sexual experience to further cement Thor's status as the less powerful partner in the marriage—as the bride, wife, and romance heroine. The author of "XVII" only gives us physical size as a significant differentiator to mark Loki as less powerful and more feminine. Because this story follows the more usual pattern of casting Loki as the heroine, we, as readers familiar with Thor/Loki arranged-marriage fanfiction, need less convincing.

But in addition to gendered elements, the arranged-marriage trope lets readers and writers think about the power implications of factors external to the relationship. Political considerations of dynastic marriages, marriage laws and customs, and characters' relationships with their families all play a role in "XVII" and "Bride" and, to varying degrees, initially tip the power balance in favor of the character cast as the "hero." In "XVII," Loki's marriage to Thor means that he is no longer considered a Jötun: he will not be able to return to Jötunheim or see his family ever again, and he is completely dependent on Thor for everything from basics like food and shelter to emotional support. Conversely, in "Bride," although Thor has to leave Asgard and is somewhat dependent on Loki, his parents repeatedly reassure him that they will continue to visit and support him. So, the consequences of a failed marriage for Loki in "XVII" are much greater than those for Thor in "Bride," and this in turn exacerbates the power differential.

Fanfiction readers and writers interpret these stories side by side with their knowledge of romance novel tropes and of the history of marriage laws and customs in Western cultures. The similarities and differences, then, highlight some of the ways in which marriage as an institution is inherently unequal. Marriage here is not a happily ever after ending but rather the beginning of a process of negotiation, with significant personal and social risks attached to failure of such negotiation. Whereas scholars such as Catherine M. Roach see risk-taking in the name of love as a key element of the romance novel, the risks in arranged-marriage fanfiction stories are often taken out of a lack of options instead. The personal, social, and legal consequences of failure—a life spent in an unhappy and loveless marriage, social isolation, or loss of legal status and the financial means for survival—are simply too great. In the face of these risks and power differentials within the relationship, the characters' options are limited.

There are, then, clear power imbalances in Thor and Loki's marriage in both "Bride" and "XVII." They are caused by factors internal to the characters (physical size and strength, age, experience) as well as exacerbated by ones external to them (marriage customs and access to material and emotional support outside the relationship). And even though characters are given androgynous characteristics, the overall picture of their relationship is still one of inequality. At the outset of the relationship, Thor has considerably more power than Loki in "XVII," and Loki has more power than Thor in "Bride." Given that we think of marriages as inherently sexual relationships, does the less powerful character in these stories—the "heroine"—really have a meaningful choice when it comes to consummating the marriage, or having sex with their spouse more generally? How are such power imbalances negotiated within the relationships in the two stories, how is the happily ever after ending achieved, and what does this mean for sexual consent?

EMOTION WORK AND THE HAPPILY EVER AFTER

If there is one feature that defines the romance novel, it is the happily ever after ending. Readers have watched the hero and heroine take risks and work hard. They have cheered for the heroine as she has tamed the hero. And now, finally, they can relax, safe in the knowledge that our protagonists have come together in a mutually loving, happy relationship—perhaps even a marriage. In marriage-of-convenience stories, of course, the marriage itself has already happened, but the heroine's hard (emotion) work has transformed it from a purely transactional arrangement into true love. The young bride (having relatively little power in the relationship, and possibly even being outright dependent on her new husband) has become skilled at reading the hero's moods. She has worked out how to please him (recall Jenny sitting up every night with Adam's favorite meal, waiting for him to return) and, by transforming his gruff personality, she has achieved happiness and fulfillment in marriage. But even the most charitable of romance scholars agree that the hero's transformation is limited at best. In many cases, he doesn't change at all: rather, the heroine (through emotion work) changes her understanding of him. And regardless of who exactly changes, the main cause of that change is the heroine's emotion work.

The happily ever after ending is important, but for many romance readers, the process of getting there is just as crucial. The expectation of the happily ever after ending is what gives us strength and helps us feel safe enough to go through the story's trials and tribulations alongside its characters. Both romance novels and fanfiction are a bit like comfort food in this way: we read them because they are familiar and predictable. Therefore, arranged-marriage fanfiction, as a close cousin of the marriage-of-convenience romance novel, has to retain that happily ever after ending. As we already know, however, fanfiction is an exercise in repetition with a difference. Minor tweaks of the originary material can lead to major changes in tone, mood, and meaning. And although they can't change the ending, fanfiction authors *can* change how we get there. So, what kinds of tweaks do they make to the development of the relationship between the protagonists, the risks that must be taken, and the emotion work that must be done for us to get that happily ever after?

Emotion work continues to play a vital role in negotiating the multiple and layered power differentials between Thor and Loki in both "Bride" and "XVII." It allows them to create a much more equal dynamic over the course of the story. But there is a key difference between arranged-marriage fanfiction stories like "Bride" and "XVII" and more traditional marriage-of-convenience romance novels, and that is in who does the emotion work. In romance novels, it is the heroine (or less powerful character in the relationship) who does the heavy lifting, but in both "Bride" and "XVII," the bulk of the emotion work falls on the more powerful partner (or hero): Thor in "XVII," and Loki in "Bride."

The first time Loki does emotion work in "Bride" is shortly after the wedding ceremony at which he and Thor meet. At the wedding feast, Loki tries to put Thor—still too nervous to eat or engage in much conversation—at ease:

> Loki has kept his hands largely to himself. He has leaned over a few times and set his hand at the small of Thor's back, pointing out the members of court with a nod of his head and breathing the best gossip about them into Thor's ear. He brushed his fingers over Thor's when he took his goblet from him to refill it with wine, but Thor wasn't certain if it was meant to be friendly or if it was incidental. They danced, but Frigga had held Thor closer when she was teaching him the steps than Loki held him as they spun through the hall. ("Bride")

Thor is surprised by Loki's considerate behavior, given that he has a reputation in this story for being cold and even cruel. And yet here he is, making an effort to set at ease the younger Thor and mitigate the culture shock he might be experiencing. When the two newlyweds are finally alone on their wedding night, Loki uses his magic to shapeshift into Aesir (or more human-like) form instead of the frosty blue skin of the Jötnar. In this way, he empathizes with Thor's position as insecure outsider and provides some reassurance and familiarity for him. This is also the first time Thor acknowledges and reciprocates Loki's emotion work:

> Loki shifts his skin to match his spouse's and Thor pauses in his pacing to stare.
>
> "Which do you prefer?" Loki asks.
>
> "The night does not compete with the day. As a Jötun you are fairest among your own folk, and as an Aesir you are lovelier than mine."
>
> "They are all our people now," Loki reminds him, and Thor nods and smiles.
>
> Loki shifts back into his blue skin, pleased with the lad's pretty speech, and pulls out a seat for Thor. ("Bride")

Loki is proactive about making Thor feel more comfortable, and this is significant: it shows that he clearly understands that Thor is feeling vulnerable and isolated. The gesture of shape-shifting is intended to reduce that feeling of isolation. It is also important that Loki asks for Thor's opinion and gives him a choice. This empowers Thor to make decisions in the relationship very early on. At the same time, however, Thor is clearly not entirely comfortable with making this choice, as he does not want to offend Loki. He retreats into diplomatic and deliberately flattering language, effectively passing the decision back to Loki. So, even though Loki's emotion work goes some way toward making Thor feel more at ease, the power imbalances between them are still there. The fact that Thor declines to make a choice shows that he may not be feeling safe yet to do so. That in turn suggests that he may also not quite feel safe to say "no" to Loki on any other topic, including sex—and if "no" is not an available option, then "yes" is not a meaningful response. This scene, then, underlines the power imbalances in the relationship and their implications for consent, but also shows the characters taking the first tentative steps toward breaking down those inequalities.

Conversely, in "XVII," it is Thor who does the majority of emotion work. He tries to read Loki, understand how he feels, and make him feel at home in Asgard, particularly early on in the story. At the same time, Loki is studying Thor and trying to understand him, but he makes no move to initiate conversation or work on their relationship. Loki expresses a desire for safety and privacy, and Thor gives him space by leaving their quarters during the daytime and bringing him food rather than making Loki join the family at mealtimes. There is a stark contrast here between Thor's behavior and an observation romance scholar Janice Radway makes about romance novel heroes and heroines:

> Because she cannot seem to avoid contact with him despite her dislike, the heroine's principal activity throughout the rest of the story consists of the mental process of trying to assign particular signifieds to his overt acts. In effect, what she is trying to do in discovering the significance of his behavior by uncovering his motives is to understand what the fact of male presence and attention means for her, a woman.[22]

So, in romance novels, the heroine cannot avoid the hero and therefore has to find a way of living with him. A reader who is familiar with the romance novel trope would realize that Loki in "XVII" is expecting to have to play the role of the heroine who has to find a way to accommodate the hero in her life. Loki is watching Thor carefully and testing the limits of any freedom he may have in this new situation. But where the heroine in a romance novel would then use any knowledge gained this way to provide emotional comfort and support for the hero in the hope of transforming him, in "XVII," Loki finds every wish he expresses respected, and Thor gives him as much space as the social and legal restrictions on the two of them allow. As a result, Loki does not need to account for and come to terms with Thor's presence in his life the way a romance novel heroine would. In "XVII," Loki could potentially avoid Thor forever. It may not be a pleasant existence, but it is definitely an option he has and a way for him to exercise agency. And although Thor may not be happy with this, he recognizes that he has the upper hand in the relationship and does his best to give Loki as much space and agency as possible within the constraints they both find themselves in.

Thor also tries to find other ways to improve Loki's life, largely by taking cues from his behavior to find activities Loki might enjoy. The first breakthrough in their relationship comes when Thor, having seen Loki read the single book he has brought with him from Jötunheim, takes him to Asgard's library. As the relationship develops, Thor and Loki reach a level of mutual trust, and the emotion work involved in deepening and sustaining it evolves to being shared equally between them. Even though the inequality of the marriage arrangement is never erased, and formally Loki remains dependent on Thor, Thor repeatedly demonstrates that he views his husband as an equal. At the end of the story, Loki has the choice to dissolve the marriage and return to Jötunheim or stay in Asgard with Thor. He now feels confident in his own status and power as Thor's husband, and so he freely chooses to stay and negotiates a reopening of the border between the two realms. Thor's emotion work has transformed the relationship to one where Loki is a loved and respected equal who feels able to make choices freely.

As readers, then, we get our safe happily ever after. But in arranged-marriage fanfiction stories, the way we reach that happily ever after ending and the ways that characters overcome obstacles differ significantly from familiar romance novel tropes. Here, it is the partner with more power in the relationship (i.e., the "hero") who takes on the bulk of the emotion work and the responsibility for negotiating and leveling the inequalities of the relationship. In a romance novel, it would be the heroine who has to struggle to understand and accommodate the hero, but here the partner with less power in the relationship has emotion work done for them. We start with a deeply unequal relationship, but, through persistent emotion work, the partner with more power levels the playing field, builds trust, and minimizes inequality in the couple's day-to-day interactions.

All of this is great. But because marriages are still thought of as sexual relationships, the genre conventions of both fanfiction and romance demand that these unequal marriages be consummated, raising two questions: To what extent and how can such a consummation be consensual? And what does it take to make "no" a safe enough option so that any "yes" given is genuinely meaningful?

MARRIAGE CONSUMMATION

Marriage consummation is a recurring feature of arranged-marriage fanfiction stories. This is hardly surprising: arranged-marriage fanfiction borrows from both romance novel and wider fanfiction tropes, and both of those often feature sex scenes. In the romance novel, a sex scene is frequently used to mark the happily ever after ending, with the couple consummating their relationship in a mutually loving and respectful way. But in both marriage-of-convenience romance and arranged-marriage fanfiction, the marriage (and therefore its consummation, especially in romance novels) comes before the love and trust. And the relationship at this stage is often so deeply unequal as to make any consent given by the less powerful partner meaningless. The heroine of the novel or the partner cast as the heroine in a fanfiction story is at this stage materially dependent on the hero. They are under pressure to make the relationship "work" by any means necessary; therefore, refusing to consummate the marriage is not really an option. Marriage-of-convenience romance novels frequently gloss over this. In *A Civil Contract*, for instance, Jenny and Adam consummate their marriage without much comment from the narrator, and by the time they actually find their happily ever after, Jenny has given birth to their first child.

The consummation scene is also a key genre convention in arranged-marriage fanfiction. Sometimes it works in the same way as the climactic sex scene in romance novels: it is toward the end of the story and marks the happily ever after ending. In these cases, most of the relationship development happens between the wedding and the consummation—frequently an extended period of time. This is already a significant departure from the scenario depicted in *A Civil Contract*. But in many arranged-marriage fanfiction stories, the consummation scene is still fairly close to the beginning of the story, as in the marriage-of-convenience romance novel. Unlike in romance novels, though, these scenes are rarely glossed over. They receive quite a lot of focus and attention, both in the text itself and in paratexts: author's notes, archive tags, and comment exchanges between readers and writers. What fanfiction readers and writers say about these scenes shows how they think about complex issues around consent, power, and inequality in intimate relationships.

Of the 10,200 works tagged "Arranged Marriage" on AO3 in July 2019, 1,630 also use a tag related to at least one of the following: "Consent Issues," "Non-Consensual," or "Rape/Non-Con." The primary function of tags on AO3 is to organize content: to allow readers to easily discover the kinds of stories they would like to read. But fanfiction readers and writers also use tags for other purposes (as we will see in more detail in chapter 7). Tags related to consent allow readers who may be upset by stories dealing with consent issues to avoid them. But they also allow the writer of the story to flag something important: "I know that this is not romantic, and I am exploring the consent issues deliberately." Unlike Jenny and Adam's story, where consummation simply had to happen and was glossed over, these stories draw attention to the problems of marriage consummation in such arranged and unequal relationships.

I read five highly popular and influential Thor/Loki stories in depth before settling on "Bride" and "XVII" as the two detailed case studies. Of those, consummation was a central feature in four, and premarital sex had a similar function in the fifth. In one story, the consummation scene was clearly and deliberately presented as an outright rape, and in another three (including both "Bride" and "XVII") the characters actually discuss consent and the arranged and unbalanced nature of their relationship in the text. They openly acknowledge that consummation is expected, both legally and culturally. Fanfiction readers and writers, then, use both the stories themselves and the paratexts around them to highlight how marriage consummation—which we tend to see as "normal"—is at least potentially problematic and coercive in some contexts. And because the sources of inequality between the partners are both legal and cultural, this recontextualization of marriage consummation as potentially coercive allows readers and writers to question both the legal and cultural foundations of marriage as an institution that they may have been taking for granted.

But as much as arranged-marriage fanfiction highlights some of the problems with romance novels, it, too, is still very much part of the romance genre. The reader demands and the writer wants to deliver a happily ever after. The traditional romance route to it—the glossing over coercive consummation practices and the heroine's emotion work to tame the hero—is barred because once we have seen the problems with that approach, we can't unsee them. So, this is where we find out exactly how much emotion work it takes on the part of the partner with more power in the relationship to create the space for their spouse to say "no," and thereby make any "yes" meaningful.

"XVII" is very direct in its treatment of the issue of consent and consummation. In this story, when Thor (who has more power in the relationship) meets Loki and finds he is not a giant, he is immediately attracted to him. Once the wedding feast is over and the couple are alone in their room, Loki makes it clear that he expects the marriage to be consummated, but also that he is not enthusiastic about this prospect. When Thor refuses on the basis that Loki would clearly not be a willing participant, Loki is both confused and angry. As Thor's husband, Loki's position in Asgard is extremely precarious: he has left his home and family, is unable to return to them for political reasons, and he is materially and socially dependent on Thor. Being married to Thor is his only way of maintaining both social status and material necessities in his new life, but that marriage is precarious at best if it remains unconsummated: Thor could choose to annul it at any moment, potentially leaving Loki destitute. Loki continues to be cold and hostile as a result, not trusting Thor's intentions in refusing to consummate the marriage, but eventually accepts that he has some agency within their relationship. This exchange clearly highlights the at least potentially coercive nature of marriage consummation, as Loki's options are extremely limited. As far as he can see, he can reluctantly accede to sex with his new husband, or he can refuse and risk being cast out. Even when Thor tries to go off-script, Loki understandably suspects underhand motives. And so rather than "just sex" that we accept as part and parcel of being married, consummation here becomes "potentially rape."

There is a similar, though far less confrontational, conversation in "Bride." This time it is Loki (again, the partner with more power in the relationship) who makes it clear that Thor's consent matters and that he will not insist on consummating the marriage unless Thor is willing. Thor, while nervous, does prove willing, though the language used in reaching their mutual agreement to have sex is rather formal and carries connotations of meeting expectations, both social and each other's:

> "I would not have you unwilling," Loki says, turning toward Thor. "I'm not a monster. This marriage was no more of my making than of yours. We needn't punish each other for it."
>
> "It is no punishment," Thor answers. "It is a gift, is it not? I mean to keep my promises. I would not rob my husband of the pleasures of his wedding night."
>
> "Nor I mine," Loki agrees, smiling. ("Bride")

Thor's phrasing here reflects and to an extent legitimizes the dominant idea of marriage as a sexual relationship: their wedding has generated an expectation that they will have sex with each other. The word "rob," in particular, implies a sense of obligation on Thor's part and an entitlement for Loki. We also see this kind of obligation/entitlement dynamic in "XVII," where Thor reflects that wedding night rape is "not an uncommon practice, but certainly no practice Thor would ever take part in," while Loki concedes that he "did not expect [Thor] to be so honorable." In "Bride," the expectation of intercourse is ultimately met, but this only happens with mutual agreement. Loki's final response in the preceding exchange picks up on the implications of Thor's phrasing and the word "rob" and puts them on equal footing: it acknowledges that the entitlement and obligation apply in reverse, too. Thus, each of them has the same rights and expectations of his husband, but equally each of them can also refuse.

Marriage is both a cultural and legal institution, and so there are also cultural and legal aspects to consummation. In the Western legal context, there are consequences for nonconsummation that may put one or both parties at risk. In many US states, for instance, nonconsummation is grounds for annulment, which has different legal implications to divorce. In the United States, annulment may have a significant negative impact on an immigrant spouse's application for permanent residence, putting them at risk of deportation. Of course, we don't know what the marriage laws of Asgard and Jötunheim look like, but fanfiction readers and writers construct and read these stories side by side with an understanding of the marriage laws in our own world. The legal complexities of the arranged marriages in the stories frequently form part of the worldbuilding. In some of the other stories I read before choosing "Bride" and "XVII" for detailed analysis, the consequences for nonconsummation ranged from immediate magical death at sunrise to being disinherited (Thor) or flogged to death (Loki) for treason and filial disobedience. In "XVII," when Loki balks at Thor's refusal to consummate their marriage with an unwilling partner, it is out of concern for his own safety: a consummated marriage gives him a degree of status and protection. As the partner with far less power in the relationship, the risks for Loki of a failed marriage are enormous. As a traditional romance "heroine," this risk would give him the impetus to try and make the relationship work—and, in "XVII," it pushes him to bring up the issue of consummation. Far from being a risk taken willingly and in the name of love, as romance scholars like Catherine Roach suggest, the risks here are clearly ones the characters are forced to take for lack of other options and, potentially, under threat of death.

For the less powerful partner in each of these marriages, then, refusing to consummate the marriage is not really an option. This is why we see Loki in "XVII" push for consummation even though he does not actually want to have sex with Thor. And that, of course, is not meaningful consent. So, what *would* it take to enable the partner with less power in a relationship to genuinely, meaningfully consent to sex if they wanted to? The answer we get from these stories is emotion work: emotion work performed by the partner with more power, to build the relationship, establish trust, and, above all, create a space where a refusal to consummate would be heard, respected, and meaningful. This emotion work continues throughout the consummation scene, where Thor in "XVII" and Loki in "Bride" both try to ensure that consent is continuous, and that their partner could say "no" at any time.

In "Bride," the conversation between Loki and Thor once they are alone in their room quickly becomes an equal exchange, both of them working toward building trust and rapport. But once they agree to consummate the marriage, it is Loki who works to read Thor's feelings, calm his nerves, and provide reassurance. In "XVII," after Thor's initial refusal to consummate his marriage with an unwilling Loki, the couple grow closer over the course of weeks, largely due to Thor's efforts to make Loki feel more comfortable and at ease with him. Their first kiss is triggered by a scuffle following a trip away from Asgard during which Loki is verbally assaulted by another character. The kiss leads on to the consummation of their marriage, but throughout this scene Thor continues to consciously read Loki's reactions and feelings, and verbally or through gestures asks for consent on several occasions:

> It gets Thor hot all over, and suddenly he has too many clothes on, and this isn't going fast enough.
>
> Thor leans back and Loki looks angry, not because Thor is kissing him but because he's stopped. The look disappears once Thor pulls him upright and leads him to the bed. Loki understands then what's happening. He keeps himself pressed very close to Thor, like he can't stand to be pulled away from him right now. Thor doesn't move them onto the bed though, not yet. He searches Loki's eyes, tries to figure out what he's thinking, what he's feeling. He made a promise before, and he means to keep it, despite the lust that grips him tight all over and threatens to drive him crazy. ("XVII")

Thor is here actively controlling his own desire. He is both the more powerful partner in this relationship, and has so far shown much greater desire for sex than Loki. But he is actively thinking about the power dynamic and consent issues, and trying to ensure that Loki has the space to deny or withdraw consent if needed. He is carefully reading Loki's facial expressions and reacting and adapting to them.

This provides a stark contrast to what we know about emotion work and sex from our own world: that women who want less sex than their partners actively work to increase their own desire.[23] Readers and writers of fanfiction are likely aware of this from their own lived experience. Rewriting both the romance trope and their own lives in a way that makes the partner with more power and a greater desire responsible for regulating their emotions and ensuring consent is meaningful is a radical act. Whereas potentially coercive heterosex is frequently constructed as "just sex" in Western culture, fanfiction readers and writers challenge and problematize it as "potentially rape." Consent can only be made truly meaningful through emotion work and a conscious effort to negotiate and manage power inequalities: "no" has to be an equally available option. The responsibility for this work falls squarely on the shoulders of the partner with more power in the relationship.

What we are beginning to see from both arranged marriage and Omegaverse fanfiction is that not all slash fiction is about equality, as early fan studies scholars thought. At least some slash is a literature of *negotiated inequality*. It asks (and tries to answer) this question: if we live in an unequal world, in a society that structurally treats some of us as lesser in various ways, what can we do in our individual intimate relationships to negotiate and minimize those inequalities? And if those inequalities affect our ability to consent, then how do we get to a place where our consent can be made meaningful again within the coercive structures we live in? Fanfiction tropes such as arranged marriage and the Omegaverse highlight and make visible (or, in Cornel West's words, demythologize) the inequalities around sex that we have been taught to believe are "natural." They make the fault lines of consent visible and ask us to think again about how much of our experience is "just sex" and how much is in some way nudged or outright coerced. So, if fanfiction readers and writers ask these questions in their fiction, to what extent do they also translate the answers to their understanding of real-world sexual violence and rape culture? In the summer of 2015, as we will see in the next chapter, I had a most unwelcome and unexpected opportunity to find out.

5 BLURRED LINES: FROM FICTION TO REAL LIFE

So when the Hawks face elimination late in the play-offs, about 50 people get together on the internet and write porn for the hockey gods. And we are all fully aware that it's completely ridiculous, but it does some things:

- it keeps us too busy to freak out too much between games
- it gives us the sense that we're doing something, that this is somehow under our control and we're doing our bit
- and it builds community.

I repeat, we're all fully aware that it's completely ridiculous. But it's our particular brand of completely ridiculous, in our corner of the internet, and we like it.

Fast forward 1,000 years. We've had an apocalypse, a dot com bubble or six, the usual. The data archaeologists are working hard on the scraps they can salvage from the early 21st century. They really wish we'd used stone tablets.

And today is a very special day for the data archaeologists because, out of the wreck of the Tumblr data center, after years of painstaking work, they've finally managed to (mostly) piece together something remarkable. "Gay porn hard" repeated like an incantation. The "hockey gods" invoked and asked for mercy, for intercession, words upon words offered in sacrifice. (Words are precious in the society the data archaeologists live in; they are bits of people's souls.) They haven't managed to trace all the links, all the offerings, because some lead to the Archive of Our Own, a mythical and vast temple of knowledge no one even knows the location of.

This surely is the high priesthood of a global religion. A religion so powerful, that had its followers so enthralled, that they would literally carve out pieces of their soul and offer them up for sacrifice. The data archaeologists are both fascinated and horrified. What awe-inspiring gods these must have been to warrant such barbaric sacrifice.

I wrote this in an email to my partner on May 31, 2015. The Chicago Blackhawks had just made the Stanley Cup Finals, and on game nights I was waking up at 4 a.m. to check the score. I had stumbled into ice hockey fandom through Hockey RPF a couple of years earlier. Hockey RPF was my fannish home, where I made friends, wrote stories, recorded audio performances (podfic) of other people's work, and just generally hung out. The focus of much of Hockey RPF fandom during those years was the Patrick Kane/Jonathan Toews pairing and the wider Chicago Blackhawks team.[1] Kane and Toews are both "franchise players"—incredibly skilled, drafted high in consecutive years by a then struggling team, and the core (both as players and as marketing vehicles) of what became an epic rebuild and turnaround that would lead to three cup wins over six years.[2] Their narrative made for good stories.[3] And then the Hawks went and won the cup—the third one for both Kane and Toews. The hockey gods had smiled on us, had accepted our offerings—and we were going to thank them with even more porn! The summer of 2015 was going to be so much fun.

On August 6, 2015, Patrick Kane's name trended on Twitter, and the first reaction of many of us in the Hockey RPF community was, "What has he done *now*?" Kane has a reputation for what is euphemistically known as "off-ice issues": public behavior that does not fit with his NHL-marketed image as a franchise player and role model. As Hockey RPF fans, we had been fully aware of various incidents, and even worked some of them into our stories. A drunken weekend in Madison, Wisconsin, in 2012 provided a convenient narrative "rock bottom" from which the fictionalized Patrick Kane in our stories could grow and emerge a better human being. (It is interesting to note which off-ice issues we picked to build narrative beats on, and which we glossed over. There were allegations, for instance, that Kane had attempted to choke a woman at a party during that Madison drinking spree.[4] And there was a well-known incident of Kane and teammate Adam Burish using blackface at a Halloween party. Somehow, neither of these ever made it into fanfiction.) For a while there, if you squinted enough, art and life seemed to converge: the media controversy died down, and the Blackhawks were able to portray Kane as having matured and refocused on hockey. Still, seeing Kane's name trend on Twitter in the middle of summer, when it wasn't his day with the Stanley Cup, was enough to ring the alarm bells, bringing back memories of all those off-ice issues for many of us. We wish we had been wrong. The story, first reported by a local paper in Kane's hometown of Buffalo, New York, was that he was under investigation for rape.[5]

Many complex things happen in a fandom when a "fave" turns out to be "problematic."[6] The community of Hockey RPF fans had collectively invested thousands of hours in Patrick Kane (both the ice hockey player and the fictionalized character) as a fan object. We had written stories, created fan art, watched games, memorized stats, made offerings to the hockey gods. We had even used the fictionalized versions of Patrick Kane and Jonathan Toews to explore our own feelings and experiences—in some cases, as survivors of sexual violence. In the wake of the rape allegations, the sudden rift that opened up between Kane's public persona, the character that the RPF community had lovingly created from that, and what now looked to be a much darker private person created a deep moral conflict: could we justify such an emotional involvement—either past or future—when the fan object was, at the very least, potentially a rapist?

It took three months for the rape allegations to come to some sort of resolution. During this time, Kane kept public appearances to a minimum. Despite the media attention surrounding the ongoing rape investigation, the Chicago Blackhawks made the decision to let him participate in training and games early in the 2015–2016 season.[7] On November 4, 2015, the DA's office announced that Kane's accuser had stopped cooperating with the investigation, and two days later the investigation was formally closed without charges being filed.[8] Almost immediately after this, the NHL and the Chicago Blackhawks resumed their use of Kane in promotional material and events; for instance, through prominent coverage of his then ongoing point streak.[9] Throughout all of this, the messy reckoning with Hockey RPF's problematic fave continued. Friends fell out, stories were deleted from archives, people quietly dropped out of the community. One common thread ran through all of this: a desire to live by feminist values, even where it might be personally painful. For me, this reckoning became a unique opportunity to understand how fanfiction readers and writers think about issues of consent, sexual violence, and rape culture in real life.

REAL PERSON(A) FICTION IN THE WIDER FANFICTION CONTEXT

RPF, almost by definition, bridges the divide between the real and the fictional. Most of us know that what we see publicly of celebrities is not the actual person. Celebrity is performance and textual construct: we piece together a star image from what we see celebrities do, what we hear them say, and what various media tell us about them.[10] But there is still a real person behind all that, and RPF readers and writers thrive on imagining what that person might be like. How much of the private person bleeds into the public performance? How do the publicly known events in a celebrity's life affect their private life and relationships? In our modern media environment, there is an endless flow of information about our favorite celebrities—from paparazzi shots to their own Instagram and Twitter posts.[11] So when we write RPF, we carefully pick and choose which of these pieces of information we accept into our version of the celebrity, and which we discard. Unlike fanfiction based on fictional material, RPF does not have an official "canon"—a complete originary work that describes events in the characters' lives that we all agree happened. Rather, RPF fans collectively construct our own canon through active choices of which events we pay attention to and which ones we discard. In this process, the authenticity of any given piece of information about the celebrity is not necessarily the deciding factor as to whether we accept or discard it. Rather, as fan studies scholar Kristina Busse argues, fan writers "shape and alter the star to their own specification, making him more interesting, intelligent, or vulnerable, and thus more desirable, identifiable, and available."[12] For most of Hockey RPF fandom, Patrick Kane had been very drunk in Madison, but he hadn't actually choked anyone, or worn blackface.

So, the RPF canon is a collectively created patchwork of pieces of information—some more authentic than others. This also means that not everyone's canon is quite the same, but a core still emerges. Readers and writers can use deviations from that core as a storytelling tool, just like Omegaverse fans use slightly different interpretations of the A/B/O setting in their meaning-making processes. Importantly, the pieces that form the core canon can also be rearranged in many different ways to tell many different stories. Different authors can shape real-life celebrity Patrick Kane's drunken spree in Madison into anything ranging from an expression of grief at an early play-off exit to a teachable moment and turnaround point for the fictionalized character Patrick Kane. Hundreds and sometimes thousands of different fanfiction stories based on the same "facts" circulate and are enjoyed alongside each other. Fanfiction readers and writers, then, are very aware that the limited information available can be interpreted in a variety of ways and, as a result, that we are not reading or writing about the real private person, or even about the celebrity public persona, but rather about a fictionalized character we have collectively created using bits of both.[13] Sometimes, however, as one fan of Hockey RPF put it in relation to the Kane rape allegations, "the RP gets in the way of the F": the real-life celebrity does (or is alleged to have done) something so irreconcilable with the fictionalized version that no amount of mental compartmentalization on the part of fans can paper over the cracks.[14] And, in the case of Patrick Kane, this point of friction between the real and the fictional is where fanfiction readers and writers' engagement with real-world sexual violence, rape culture, and questions of consent became most evident.

RAPE: CULTURE, PERCEPTION, AND THE LAW

To understand how the Hockey RPF community engaged with the rape allegations against Patrick Kane, it is helpful to examine how media and the law shape our ideas of rape, sexual violence, consent, and what a victim looks like. Feminist theorists and activists have long argued that we live in a rape culture: a culture that enables, supports, minimizes, and renders invisible sexual violence; that finds excuses for perpetrators and blames the victims.[15] The law—both legal definitions of rape and how they are put into practice through the criminal justice system—plays a significant role in rape culture. The feminist sociologist and legal theorist Carol Smart argues that the law holds a special status in our society: it is able to completely disregard other ways of seeing things and define its own version of the truth.[16] (Or, using the framework of French philosopher Michel Foucault, the law is a special discourse with its own regime of truth, and it has the power to dismiss and invalidate other discourses.) So, for instance, if a woman claims a man raped her, and he is found not guilty in court, then legally, a rape was not committed. Regardless of the woman's experience, as far as the law is concerned, she was not raped. The law here is the arbiter and ultimate knower of whether a rape occurred. This is made worse by the popular perception of the law, which gives it even more power than it already holds. In strict legal terms, for instance, a "not guilty" verdict means that the prosecution could not prove to a jury "beyond reasonable doubt" that the accused committed a crime. Yet, in common parlance, we tend to take "not guilty" to mean that the accused did not commit the crime. Thus, the law becomes the arbiter of whether a rape occurred not only in criminal court but also in the court of public opinion, allowing society to systematically dismiss and disbelieve victims. Carol Smart goes as far as arguing that traditional feminist campaigns for legal reform only strengthen the law's power in this regard. She shows, for instance, how successful campaigns to reform legislation have led to even worse outcomes for women when the law has been put into practice.[17] Instead of calling for legal reform, she suggests that we should decenter the law in feminist political action and find other ways to tackle key feminist issues including sexual violence.

There are some important ways in which the law's special ability to determine "truth" hurts victims and survivors of sexual violence beyond the aforementioned example. One is the way the criminal justice system handles forensic evidence collection from rape victims, commonly known as "rape kits." Rape kits are seen as decisive for the outcome of rape trials both among legal professionals and in the public imagination. A never-ending series of crime shows tell us that they can identify the unknown attacker and prove in court (beyond reasonable doubt) that a rape has occurred and who the rapist was. By and large, law enforcement professionals (police, prosecutors, etc.), medical professionals (forensic medical examiners, forensic nurses, and forensic scientists), and even victims of sexual violence who report their experiences to the police believe that rape kits are vital to securing a conviction. In reality, the majority of rape cases, even those that get to court, are not about the stranger who sprang from the bushes and needs to be identified. The majority of rapists are known to their victims, and the question a jury needs to answer (beyond reasonable doubt) is not "Who did it?" or even "Did sex happen?" but rather "Was the sex that both parties acknowledge happened consensual?" Forensic evidence can rarely shed light on that. Because of the widespread belief that it is vital, however, victims of sexual violence continue to be subjected to what is an extremely invasive, demeaning, and traumatic process in the immediate aftermath of the trauma they have already experienced.[18]

Both among the general public and in courtrooms, we also see a high degree of victim blaming. Even in the wake of #MeToo, a range of rape myths still persist. If she was wearing a short skirt, she was asking for it. If she hadn't been drunk, she would have been able to protect herself. Oh, women always put up *some* token resistance. If she didn't scream, kick, fight, or try to run away, she must have really consented.[19] These myths and judgments are even harsher when it comes to victims and survivors who are not White, who are men, who are queer.[20] And defense lawyers frequently leverage such rape myths in court.[21]

These are the legal and cultural attitudes to sexual violence that we are all steeped in. They are dominant ideas that shape how we see victims and rapists, and whom we deem guilty and innocent. Feminist theorists and campaigners have worked very hard over decades to shift some of these perceptions (most recently with the #MeToo campaign), but in wider society, rape myths have proven remarkably resilient. This is the backdrop against which the Hockey RPF community had to grapple with the idea that one of our favorite fan objects was allegedly also a rapist. So, how useful were the insights that fanfiction readers and writers create about consent in their fiction when it came to dealing with sexual violence in the real world?

HUMANIZING THE LAW: THE COMPLAINANT

Patrick Kane's career has not suffered as a result of either the rape allegations of 2015 or his previous off-ice incidents. For Hockey RPF fans, however, the events of the summer of 2015 became impossible to either incorporate into the shared and collectively constructed canon or completely discard and ignore. The real Patrick Kane created an unfillable gap in the story of the fictional Patrick Kane while at the same time inextricably tying the fictional character to issues of rape culture. Later in this chapter, I will address the implications of this for the community's fiction output and other fannish engagements with Kane as a fan object.

But Kane was not the only person of interest in the Hockey RPF community's attempts to process the allegations. Hockey RPF fans looked for and discussed information about two other key figures: the complainant (i.e., the woman who had made the allegations against Kane), and the district attorney (DA) in charge of the investigation. But the DA was a much less public figure than Kane, and the complainant had the right to anonymity (which community members repeatedly advocated respecting). So, a group of people who are used to building thoroughly fleshed out characters and elaborate stories from a handful of pieces of information did just that. They[22] took what little they knew about the individuals, combined it with what they knew of rape culture, the law, and the experiences of sexual violence survivors, and used this to think their way through likely scenarios, motivations, and possible outcomes. In the process, they gave a human face to the operation of the law and created complex, nuanced new understandings of rape culture. They questioned the special, privileged status of the law in determining truth and opened up new spaces for alternative ways of seeing what might have happened and how the power of the law might enable it to trample over survivors and let perpetrators get away.

The first key figure Hockey PRF fans tried to engage with and understand was Kane's accuser. There is of course a key difference between the accused and the accuser in a rape case, particularly a high-profile one: the accused is named and in the public eye, whereas the complainant has the legal right to anonymity. This significantly affects the public's perception of them. Accused and accuser are also systematically treated differently by the criminal justice system. In 1993, British feminist academic Sue Lees dubbed what happened to rape victims in courtrooms "judicial rape." The victim, she said, was "put on trial, her reputation attacked, her credibility doubted."[23] This process makes the complainant relive the original violation and even makes it worse while letting perpetrators get away. Despite a range of reforms since then, there is much evidence to suggest that little has improved in practice.[24] Another asymmetry in the treatment of accuser and accused is that the accused generally has a defense lawyer or team working directly in their interest. The complainant, however, does not. The prosecution represents the state, and the complainant is relegated to the role of witness for the prosecution, for which they get little to no preparation. Many cases do not even get as far as the courtroom; police and prosecutors only take forward the ones most likely to secure a conviction—that is, those that most closely conform to rape myths about who is a deserving victim, who is a likely perpetrator, and what a rape looks like. To determine this, they probe a complainant's character, criminal record, and even past sexual experience. Again, the complainant ends up as the one being put on trial.[25] This asymmetrical treatment is made even worse when the accused is a public figure who, in many cases, can garner public sympathy, whereas the accuser remains anonymous for their own protection. The protection here is a double-edged sword: the rape complainant is faceless, voiceless, and anonymous, and this generally allows public opinion to side with rape myths and prejudice: *He is such a nice boy. She must be out for his money.* But this is where the Hockey RPF community was able to change that narrative. In the absence of information about the complainant, they brought other sources of information to bear on their evaluation of the case. Most notably, these included accounts and experiences of rape survivors within the community, and a feminist understanding of rape culture and the inadequacies of the criminal justice system.

There were several prominent survivor voices within the community. These individuals shared their own experiences of sexual violence and encounters with rape culture and, where applicable, the criminal justice system. A key focus of these discussions was the rape kit process. Once it emerged that Kane's accuser had undergone a rape kit exam, community members repeatedly highlighted the physical and emotional invasiveness of this process. One anonymous commenter said:

> One thing I think tumblr and a lot of people need to learn about is rape kits. The false information being spread of them is painful. But the biggest thing, is if you haven't been through one or know someone who has (and they have told you about them), they are one of the most demeaning, invasive, embarrassing, and cold things to go through. I speak from personal experience. Anyone who goes through one of those who wasn't raped . . . yeesh. (anonymous comment submitted to pidgey's Tumblr)

Rather than speculating about Kane's accuser as a person, this commenter instead brings their own experience of a rape kit into the discussion. They describe it as "demeaning, invasive, embarrassing, and cold," and crucially compare it to the experience of rape itself. This opens up a new space where, even without knowing anything about the complainant as a person, we can think about her lived experience and emotions: what is it like to be raped and then to have to face the cold invasiveness of the criminal justice system? Is it likely that someone would volunteer to undergo this unnecessarily?

In more common RPF practice, readers and writers use snippets of a celebrity's public persona to construct elaborate stories that give them a rich and complex internal life. In this way, they make the celebrity more vulnerable, more relatable, and more human: they suggest an insight into the possible thoughts, feelings, and experiences of the person behind the persona. This is impossible to do for an anonymous complainant in a rape case, who has no public persona. Instead, the Hockey RPF community here used external pieces of information, such as what a rape kit exam actually feels like, to fill the gaps and humanize Kane's accuser. The anonymous commenter here argues that no one would voluntarily submit to a rape kit examination if they had not already undergone the more traumatic experience of being raped. This serves to strengthen the credibility of the accusation in the face of a rape culture which systematically disbelieves victims and survivors of sexual violence. We know one tiny piece of information about Kane's accuser: that she had a rape kit done. We weave that in with a much more detailed account of what that feels like, and so the nameless, faceless, voiceless complainant suddenly acquires an inner life that we can relate to and empathize with. This empathy is produced not through an emotional attachment to the victim herself (as is the case for the emotional attachment to Kane's celebrity persona) but through the intertextual meanings brought into the discussion. Hockey RPF community members read the commenter's account of her rape kit experience side by side with developments in the investigation. One effect of this reading is that, like a more conventional RPF character, the complainant here is humanized despite the relative lack of publicly available information about her. Commenters map their own experiences of the criminal justice system onto her, giving her a face and a voice composed of those elements.

Hockey RPF community members also extensively discussed their understanding of rape culture and its prevalence in the criminal justice system in relation to the Kane allegations. We can see these in the following tags added to a Tumblr post:

> Tags: BASICALLY reblogging because "neutrality" isn't really neutral in rape culture and I've picked my side I'm done with Patrick Kane now (tags on a Tumblr reblog by snorlax)

Here, snorlax argues that because we live in a rape culture, there is no way to be neutral when it comes to sexual violence: you are either on the side of the accused or the accuser. Any notion of "neutrality" is tantamount to siding with the (potential) rapist, because of the way it plays into how rape culture leads us to systematically disbelieve victims and excuse perpetrators. Many community members expressed similar sentiments with specific reference to the complainant and how she was likely to be treated by the press, the criminal justice system, Blackhawks fans, and the general public. Like the account of the rape kit experience, these comments also generate a relatable inner life for Kane's accuser. They invite the reader to consider the emotional and material impact that the rape and the resulting experiences are likely to have on the complainant.

The discussion of the Kane rape allegations in the Hockey RPF community was highly emotionally charged. Community members had a personal emotional stake in their involvement with Kane as a fan object. Despite this, they foregrounded the complainant throughout their discussions and found ways to generate empathy with her rather than Kane. Even in the absence of a face and public image, they used RPF techniques to humanize the alleged victim. This stands in stark contrast to rape culture, where—particularly in high-profile cases like this—media reporting and public debate urge us to empathize with the alleged perpetrator and dismiss and disbelieve the complainant. Community members highlighted the failings of both culture and the law when it comes to supporting victims and survivors of sexual violence. They brought in their own experiences of sexual violence and encounters with the criminal justice system to help each other better understand what might have happened and what was at stake. For those who did not have such experiences, these discussions opened up new ways of thinking about the law and its role in sexual violence and rape culture. These ways of thinking were based not on legal definitions and principles but rather on internal realities and subjective experiences of sexuality and sexual violence. Fannish and social engagement, the personal and political, were inextricably intertwined in these discussions.

HUMANIZING THE LAW: THE DA

The Hockey RPF community, then, counteracted rape culture by humanizing Kane's accuser. But they also engaged extensively with another prominent figure in the case: Frank Sedita, the district attorney for Erie County, New York, whose department was in charge of the investigation.

Unlike the complainant, Sedita was a public figure in the sense that he was an elected official, but he did not have the mass appeal of Kane. During the investigation, however, he was considerably more visible than either Kane or his accuser, as Kane made no public statements on the allegations and minimized his public appearances. Sedita, on the other hand, made a number of public statements throughout the case as there was intense media interest. These included his first public statement after news of the investigation broke, in which he expressed concern for Kane's reputation,[26] and an in-depth interview after announcing the closure of the investigation, in which he cast doubt on the complainant's credibility.[27]

In the Hockey RPF community's discussion of the Kane allegations, Sedita became the human face of the law. In an attempt to make sense of the outcome of the investigation and his statements, community members researched Sedita's background and record as a prosecutor and interwove this information with their understanding of rape culture and the criminal justice system. This worked much like the textual processes that turned the star Patrick Kane into the fleshed-out, complex fictional character Patrick Kane, and that gave an internal life and voice to the anonymous complainant. But the community could not agree on a single core "canon" for Sedita. Rather, three different versions of him emerged from this process. Some members of the community were satisfied with the thoroughness and integrity of the DA's investigation and this served to convince them of Kane's innocence. Another set did not question the thoroughness of the investigation or the impartiality of Sedita and the police, but raised issues of rape culture and the inadequacies of the criminal justice system to justify their continued belief in Kane's guilt. Finally, a significant part of the community questioned Sedita's integrity and motivation as part of a wider discussion of the failings of the criminal justice system in sexual violence cases. Using RPF techniques to give Sedita an inner life and establish him as a fully realized character allowed community members to put a human face on the law and its operation. These three different versions of the DA—thorough, impartial, and competent; impartial, but steeped in a wider rape culture; and openly biased—mirrored three different approaches to the criminal justice system.

This exchange between an anonymous commenter and oddish, posted on Tumblr shortly after the closure of the investigation, shows the first two versions of the DA:

Anonymous: 1) The DA is known for being tough on rape suspects. 2) It's not about different accounts from two people in the room. They are not arguing about whether the sex was consensual or not. There was no sex. The evidence doesn't support the woman's story. So, you are twisting the facts to support your point of view. . . .

oddish: The evidence doesn't disprove her story, nor does it definitively confirm it. If evidence comes to light that she made a false charge, fine. But the current evidence does not establish such a claim as fact, and it does not disprove her claim of being sexually assaulted.

But let's be honest—the problem is less about knowing the full facts of the case (which will never even have a chance to happen) than it is about how society reacts on the basis of the limited facts known. That so many people incorrectly identify "not being charged" as "being innocent" and are willing to attack a woman who claims to have been assaulted is a problem on a disgustingly grandiose scale. . . . (anonymous commenter and oddish)

The anonymous commenter uses   the DA's reputation for "being tough on rape suspects" to bolster the case for Kane's innocence. The implication here is that if Sedita is indeed "tough" in sexual assault and rape cases, then the investigation conducted by his department and the police must have been thorough and the resulting lack of evidence for Kane's guilt must mean that Kane is, in fact, innocent. The commenter also interprets the DA's final statement to mean that no sexual contact took place between Kane and the complainant to begin with, thus completely ruling out the possibility of rape. As in any other RPF story, this commenter selects some of the available information about Sedita's background and track record as a prosecutor and uses it to create a more fleshed-out character. They put a relatively small piece of information with relatively little factual underpinning—Sedita's reputation as a prosecutor—into the wider context of the of the story of the Kane rape allegations. At the same time, this commenter also discards other potentially relevant pieces, such as the DA's political ambitions.[28] In this way, they create a fictionalized Sedita who is beyond reproach, and this characterization also becomes the face of the law: if Sedita is tough on sexual assault and a good prosecutor, and no charges were filed, then Kane must be innocent. These arguments ultimately hinge on accepting the law's special status in defining truth, and on the idea of "innocent until proven guilty," in particular. Following this line of reasoning, a lack of evidence of guilt, or the existence of "reasonable doubt," becomes evidence of innocence. The legal system gets a human face in the form of the DA, who is tough on sexual violence and beyond reproach, and this bolsters the power of the law even further.

By contrast, oddish's response to the anonymous comment foregrounds the experience and expertise of RPF writers and readers in constructing multiple versions of events from the same information. She applies this expertise to the outcome of the Patrick Kane rape investigation. Without questioning the DA's credibility and integrity or the outcome of the investigation, oddish highlights that multiple valid interpretations of the available information are possible, and that there is no certainty about Patrick Kane's innocence or guilt. She also goes a step further: she openly critiques the way a lack of evidence or "reasonable doubt" in rape cases is generally taken to mean that the accused is innocent. Here, oddish's criticism of the anonymous commenter's views becomes a critique of wider rape culture. She sets aside the issue of Sedita's character in favor of focusing on systemic issues of rape culture and the law.

Other community members who took a similar approach conceded that, within the narrow framework of the criminal justice system, it may be appropriate to prioritize the accused's potential innocence over other considerations. But they also argued that in other contexts, it was reasonable and appropriate to make judgments based on the preponderance of evidence and the balance of probability, or even on wider considerations such as the statistical improbability of a false rape allegation. These arguments make nuanced distinctions about when the presumption of innocence and the "beyond reasonable doubt" standard of proof are and are not appropriate. The key distinction here is what possible consequences there could be for the accused from a particular judgment. A judge or jury have the power to imprison or otherwise punish the accused; for these community members, then, it was appropriate to require a higher standard of proof in a court of law. Here, the accused is innocent until proven guilty beyond reasonable doubt. But an individual's private opinion of Kane's guilt or innocence does not have such power, so deciding whether you believe Kane or the complainant on the balance of probability is appropriate here.

Just as oddish brackets the question of the DA's integrity, then, she and other proponents of this view bracket the special status of the law in determining what is and is not true. These commenters acknowledge that in certain contexts the law does—and perhaps even should—have that power. At the same time, these Hockey RPF community members challenge the universal applicability of this special status of the law. Instead, they make nuanced distinctions based on the relative power of those making judgments about guilt or innocence. These arguments maintain the special status of the law to some extent, but they go a long way toward denying its power to determine an official version of events beyond the very narrow context of the courtroom and the criminal justice system. They bracket the legal version of events as one possible interpretation; a necessary evil, perhaps. But they also argue for a wider understanding of reality that is more sympathetic to victims of sexual assault. They accept that ideas such as "innocent until proven guilty" and the necessity for guilt to be "beyond reasonable doubt" are there to protect us from the overreach of the law. In that sense, letting potential perpetrators go free is preferable to not having safeguards against arbitrary enforcement and other legal overreach. But they also demand that we acknowledge and address the cost of these safeguards in terms of how we treat victims and survivors of sexual violence. These arguments build on the experiences of sexual assault survivors within the group as well as the work done collectively by the community to give the voiceless, faceless complainant in the Kane case a more relatable inner life, much like an RPF character.

Here, fanfiction readers and writers use the way they would normally construct an RPF "canon" to think through real-life issues of rape culture and the law. They shift the focus away from the law's special definition of truth and toward what the people involved—the complainant, individuals within the criminal justice system such as the DA, and, to a lesser extent, Kane—might be feeling and experiencing, what might be motivating or influencing them. This is a process of bracketing: accepting that the law has its place in society, but that it is not all that can be said on the subject. This creates a space where alternative truths not legitimized by the law can exist alongside the official legal version. It highlights that the law offers only one version of events constructed for a particular purpose (deciding whether an alleged perpetrator should be punished), and not the absolute truth. It allows us to acknowledge that even if we cannot be sure enough that Kane committed a rape to lock him away, in all likelihood there is still a woman who was harmed by his actions, and who is being further harmed by the criminal justice system.

The final approach to the district attorney within the Hockey RPF community's discussions of the Patrick Kane rape investigation is illustrated by this Tumblr post on Sedita's end-of-investigation statement by Hockey RPF community member vulpix:

> The DA's statement was full of incredibly loaded language. It was uncomfortable to read. It literally used scare quotes (this so-called "case"); it used "well he didn't act guilty" as an apparently legitimate reason to disbelieve the alleged victim. And this is what he thought was appropriate to put out to the public in an official statement, so no, I'm not inclined to think anyone in this case went into it with no bias, even before you consider the hometown hockey hero who has made mistakes but is a reformed character who is friendly with the police narrative. (vulpix)

Taking issue with both the language of the DA's statement as well as the reasons he cited for closing the investigation, vulpix implies here that Sedita's words were deliberately chosen in an attempt to discredit the complainant. Rather than simply stating that there was "reasonable doubt" or "insufficient evidence to prosecute," which would be common phrasing for statements in these circumstances, the DA used language dismissive of Kane's accuser. He also unnecessarily—and perhaps selectively—outlined details of the investigation. Other community members offered similar analyses and brought other pieces of information about Sedita into the discussion, including the fact that in his first public statement about the case he had expressed concern for Kane's reputation,[29] and the fact that he was running for election to a judgeship for nearly the entire duration of the Kane investigation.[30] Using this information, community members gave the DA an inner life and highlighted his humanity over his function as a part of the criminal justice system. The fictionalized Sedita who emerged from this process was biased, more interested in upholding the reputation of a hometown sports hero than ensuring justice for the complainant, and unlikely to have presided over a thorough and impartial investigation. In this way, a characterization of the DA was again used to make broader points about the law and the criminal justice system: if individuals within the legal system are steeped in rape culture and personally biased in sexual assault cases, then the system itself cannot be seen as just and impartial. Commenters who took this approach were frequently sexual violence survivors themselves, or had previous experience with the criminal justice system; for instance, from reporting (or deciding not to report) sexual assault, or from supporting friends and family through similar decisions and legal processes.

Community members also raised issues of rape culture, victim blaming, and rape myths. They highlighted the fact that Kane is rich, White, and privileged, and that he had connections with police in his hometown, where the alleged assault took place. They also discussed the effects of and outright challenged common rape myths. Believing that the accused is innocent until proven guilty, they argued, was irreconcilable with believing the victim. They quoted statistics on low conviction rates as well as the extremely low rates of false allegations, and highlighted the need to believe and support victims in the face of an actively hostile criminal justice system. The RPF canon construction work done by the community for both the complainant and the district attorney is crucial in these debates. Sedita is cast as actively complicit in an unjust and ineffective system. At the same time, comments invite readers to identify with the complainant's experience of both the assault and the criminal justice system's response. Ideas such as "innocent until proven guilty" and "beyond reasonable doubt" are challenged outright: they tilt the system in the favor of rapists. This, in turn, brings into question the very legitimacy of the law in cases of sexual violence. These challenges extend far beyond the bracketing of the law we saw earlier. They show us how the law systematically excludes and invalidates the experiences of victims and survivors, and how it sides with the alleged perpetrator by default. Feminist legal scholars, of course, have long argued this.[31] Yet, we have seen the Hockey RPF community circulate and further develop these arguments in ways that legal scholars cannot. By using the textual processes of real person(a) fiction to think through issues of sexual violence, rape culture, and the law, Hockey RPF community members emphasize the lived experience of sexuality, consent, and sexual violence over the definitions of the law. This also makes these arguments much more broadly accessible than feminist legal scholarship.

The Hockey RPF community used a range of RPF canon construction techniques in their evaluation of the rape allegations against Patrick Kane. By bringing in community members' own experiences of sexual assault and the criminal justice system, they constructed a version of the complainant—left nameless, faceless, and voiceless by measures ostensibly intended to protect her—that they could empathize with and whose credibility was bolstered. The district attorney's professional reputation, use of loaded language, and possible political motivations were used to construct three different versions of him. All of these characterizations were used to humanize and give a face to the law, allowing Hockey RPF community members to engage with and challenge the criminal justice system in complex and nuanced ways. Ultimately, the community's RPF canon construction processes created new ways to think about rape, consent, and the law, based not on legal principles and precedent but rather on affective and emotional engagement with issues of sexuality, agency, and bodily autonomy and how they intersect with the legal system. Although a minority of community members placed a high degree of trust in the criminal justice system and interpreted the lack of criminal charges as evidence of Kane's innocence, the majority used RPF canon construction processes to challenge the law. They either bracketed it, acknowledging its power in a specific context but questioning it outside of that context, or rejected it outright. Both bracketing and outright challenging the law are powerful acts of demythologization and demystification, opening up spaces for alternative truths and discourses to exist either alongside or in place of the law.

LIVING OUR VALUES

The Hockey RPF community used their discussions around the Patrick Kane rape allegations to think in new ways about rape, consent, rape culture, and the law. Yet, as the Kane investigation developed, another question arose: in light of this understanding of rape culture, and of what many community members saw as the impossibility of determining Kane's guilt or innocence with any certainty regardless of the legal version of truth, could they justify further fannish involvement with Patrick Kane? Three approaches to this question stood out in particular: ending involvement with the fandom, or at least with Patrick Kane and the Kane/Toews pairing; deleting existing work from AO3; and finding ways to justify continued involvement. What drove these seemingly contradictory approaches?

Questioning, suspending, or outright ending involvement and activity in the Hockey RPF or Patrick Kane fandoms was a common reaction from many community members very early on. Even before any details were known beyond the fact that a rape investigation was being conducted, many readers and writers declared their intent to withdraw from the community.

> It almost doesn't matter whether he did this thing or not—I believe he could have, and that realization makes me sick to my stomach. It might not be enough to convict him in any court, but it's enough to make me put down my pen where he's concerned. (oddish)

This comment clearly acknowledges the uncertainty around the case, and in fact, oddish's full Tumblr post deals extensively with the problem of uncertainty in rape allegations in general and the Kane case in particular. As discussed in the previous section, she also makes a clear distinction between any judgment she as an individual makes based on information she has, and what may or may not be enough to convict a person of rape in a court of law. Crucially, it is the realization that she believes—based on what she knows—that Patrick Kane (the celebrity athlete) is *capable* of rape that ultimately drives oddish's decision to no longer write about Patrick Kane (the Hockey RPF character). Elaborating further in another post, oddish writes:

> I need to own that as an RPF writer, I have two very different Patrick Kanes in my mind—one, the character that I see when I read or write who is a flawed but loveable idea that we have cooperatively created. The other is a real

human being who for all the media attention he receives is unknowable—and deeply problematic. In fiction, we can create scenarios that suggest favorable interpretations and allow for character development . . . but those scenarios are clearly fiction.

Where life seemed to be imitating art, and Patrick Kane seemed to be improving himself as a human being, I was selfishly pleased, because it allowed me to enjoy my fiction all the more. But the recent accusation of sexual assault changes things. (oddish)

This comment echoes the analysis of fan studies scholar Kristina Busse of how RPF writers shape and mold the celebrity persona in their stories. It also clearly references the way RPF constructs canon from selecting, arranging, and interpreting publicly available pieces of information about the celebrity.[32] The way RPF uses the celebrity's public self to create versions of a private self poses a particular problem for oddish and other Hockey RPF writers: the fictional private self is often presented in the most favorable light and depicted as capable of learning, development and overcoming the celebrity's publicly known character flaws. Fans read the fictional Patrick Kane and the celebrity Patrick Kane side by side. This, in turn, leads to a changed perception of the celebrity within the fandom—a perception now at odds with the new information emerging about the celebrity. Rather than placing the fictional character and the celebrity persona side by side and constructing meaning from the similarities and differences between the two, the knowledge of what the real Patrick Kane is alleged to have done overwhelms any possible fan interpretation and imposes meanings that many Hockey RPF fans find distressing. A number of community members shared comments about the highly personal stories they had told through the character of Patrick Kane—including stories about surviving sexual assault. In light of the rape allegations against real-life Kane, they now felt that the fictional character was in some way tainted for them.[33]

The conflict generated by side-by-side readings of Patrick Kane—the celebrity athlete accused of rape—and the RPF character Patrick Kane is so deep and significant for the Hockey RPF community that oddish characterized it as a struggle to "live our values." Hockey RPF fans understand how rape culture operates in the criminal justice system and celebrity culture, so here the discussion moves toward what fans can personally do to disrupt and no longer reproduce it. What would a world that wasn't dominated by rape culture look like? One small part of the answer to that—the part that is within this community's control—is that we would not be fans of celebrities accused of rape. Cultural activism theorists call this an "exemplary gesture"—an act that shows us what a better world might look like in practice.[34]

The rape allegations against Kane not only changed the meaning of any possible future fanfiction about him, but also the meanings of existing works for both readers and writers, leading to discussions of whether such fanfiction stories should be deleted from AO3:

> I have been thinking hard about pulling the only fic I wrote with him. Or changing it to a different pairing. I just—the things people have said about this fic, how it helped them process stuff in real life, I don't want to delete it. But I don't think I can present him as a sympathetic character anymore. (scyther)

From scyther's comment, we can see that her Kane-centric fanfiction has acquired meaning for her (and her readers) beyond the immediate connection with Kane. In this case, her readers found the story helpful in addressing issues in their own lives, which in turn made it more meaningful and valuable for scyther. This is only one example of how fanfiction stories acquired additional meanings for their readers and writers. Community members also discussed the emotional investment and labor involved in writing stories and engaging with the community, as well as the pleasure and joy they got from reading and writing stories and discussing them in the comments section. All of these meanings became part of their involvement in Hockey RPF fandom, and therefore became a part of their own personal attachment to Hockey RPF or Patrick Kane, to an extent. These meanings needed to be reevaluated against the meanings now imposed by the rape allegations, as scyther's comment demonstrates. Her desire to make an exemplary gesture is taken beyond ceasing involvement with the fandom to actively removing existing fanworks about Patrick Kane from AO3. For many commenters, this approach was driven by a kind of "scorched earth" policy—the intention to not only remove themselves from the fandom but also prevent potential new fans from joining. This again shows a conscious desire to stop the reproduction of rape culture within the Hockey RPF community.

The process of reevaluating the meanings of Hockey RPF and Patrick Kane stories was common to many community members, but not all reached the same conclusions. Community member voltorb posted a long reflection on Tumblr expressing a different view:

> A huge part (the overwhelming portion, really) of my delight with hockey is rooted in the fantastic irony of a bunch of intelligent, sassy, powerful women taking a hegemonic male structure and turning it on its head: refashioning this world and these people to our purposes. It's a subversive act. (voltorb)

Here, voltorb is weighing the meanings Hockey RPF has accrued for her over time against those imposed by the rape allegations against Patrick Kane. But the outcome of this process is exactly the opposite of scyther and oddish's reevaluations. Rather than finding other meanings overwhelmed by the rape allegations, for voltorb, the subversive meanings she finds in Hockey RPF directly challenge rape culture and hegemonic masculinity. A cornerstone of this argument is the observation that Hockey RPF characters are better, more compassionate human beings than their respective celebrity personas are. For voltorb, the contrast between the fandom community's perception of and depiction of hockey culture is what attracts her to Hockey RPF. For her, Hockey RPF only acquires meaning because it shows a kinder, gentler, less harmful version of the hockey culture she experiences in real life. Elsewhere in the post, voltorb also acknowledges—in language very similar to oddish's "live our values" comment—the conflict she experiences in enjoying a sport so deeply mired in rape culture. But voltorb argues that it is Hockey RPF, through what she perceives as its subversiveness, that helps her reconcile some of these tensions because it changes how she views the sport of hockey itself. What is important here is that even though voltorb is arguing for precisely the opposite action to oddish and scyther, she is also basing that argument on a desire to challenge rape culture. The disagreement here, then, is not about the end but rather the means. At the heart of both sides of this argument is the desire to make an exemplary gesture, to find ways of challenging rather than reproducing rape culture, to start creating a better world here and now. The actions proposed by different members of the community in response to the Patrick Kane rape allegations are all intended to enact the community's beliefs and understandings of rape culture in ways that point to a world where rape culture no longer exists.

These discussions show that many Hockey RPF readers and writers felt deeply conflicted, weighing their emotional engagement with the fandom against their desire to challenge rape culture. Ultimately, however, voltorb's argument in favor of continued engagement with the fandom as a way of subverting rape culture was rejected by the majority of the community. The emotional conflict community members experienced translated to significant levels of disengagement with the fandom. To understand the exact levels of turnover and disengagement in the fandom, I looked at both the number of works posted to AO3 featuring "Patrick Kane" as a character tag or "Patrick Kane/Jonathan Toews" as a relationship tag, and the number of active authors producing stories with these tags before and after the rape allegations became public (table 5.1). Between early August 2015 and the end of January 2016, a total of 134 works featuring one or both of these tags were posted on AO3. In order to obtain a comparable sample for the period before the rape allegations, I also took into account the 134 works posted to AO3 prior to August 6, 2015 (the day news of the allegations broke).[35] Two key metrics in this data are the rate of posting of new works, and the number of authors active in the fandom during the relevant time periods. I also took into account key milestones of the rape investigation, splitting the period after the allegations became public into two around the official closure of the investigation. Finally, I wanted to understand how individual authors' activity patterns had changed over the course of the investigation.

Immediately after the rape allegations, the Hockey RPF community's output of fanfiction about Patrick Kane stopped almost completely. In the three months between August 6 and the date the investigation was formally closed, November 5, only 40 works were posted in the Patrick Kane or

Table 5.1: Number of active authors and works posted in Patrick Kane–related tags on the Archive of Our Own in the months leading up to, during, and following the rape investigation (June 2015–January 2016)

Time period	Total works posted	Average works posted per month	Total active authors	Authors active in this period and pre-allegations	New authors in this period
June–July (Pre-allegations)	134	67	84	n/a	n/a
August–January (Post-allegations)	**134**	**22**	**66**	**19 + 4**	**43**
August–October (During investigation)	40	13	28	12 + 4	12
November–January (After investigation)	94	31	51	14	31

Patrick Kane/Jonathan Toews tags on AO3. By contrast, the 134 works included in the pre-allegations sample were posted within a two-month period (June and July 2015). In the three months after the investigation was concluded, the rate of new works doubled compared to the August–October period, with 94 works posted to AO3, but it was still only half the monthly rate of new works produced before the allegations. The overall number of authors active in the fandom decreased from 84 in the two months before the allegations to 66 in the August–January period. Of the 84 authors active in June and July, only 19 (less than a quarter) remained involved after the rape allegations became public, with the remaining active authors being new to the fandom.[36] Another four authors were active before June and then again after August, though two of them posted works which had largely been completed before the allegations and then withdrew from the fandom entirely. Of the 66 authors active between August and January, 43 (nearly two-thirds) joined the fandom after the rape allegations. These numbers show three key developments: a mass exodus of long-term fans from the fandom; a significant slowdown in the creation of new fanworks; and, ultimately, an overall smaller community made up largely of individuals who joined after the rape allegations became public—more specifically, after the police investigation was concluded.

What the Hockey RPF community did in the wake of the Kane rape allegations—their disengagement with the fandom, resulting from extensive discussion about the best way to live their values—is an exemplary or prefigurative gesture. This kind of gesture shows us the way toward a world free of rape culture. It tells us that it is up to us, at least in part, to stop reproducing that culture; stop buying into the dominant narratives about pretty, rich White men; and start believing victims and survivors. It is up to us to do whatever is in our power within whatever small sphere of influence we might have to start creating a culture of consent. For the Hockey RPF community, something they could do within that sphere of influence was to stop being fans of Kane. But that was not all: the community used their expertise in RPF to find new ways of looking at the law and the criminal justice system. They used fanfiction techniques to put a human face on the law, and to find strategies of challenging a legal and criminal justice system that is mired in rape culture. Community members helped each other translate insights about sex, rape, and consent developed through fanfiction into insights about how these things operate in the real world. These challenges to rape culture may be on a small scale, but they are powerful nonetheless. They make visible the problematic aspects of the law and give community members new ways of collectively thinking and knowing about sexual violence, consent, and rape culture. This is how activism— and change—begins.

6 "TAB A, SLOT B": LIVED EXPERIENCE AND KNOWLEDGES OF CONSENT

THE EPISTEMOLOGY OF CONSENT

We saw in chapter 5 how fanfiction readers and writers found ways of bracketing and challenging the law and the criminal justice system on questions of sexual violence. They saw that the law was dismissing an event as "not rape" and found ways to continue discussing it as rape and sexual violence, regardless of what the law said on the subject. Why is this necessary?

We know that the majority of rapes do not get reported to police, and of those that do get reported, only a tiny fraction ever result in the conviction of the perpetrator.[1] And those of us who are survivors of sexual violence know that, regardless of whether our rapist was convicted or not, what we experienced was rape. And yet, if our rapist was acquitted, society at large is likely to believe that they are innocent. This is what Carol Smart means when she says that the law has a special status in society that allows it to dismiss other discourses and ways of knowing and impose its own truth on us.[2] It is not only survivors of sexual violence who understand this disconnect between what we have experienced and what the law tells us did or did not happen. Generations of feminist scholars have shown how we as a society tend to give the law too much power and credence, particularly in cases of sexual violence.[3]

Something else we are beginning to see from both sex-critical approaches to sex and fanfiction readers and writers' engagements with issues of consent—from tropes like the Omegaverse and arranged marriage—is that consent is not always clear-cut. Our culture normalizes so many coercive practices as "just sex" to the point where it is difficult for us to think of them otherwise. Sexual scripts[4] at the cultural level tell us that sex happens between exactly one nondisabled cisgender man and one nondisabled cisgender woman, that it starts with kissing, progresses through touching and undressing to a penis going in a vagina, and ends when the man ejaculates. How we see ourselves or want to be seen by others also shapes our behavior when it comes to sex. Unwanted sex is common in casual situations where, for instance, a woman wants to be seen as sexually liberated.[5] It also happens in long-term relationships where we see the amount of sex a couple is having as a metric of relationship quality, thus making sex into a relationship maintenance activity.[6] Our society's dominant ideas of (hetero)sex tell men they should be wanting and initiating sex all the time, while trapping women between the roles of gatekeeper and sexually liberated agent.[7] All of these ideas mean that it is difficult to truly and meaningfully exercise our agency when it comes to sex and consent because we don't even know (or don't believe) that "no" is an option. Sometimes, agreeing to (or even initiating) unwanted sex is our least bad option for exercising agency,[8] but our choices in these situations are limited by dominant ideas of what we *should* be doing. And because we are so steeped in these ideas—because they seem natural to us—naming some of these experiences as nonconsensual becomes unthinkable. If we initiate sex to conform to societal expectations, is that sex in any way meaningfully consensual?

In the face of this kind of overwhelming, all-encompassing operation of power, where does meaningful resistance begin? What does it look like? And how can we conceptualize forms of activism that begin to challenge what seems perfectly normal and natural? Questions about making the unthinkable thinkable are ultimately questions about epistemology: how do we *know* consent? How can we expand our knowledge of consent? How do we know if an encounter was consensual? How do we know that consent was indeed freely given and as unencumbered by the multidirectional pervasive operations of power in our society as it is possible to be? And who, exactly, is a qualified knower of this? These are questions of epistemic (i.e., related to knowledge and ways of knowing things) justice and injustice. We already saw in chapter 2 that knowledge and power are intimately related. In our society, we consider some ways of knowing things valid and others not, and declaring a way of knowing things as not valid is a key way of exercising power and marginalizing people. This is what the law does when it declares survivors' experiences as "not rape."

Philosopher José Medina conceptualizes issues like these through the idea of credibility.[9] How much credibility do we as a society give to particular institutions, or people, or groups of people? When the law systematically disbelieves marginalized people (including survivors of sexual violence) and we take our cue from it, it has a credibility excess. The people whom we see as less credible, on the other hand, have a credibility deficit. So, a rape survivor's testimony alone is generally not considered enough in the eyes of the law to convict a perpetrator. Lawyers, judges, and juries want to see corroborating evidence such as witness statements or forensic evidence. They also often seek to challenge and undermine the complainant's credibility further by probing their past or their character. Defense lawyers often reword or reinterpret the complainant's testimony to suggest that they, in fact, consented. A judge may instruct a jury to take some pieces of evidence into account and ignore others. In this way, both the law as an institution and the individuals who serve it claim for themselves an epistemic authority over victims and witnesses: they not only claim to know better but also claim to be better equipped to decide what counts as knowledge in the first place. Credibility deficits and excesses like these are crucial to the law's special status in our society and its ability to outright determine truth and dismiss other kinds of knowledge. And because of the massive credibility excess we tend to afford the law, it effectively becomes the arbiter of consent: what the complainant says happened, or what actually happened does not matter anywhere near as much as what the law says happened. In our simplified common-sense understanding, if the law says it was not rape, then it was not rape. This is despite the fact that the law's declaration of "not rape" generally comes with small print explaining that what it actually means is that there was not sufficient evidence, or that a jury was not convinced beyond reasonable doubt—which are, of course, very different statements from "a rape did not occur."

Feminist scholars and activists have for years argued that the law is both structurally and epistemically unqualified to be the arbiter of consent. To use a meme way past its use-by date, when it comes to ways of knowing, the law simply does not have the range. The law tends to operate in binary opposites: true or false, guilty or not guilty. If it declares something not rape, as sociologist Lynn Jamieson points out, the law does not have to go on and answer, "What is it then, if not rape?"[10] This kind of binary thinking, combined with safeguards from legal and state overreach such as the "innocent until proven guilty" burden of proof and the "beyond reasonable doubt" standard of proof, results in a structural credibility deficit for sexual violence survivors. It also makes vast swaths of experience between "rape" and "consent"—those experiences fanfiction readers and writers label "dubcon"—completely unintelligible and unthinkable.

Feminist scholarship and activism has only really found the tools to grapple with these vast gray areas since the rise of the sex-critical approach over the last ten to fifteen years. Nicola Gavey's ideas about a continuum of sexual violations, most of which we still tend to subsume under the idea of "just sex," have been crucial here.[11] But our conceptualization of normal sex continues to include many arguably coercive practices and, for many of us, continues to be deeply ingrained. Outside of fanfiction circles, we don't really even have a word for the experiences that lie between rape and consent, and so many of us are still stuck in the law's binary way of thinking. Outside of fanfiction, we have only recently started even mapping out what might fall into that space between. In her 2018 book *Rape and Resistance*, philosopher Linda Martín Alcoff, building partly on Gavey's work and partly on her own experiences and other firsthand accounts of sexual violence, outlines a range of experiences that do not neatly fit into the rape/consent binary.[12] But where in the 1980s Carol Smart (despite having no clear concept of "dubcon") was calling for an outright decentering of the law from our efforts to combat sexual violence,[13] Alcoff merely seeks to open up a still necessary parallel conversation that takes into account the lived experiences of survivors and that might, in time, inform legal conversations. By better understanding what lies between rape and consent, we can extend what is *knowable* about sexual violence, and we can start challenging the credibility excess we afford the law as a knower and arbiter of consent.

But if the law is epistemologically unqualified to know about consent, then who or what is? We have already seen how deeply ingrained dominant ideas about what "normal" sex looks like are. We think it's normal to push past the first "no" in the name of seduction. We think it's normal to initiate unwanted sex to maintain our relationship. We think there is only one normal way to have sex. Our society's dominant ideas and regimes of truth (i.e., what can and can't intelligibly be said) about sex are deeply problematic. And we filter our experiences and interpretations of them through those dominant ideas. To what extent can we trust our own experiences and interpretations if what passes for normality isn't actually consensual? How do we grapple with experiences that feel "off" when we lack the words to explain why? In the current regime of truth, it is almost impossible to articulate them as violations. We are so steeped in the idea of these things being normal that we cannot even imagine an alternative.

However, we also cannot completely discount our experiences as a source of knowledge about consent. Yes, they are filtered through the dominant ideas of our society, but still, even when we don't have the words for them, some experiences still just feel "off." If nothing else, those situations can provide an impetus to start challenging those dominant ideas. Linda Martín Alcoff gives an example from her own lived experience, describing an occasion in college where her partner initiated intercourse with her while she was asleep. Although she says the incident left a "bad taste" for her, and that she "would like to have been asked," she shies away from calling it a rape.[14] She also talks about the time and distance it has taken her, as it has many other survivors of sexual violence, to even process that experience as something that wasn't quite right. And yet, Alcoff points out, within the criminal justice paradigm, "it continues to be a mark against the credibility of an accuser . . . if there is even a whisper of change in their assessment of an event."[15]

Alcoff's account is, in fact, a perfect illustration of how important both time and distance are in our processing of experiences, and of the role that dominant ideas and regimes of truth play in our interpretation of our experiences. The incident she hesitates to name a rape is likely to sound familiar to anyone following US, UK, or Swedish politics since 2010: the allegations against Wikileaks founder Julian Assange are very similar.[16] Assange's supporters and many conservative voices would indeed deny that the behavior he is accused of constitutes rape. But in contemporary feminist circles and conversations, there is very much a consensus that initiating sex with someone who is asleep and thus unable to actively give consent is indeed rape.[17] At some point between Alcoff's college days in the 1970s and now, we have developed the words and ideas to be able to name that experience as a violation. In fact, dominant ideas about what counts as normal have shifted so far as to make that experience intelligible and nameable as a violation even within the context of the Swedish criminal justice system.

To make this kind of change, the first step is to make sense of and reinterpret our own experiences—to take them outside the dominant regimes of truth and make them intelligible to ourselves. This is frequently a fraught process. We may struggle to find the words. We may only have part of the picture. We may take wrong turns. And even once we find the words for ourselves, explaining what we have found out to others can seem almost impossible. To make the process possible, José Medina argues that "it is crucial to develop *a hermeneutical sensibility with respect to embryonic and inchoate attempts at communicating* about experiences that do not yet have standard formulations."[18] We have to learn to pay attention to our own and others' attempts to make sense of our experiences in the face of dominant ideas and regimes of truth.

There is (or there can be) friction, then, between our experiences and our society's dominant ideas. Such friction is both difficult and productive—it is from this kind of friction that change may ultimately arise. Change starts with making sense of our experiences *to ourselves* before we can communicate them to others who have had such experiences and, later, to those who have not.[19] When it comes to our experiences of consent and sexual violence, friction and uncertainty do not fit well with the binary certainty that the law demands. Yet, as Alcoff argues, uncertainty is also vital if we are to create spaces where survivors—and society as a whole— can move beyond and dismantle the dominant ideas and regimes of truth:

"Our capacity to critique is related to a capacity to imagine things differently, and thus to participate in transformations."[20]

Acknowledging that experience is always filtered through the available dominant ideas means we cannot look to it as the sole arbiter of consent, much like we cannot trust the law because it is too binary. The way our interpretations of our experiences are filtered through the dominant regime of truth means that we are likely to overlook or be unable to name violations. At the same time, understanding that the current dominant ideas are likely to have this effect—to tilt the playing field toward obscuring sexual violation and nonconsent and casting them as consensual—can be a starting point. It means that we can look to our experience as a reliable arbiter of *nonconsent*: given the difficulty of making sexual violation intelligible to ourselves and others, we are likely to be able to trust that someone who articulates a particular experience as nonconsensual on their part has the credibility and epistemic authority to make that claim. They have, after all, had to do a lot of work in understanding and interpreting their experiences against the dominant ideas of our society. Challenging the law's need for certainty and living with discomfort and uncertainty while also understanding how dominant ideas shape our interpretations of our experiences are the foundations of an epistemology—a way of knowing—of consent.

Dominant ideas of sex, sexuality, and consent are so totalizing—so deeply internalized that they have come to seem natural—that naming the problem is the necessary first step in finding ways to resist them. It is a problem of creating and legitimizing new knowledges and new sources of knowledge, and extending credibility to qualified knowers who have historically been denied it: believing victims and survivors of sexual violence, holding a space for uncertainty, revoking the special status we give the law on these matters. This kind of discursive resistance names the problem and creates possible solutions: we can show that the current state is not the only way for things to be, and that alternatives are possible. But discursive resistance is a communal activity. As Black feminists like bell hooks and Patricia Hill Collins remind us,[21] we can only find our critical voice in conversation with others. By allowing us to compare our experiences with those of others, these conversations help us see wider patterns that we might not be able to see on our own. In this way, they help us make the leap from articulating our own individual lived experience to structural analysis. They create new knowledges at the margins (subjugated knowledges, if you will). They enable us to shed internalized oppression and naturalized dominant ideas and view ourselves and our experiences in a new light. The next question, then, is this: How do we move from discursive resistance to making a material difference in the world?

To start understanding how discursive resistance on issues of sexual consent may permeate into the real lives of fanfiction readers and writers, I spoke to eight fans at the Nine Worlds convention in August 2016.[22] In these conversations, interviewees told me about the kinds of new knowledges of consent they had been able to develop through their involvement with fanfiction communities, and how they had put those knowledges into practice in their own lives.

EXPLORING EXPERIENCE

One important theme arising from my interviews with fanfiction readers and writers is that sex, and by extension consent, is inextricable from feelings and emotions. Our internal experience is a key factor in how we understand consent. In her interview, Magmar talked at length about the emotional aspects of sex and sexuality, and the sometimes contradictory feelings they can generate. She described how reading and writing fanfiction allowed her to process those feelings both before and after new sexual experiences:

> I know that when I discover new kinks, I . . . think about the way I would feel about them as well as the characters. And some things, like questions about in that moment you really want to do that . . . but afterwards you're like feeling guilty you wanted that or something, so like those are aspects that I really like to discuss with the characters I have. (Magmar)

Here, Magmar acknowledges that the exploration of our sexuality can make us feel a range of positive and negative emotions: desire, pleasure, guilt. She does not judge those feelings, either in herself or in her characters. Instead, she takes the time to explore and understand them, using fanfiction's focus on the characters' internal lives and experiences. This focus on emotions and lived experience also sheds a light on the limitations of our dominant understanding of consent. When we talk about consent negotiation, we tend to think of a rational exchange. We assume that all parties know exactly what they do and do not want, and can put that into words and come to some sort of negotiated agreement that makes everyone happy. But, like all aspects of human sexuality, consent is deeply affective and emotional, and our understanding of it has to take that into account. We may not know what we want. Our feelings about the situation may change as it progresses. We may struggle to say what we do and do not want because our society teaches us that talking about sex is not something we should be doing. Magmar highlights this further in talking about fanfiction as a tool for consent negotiation:

> What I really enjoy is, like, two characters, for example, sitting down and talking about fantasies. Like, "There is this woman, she is doing this and that, what will she do next, how will she react if I would do something or . . . ?"— like in the third person, and you can think about it and it feels like a safe way to explore because the character—who's telling the dominant one, for example, what he or she wants and doesn't want—doesn't have to say "I don't like that," it's just "Hmm, I don't think the character would react positively to being bound or something." You don't have to say, "I can't cope with that," but more like, "They wouldn't like that." So that feels—and you can, at the same time you can have a really sexy fantasy—so, it's fun. I really like that. (Magmar)

For Magmar, the exploration of sexual fantasy and, ultimately, our own sexuality through fictional characters whom we can talk or write about in the third person is safe: there is less exposure and less vulnerability involved than in talking about our own desires in the first person. Importantly, for her, it makes refusing or withdrawing consent easier because it is less of a direct refusal. We generally don't like saying "no" to people: direct refusals are socially stigmatized and conversationally "dispreferred."[23] Saying "yes" to things is socially much easier. In everyday conversation, we tend to refuse things indirectly. We might qualify them ("not right now"), justify them ("I'm too busy"), or find a whole range of other ways to soften our refusals ("I'd love to, but," "sure, some other time," "you're really nice, but," etc.). When talking about anything other than sex, most of us are also perfectly capable of understanding this kind of phrasing as a refusal. And because talking about sex is difficult, and people's feelings are involved, we tend to be extra gentle when we refuse sex. But for a long time, rape-prevention work focused on teaching women to say "no" differently, more forcefully, or more directly: a whole series of campaigns in the 1990s kept telling women to "just say no." This doesn't work for a number of reasons. A direct refusal can have a range of negative consequences. In social situations it might lead to mild disapproval. In sexual situations, it may expose a woman to anger and increased violence. Magmar's description of negotiating consent and performing refusals in the third person, through a fictional character, shows a clear understanding of how tricky refusals can be in sexual situations. Her approach allows both parties to minimize the additional vulnerability and exposure of talking about sex and possibly having to say "no" to your partner, or accept a "no" from them. It also emphasizes the gray areas of emotion and desire. Thinking through the emotional implications of sexuality in this way allows for ambiguity and complexity, making consent more than a yes/no binary.

There is a second important element of Magmar's approach to consent negotiation through fiction: pleasure. This way of talking about sex and thinking through the things we might want to do is not only safe, but also fun. Other interviewees also talked about the importance of portraying consent negotiation as fun or sexy in fanfiction. They often brought this up in contrast to how we see consent discussed in mainstream media, news, and commentary. We have seen this especially since the rise of the #MeToo movement: complaints, usually from men, that having to think and talk about consent would somehow require a legal contract to be signed, or would otherwise be too cumbersome or even ruin the mood.[24] For the fanfiction readers and writers I interviewed, fanfiction offered alternative templates to follow in their own consent negotiation to those presented by mainstream media: templates that allowed them to find socially acceptable ways of refusing or withdrawing consent, but also to make negotiation a pleasurable and fun activity in its own right. These ideas allow us to move away from a mechanistic, legalistic view of consent negotiation and focus instead on how we (or our characters) experience sexuality and consent internally. In this way, fanfiction readers and writers create a space for emotion, vulnerability, and ambiguity in sexuality and consent. This approach might highlight the situations where we feel we *should* be having sex, but also the moments of pure desire. It allows us to think of a wider range of sexual experience as consensual, nonconsensual, or perhaps somewhere in between. Experience and emotion—both those of the characters but also those of fanfiction readers and writers—become a key source of *knowledge* about consent.

Some of my interviewees also told me about how they took such knowledge from the fanfiction context and applied it to their own lives. Ekans, for instance, spoke about applying the templates of consent negotiation they had learned through fanfiction directly to their own relationship:

> In my own marriage, it's sort of been very much like—constant communication, constant negotiation, and understanding each other's boundaries, and I think that's very much something I picked up from fanfic. . . . It's sort of an ongoing cycle because I take the stuff that I've learned in my own relationship that I've learned from fanfic in the first place, and then put it back in my own fanfic, so it's a sort of ongoing cycle of learning about negotiation and learning about consent. (Ekans)

Here, Ekans describes a cycle of learning about consent from fanfiction, putting this knowledge to use in their own relationships, and putting knowledge gained from their relationships back into their fanfiction. Fanfiction has two functions for Ekans. On the one hand, it is a source of knowledge about consent—and this knowledge is created by the whole community and focuses on lived experience and emotions. On the other hand, it is also a space where they can creatively explore the issues they come across in their own life—and make their own contribution to the community's knowledge. Ekans reads their own lived experience side by side with their fanfiction, and this process allows them to see both in a new light.

Fanfiction readers and writers, then, clearly recognize the role of lived experience in knowledge creation and use both their own experience and the imagined internal lives of their characters to explore questions of sex, sexuality, and consent. Knowledges generated through fanfiction can be practical—such as new scripts and templates for consent negotiation, as recounted by Ekans and Magmar. But the focus on experience and emotion also allows fanfiction readers and writers to open up gray areas between yes and no—to admit the possibility of ambiguity toward sex and consent, as Magmar suggests. The knowledges of consent these communities generate both anticipate and answer Alcoff's calls for recognition of gray areas and ambiguity, and for recognizing the importance of experience as a source of knowledge.[25]

THE FRICTION OF DISCOURSE

Lived experience is only one aspect of our understanding of consent and, as we saw in chapters 3 and 4, fanfiction readers and writers know this. Our lived experience is filtered through and shaped by the dominant ideas in our society. If marriage consummation is the done, expected thing, and if, in order for my marriage to be valid, I need to consummate it, then—no matter how off or uncomfortable that experience might feel—it is very difficult to actually name the practice as nonconsensual. Some ideas about sex are so ingrained in our society, so "natural" and invisible, that even imagining that things might be different is almost impossible. The stories we looked at in chapters 3 and 4 make some of these dominant ideas visible and ask questions about how we can still exercise agency and meaningfully negotiate consent in the face of them. The fanfiction readers and writers I talked to also spoke about how dominant ideas of sex had affected them, and how fanfiction had allowed them to see past these ideas and create alternatives for themselves.

Several interviewees brought up the ability of fanfiction to challenge defaults and norms of what not just consent negotiation but sex more broadly "should" look like. Challenging default scripts in this way and providing alternative templates is a key focus of the community's knowledge creation around sexual consent.

> I think actually fanfic has taught me a lot about consent—in and of itself. Like, first of all, that it's a thing that, that can, like—that negotiations are a thing that can and should happen. That negotiation can be sexy. That—I'm just trying to think how to word it, that—that sex isn't a sort of linear path that goes from kiss to touch to another kind of touch to another kind of touch to, you know, Tab A, Slot B—that it can take sort of all different kinds of directions. (Ekans)

Here, Ekans uses knowledge gained from fanfiction to challenge a series of dominant ideas about sex and consent. Their description of the "linear path that goes from kiss to . . . Tab A, Slot B" is a rearticulation of the dominant idea that there is only one right way to have sex: you start with kissing and touching, move to undressing, a penis goes in a vagina, and it all ends when the cisgender man ejaculates. For Ekans, fanfiction has helped make this model of consent visible in both culture and their own day-to-day interactions, and exposed how they themselves have bought into it. But fanfiction has helped Ekans realize "that negotiations are a thing that can and should happen"—and that disrupts the standard script we have for how sex should work. Feminist sociologist Lynn Jamieson analyzed how "normal sex" is talked about in criminal trials: "The shadow of 'normal sex' cast by these [courtroom] contests, when the defense and prosecution portray events and their aftermath as 'not rape' and 'rape,' is typically far removed from mutually negotiated, mutually satisfactory sex between equals. Rather, 'normal sex' [in rape trials is constructed as] encompass[ing] women acquiescing to sexual use by men. *Mutual negotiation is not a test of normality.*"[26] And if the law (in practice, if not technically as written) tells us that mutual negotiation is not required, not normal, that idea seeps into our culture and we come to internalize it. Ekans, on the other hand, has realized through their engagement with fanfiction that mutual negotiation very much *should* be a test of normality.

But this is only the start of the knowledge of consent Ekans has gained from fanfiction. Importantly, fanfiction has given Ekans, like Magmar and other interviewees, alternative templates to follow in their consent negotiation and sexual practice. They have learned not only *that* "negotiations are a thing that can and should happen" but also *how* such consent negotiation can happen. These alternative models make consent negotiation not just normal but also sexy (or, as other interviewees described it, funny, caring, or affectionate). Finally, once aware that consent can and should be explicitly negotiated, Ekans is now in a position to start challenging the dominant definition of "sex" as penile-vaginal intercourse: rather than "Tab A, Slot B," sex can now take "all different kinds of directions."

In discussing what they have learned about sexual consent from fanfiction, Ekans describes a kind of layered effect to seeing for the first time our society's dominant ideas about sex and offering alternatives: first, you realize the dominance of the standard penis-in-vagina script and the extent to which you have internalized it; then you realize that negotiation "can and should happen" and learn how to make it happen; and then you come to the understanding that what you have been taught to think of as sex is actually only a limited selection of available options: that the penis can but doesn't have to go into the vagina, and you can still have mutually negotiated, consensual, fun sex.

This layering in itself makes visible the ways in which our dominant ideas about sex and consent might in fact be coercive. It shows us how what we have come to think of as the "natural" way sex works makes statements such as "kissing requires consent in its own right" and "there are other ways to have sex than penile-vaginal intercourse" nearly unintelligible. This combination of defining sex only as penile-vaginal intercourse, and mapping out a clear path to be followed from kissing to "sex" without opportunities for variation, negotiation, or even stopping is precisely what Nicola Gavey[27] describes as the "cultural scaffolding of rape." Every time we try to negotiate consent, we are enmeshed in these dominant ideas of what is "natural" and "normal." Both the "no means no" and "yes means yes" strands of feminist research and activism on consent struggle to account for this as they focus exclusively on interpersonal interaction without paying attention to how our society shapes that interaction. Ekans and other fanfiction readers and writers, by contrast, are actively making visible the way dominant ideas limit and shape how we can act. Critically, they also offer alternative approaches in their fanfiction: negotiation "can and should happen," and what we are negotiating is a much bigger and more open space than what society tells us "sex" is.

Other interviewees also highlighted the range of dominant ideas about sex and consent that they have become aware of, and how this has affected their ability to negotiate consent.

> Having, you know, a couple actually talk about not having sex yet, not doing it, it's interesting to me cos it—almost without explicitly doing it, it kind of tackles that assumption that they're just gonna fall into bed as soon as they decide they like each other. And that kind of brings us back to consent in a way that is a little bit different to the sort of standard talking about, asking about it, because it's agreeing, it's not just sort of saying, "Do you consent?" "Yes, let's go for it"—it's actually agreeing to stop at a certain point. (Nidorina)

Nidorina here is talking about couples and relationships as we see them in mainstream media. There is a default assumption that sex (i.e., intercourse) will happen, probably sooner rather than later. It is a defining feature and key milestone of a romantic relationship after all, and the ultimate endpoint of a progression of intimacy in any relationship. It is enmeshed in how we think of ourselves: as part of a couple, as husband, wife, girlfriend, boyfriend, romantic partner, mistress. Our dominant ideas about all of these roles we play require us to have sex. We also saw in chapter 4 how fanfiction reflects some of this in the arranged-marriage trope. Ideas of "husband," "wife," and "bride" all come in a discursive package that includes having intercourse. Nidorina, then, shows how important it has been for her to see consent negotiation in fanfiction that does not result in consent being given, or results in consent being withdrawn before that assumed endpoint of penile-vaginal intercourse. For her, fanfiction has been a key contributor to the realization that it is possible to be in a sexual or romantic relationship without necessarily having intercourse. Something that was previously unthinkable has become thinkable. Not only that, but we can see the impact of that unthinkability: if we can't imagine a romantic relationship without intercourse and we want to be in a romantic relationship, then we must have intercourse. The things we can think, the things we can imagine, shape what we can and cannot do. Fanfiction has allowed Nidorina and other readers and writers to see this. They have started making sense to themselves of how their own experiences of sexuality are filtered through dominant ideas of what sex and relationships should look like, and are finding ways of removing those filters.

Magmar goes a step further than Nidorina in her account of what she has learned about consent from fanfiction:

> It has made me more aware of the fact that some things—like kissing, for example—that are generally portrayed as completely OK for everyone don't necessarily have to be. So, for me, it's more like I'm not assuming just someone is OK with something because it seems like the normal stuff to do. So, yeah, I'm more aware of little details, little, like, breaking the whole act down into little steps. And just because you're perfectly all right with having sex doesn't mean you're perfectly all right with holding hands afterwards or something. (Magmar)

Here, Magmar takes apart the default sexual script according to which we start with kissing and touching and end up with penile-vaginal intercourse, and every action we take that conforms to that script is seen as an indication of consent to the next step. Instead, she suggests that we don't have to be OK with any of the individual elements of this script, or with other things we commonly associate with romantic relationships, such as holding hands. We can opt into and out of—consent or not consent to—each of these actions individually, with no other implications for the status of our relationship or for what else we might want to do with this person. She highlights that we cannot simply assume consent for acts such as kissing or holding hands simply because they are the done thing, just as we cannot assume that those acts say anything about our consent to other types of intimacy. She both advocates for more open consent communication and acknowledges the role of dominant ideas about sex and relationships in limiting the communication options available to us. Fanfiction, with its focus on experience and characters' internal thoughts and feelings, has allowed Magmar to see the disconnect between the dominant idea that kissing or holding hands are "completely OK for everyone" and the fact that some people might actually be deeply uncomfortable with such acts and find it difficult to articulate that. As a result, Magmar is able to dismantle and challenge these otherwise normalized and naturalized discursive constructions in her own life and practice.

In our conversations, Ekans, Nidorina, and Magmar all highlighted how fanfiction has helped them see sex, relationships, and consent in a new light. It has helped them identify and question dominant ideas about how sex and relationships work, and develop alternatives that work better in their own lives. These conversations begin to paint a picture of a discursive resistance and cultural activism that operates on two levels. Within the community, it is directed at dismantling community members' internalized ideas of what "normal" sex looks like—their internalized oppression. Cornel West would call what is happening here the demystifying and demythologizing of these dominant ideas: showing that they are not natural but rather socially constructed, and finding alternatives.[28] As we saw in previous chapters, fanfiction stories also explore how dominant social institutions such as gender, marriage, and the law play a significant role in reproducing and shoring up the power of prevailing ideas of sex and consent. Understanding that these ideas are socially constructed and knowing how they are reproduced is vital if we are to stop thinking of them as natural, if we are to make space for alternatives to become thinkable and imaginable. On a second level, fanfiction readers and writers take the knowledges they have made through their fanfiction and discursive resistance and use them beyond the boundaries of the community, in their own day-to-day lives and relationships, and in their engagements with the social institutions that reproduce dominant ideas, such as the law. By challenging the dominant regimes of truth—what is thinkable and sayable—around sex and consent, fanfiction readers and writers can reevaluate their experiences. They can make sexual encounters that felt "off" for one reason or another intelligible as coerced or nonconsensual, and, perhaps most importantly, they can develop a much more intentional approach to issues of power and consent.

This is the kind of knowledge created through the interaction between fanfiction and readers' and writers' own day-to-day sexual practice. What emerges here is a fundamental epistemological conflict between two different orders of knowledge about consent: the binary approach of the law, and the one fanfiction readers and writers create by questioning dominant ideas, focusing on the physicality and affect of sexual experiences, and providing alternative templates for sexuality to follow. Experience—both that of readers and writers themselves, and that of the characters they write about—is central to this kind of knowledge creation. At the same time, fanfiction readers and writers are finding ways to interpret that experience through lenses other than the dominant regime of truth. In this way, they create a space for uncertainty, ambiguity, sometimes discomfort, and making sense of the otherwise unintelligible.

CHALLENGING THE LAW AS A KNOWER OF CONSENT

Fanfiction readers and writers are keenly aware of the contrast between the way the law understands (or perhaps does not understand) consent, and the understandings they have developed from their own lived experience and creative work. They also see how society at large prioritizes the law's interpretation of consent rather than those of victims and survivors of sexual violence, or interpretations otherwise built on experience. The fans I interviewed repeatedly brought the law into our conversations and discussed these contrasts at length. Magmar spoke to me about a story she was writing in which the main character had consented to sex with her partner but found she had mixed feelings about the experience afterwards. Writing the story had allowed her to explore the emotional impact of the situation and reflect on the implications of such a scenario in the context of the law and the criminal justice system:

> I think that some things you have to be aware for yourself as well, and you don't always know them beforehand. So even consenting to something can result in having problems afterwards. And I think that's one of the problems we have with this whole discussion of consent and that people are, "Do I have

to get a written permission to do this to you?" Because, uh—if you think you're fine beforehand and afterward you realize you *aren't*, that is where the legal stuff, I think, gets in. Because then people can say, "I didn't want this and I don't want to talk or think about the fact that I did want it before." And suddenly then this legal position where you apparently did something without the consent even though you had it at that moment. And I think we can't really solve that by just putting our names on papers because it's about emotions. And I've no idea how to sort that out legally, but at least I can discuss it with my characters. (Magmar)

This situation also echoes some of the elements of "Sure to Lure Someone Bad" (see chapter 3), where the omega character reframes some of his past sexual experiences as coercive. Such reframing is common for survivors of sexual violence: whereas some of us know in the moment that our consent is being violated, for many it takes time and emotional distance to understand that something about an experience was not quite right. This may be because of the trauma of the event itself, but frequently it is because the dominant ideas we hold about sex in our society tell us that what we experienced was normal, and so it becomes very difficult to intelligibly name it as nonconsensual. The woman who consented but changed her mind afterwards is a trope of rape culture: a story we hear in popular culture, from defense lawyers, and even from our friends and acquaintances with the underlying message of "women's testimony on sexual violence can't be trusted." This trope is in fact so successful that, in an effort to counteract it, some feminist campaigns for legal reform will outright deny that victims and survivors of sexual violence only come to understand their experience as nonconsensual at a later date. Magmar's comments are a powerful response to the rape culture myth of "the woman who changed her mind afterwards." Feminist legal scholar Sue Lees discusses at length the issues around determining consent or the absence thereof in rape trials, and the role these play in the low conviction rates for rape. Defense lawyers consistently use arguments ranging from "she didn't fight back hard enough" to "she was wet" to paint a picture of rape complainants who make false allegations after actually consenting to sex and then changing their mind. On the other hand, as Lees points out, the vast majority of rapes are never reported to police as "forced sex is far more common than imagined and . . . women who are forced into sex often do not name this as rape."[29] The pervasive myth of women who make false allegations after consenting to sex makes conviction more difficult. It also strongly discourages victims and survivors who only later come to understand their experiences as nonconsensual from ever reporting them. And feminist scholarship and campaigns for legal reform have a strong incentive to erase and minimize such cases as a preemptive defense against the myths of rape culture.

In contrast to this, Magmar's comments, rooted in her exploration of consent through fanfiction, focus on the emotional issues of reframing our experiences after the fact. Rather than denying that this happens, Magmar demands that we open up a space where we can acknowledge and discuss such experiences. She also actively challenges the law's inability to accommodate emotional complexity. She openly says that she is unable to offer a legal solution but shifts the focus away from the law and onto other ways of knowing and understanding nuances that both rape culture and feminist legal reform campaign frequently erase. In this way, she decenters the law, and exposes an epistemological conflict between legal knowledges of rape and those based on lived experience and emotion, which she has developed through her involvement in the fanfiction community, highlighting the credibility excess of the law and credibility deficit of lived experience.

This epistemological conflict and credibility differential is particularly visible when we consider the relationship between the law as a discourse that has the power to determine truth and invalidate other discourses and our dominant ideas about sex, which construct potentially coercive sexual practices as "just sex."[30] These two forces work together and reinforce each other within rape culture. Low conviction rates for rape and routine courtroom practices casting even the most egregious violations as "consensual" reinforce rape myths as cultural norms.[31] In addition, the cultural construction of "normal" sexuality is one factor that renders the law unable to recognize more subtle violations of consent, or power relations that make consent dubious at best. If we try to position our own experiences of "dubcon" within these ideas, we are left with little choice but to continue to construct them as "just sex" or, alternatively, to go up against the regime of truth created by the combined force of the legal and cultural constructions of "normal" sex. Statements naming these experiences as anything other than "just sex" may not even be intelligible to ourselves.[32] By focusing on characters' emotions and experiences, fanfiction readers and writers are able to engage with dominant ideas of sex and consent in much more nuanced ways. They make harmful naturalized ideas visible and show us that they are anything but natural. This in turn makes it possible for readers and writers of fanfiction to expose the inadequacies of the law, as Magmar does here.

Another such challenge to the law came from Lapras when discussing the case of Welsh footballer Ched Evans who was initially convicted, and later acquitted on retrial, of rape.[33]

> But the fact is, she is telling you, she did not consent to have sex with you. So even if you, at that point in time, did not believe you were raping her, the correct and moral thing to do is to be like, "Oh my god, I am sorry, I did not mean to have sex with you against your consent, this has happened, how do I pay for your counseling and support and help you?" instead of being like, "No, it was consensual." And it's like, "Well, she's telling you it isn't." The correct response, if you genuinely did not intend to rape somebody but you did—and I do think that happens. I think some people are drunk, they don't go back to a hotel or something intending to rape somebody, but actually, maybe, they just—they're themselves drunk, and they're not aware of how out the person is. But the correct response to that is actually, check themself and maybe change the way they're living their life that this is happening. (Lapras)

Lapras's comments touch on several aspects of rape culture. Once a rape allegation is made, the criminal justice system structures all further interactions between accused and complainant as adversarial: this is a zero-sum game in which only one party's version of events can be accepted as true.[34] Lapras challenges this adversarial structure. Instead she appeals to morality and compassion and proposes an alternative approach rooted in ideas of transformative or restorative justice.[35] If we are steeped in rape culture and the view that there is no alternative to the criminal justice system, as many of us are, this complete brushing aside of standard criminal justice processes in favor of reducing and repairing harm done is almost unthinkable. For Lapras, this alternative has become imaginable, at least in part, as a result of her engagement with consent issues in fanfiction, as becomes evident from her account of how fanfiction has shaped her views on consent in real life: "I think it is interesting. It gives an interesting safe space to actually explore consent violation and actually write it when consent goes wrong or kink negotiation goes wrong."

Similarly to Magmar, fanfiction enables Lapras to explore the emotional aspects of consent issues, creating what she describes as a safe space. The safety here is created by the emotional distancing from possible real-life experiences of sexual violence, but also by the ability to explore scenarios that cannot unfold in the context of the criminal justice system as it currently exists. This is a key factor that allows Lapras to challenge the adequacy of the law and offer possible alternatives. It also enables her to envision fundamental social change and the dismantling of rape culture: "You should be able to walk down the road naked and people should think 'Why is that person naked? Let's maybe consider that maybe they need help.' We shouldn't look at a naked person and be like, 'Oh, that's permission to rape.'"

Both Lapras and Magmar here provide powerful alternative visions not only of how sexuality and consent *should* operate but also of how institutions such as the law should handle them differently. They highlight and challenge the credibility differential between different knowers and knowledges of consent. In the words of cultural activism theorists Michael Buser and Jane Arthurs, these are "alternative socio-political . . . imaginaries,"[36] or what Linda Martín Alcoff would call the "capacity to imagine things differently."[37] Magmar imagines things differently by demanding a space in law for the complexity of human emotion and sexuality. Lapras seeks to open up spaces within the law that center survivors of rape and sexual violence over the adversarial mechanics of the legal system, and spaces within wider society that value compassion for human vulnerability over the immediate sexualization of bodies. Fannish spaces and fannish engagement with sexuality and consent make it possible to create these different kinds of knowledges, rooted in both lived experience and a dismantling of the dominant regimes of truth. Lynn Jamieson argues for continued feminist efforts at legal reform: "I do not accept that to make such arguments within the legal discourse merely serve [*sic*] to strengthen the law. Let those who speak within legal discourse make these arguments while those of us who are outsiders resist phallocentrism by whatever other means are available."[38] I must admit that I am much less well disposed toward the law than Jamieson is. And what we see the fanfiction community provide here are those "other means": ways of understanding issues of consent that center, value, and give credibility to human subjectivity, emotions, and sexuality in ways that the law is, at least at present, unable to do.

7 "LIVING OUR VALUES": A PRAXIS OF CONSENT

SCHRÖDINGER'S AUTHOR: DEAD AND ALIVE

From the birth of fan studies, fans have been celebrated as the ultimate active audience. Henry Jenkins, one of the founders of fan studies, describes fans as "active producers and manipulators of meaning . . . articulating concerns which often go unnoticed within the dominant media."[1] We see fans—particularly those actively engaged in the production and circulation of fanfiction—as the epitome of the "Death of the Author." In his influential essay on literary criticism, French literary theorist Roland Barthes argues that the meaning of texts is not determined by the author, their experiences, or their intent; there is no message from the "Author-God" to be deciphered by critics. Rather, the meaning of the text is made by the reader: your or my interpretation of any given text is no more or less valid than that of the person who wrote it.[2] Hence, the author is dead.

We could expect that fanfiction readers and writers, who constantly poach and repurpose texts for their own ends, would themselves fervently declare the death of the author. To an extent, this is true, particularly with regard to any claims of ownership of meaning in the originary work. Fanfiction readers and writers claim for ourselves the right to read, reread, and rewrite any text in any way we see fit. J. K. Rowling may have intended only for Dumbledore to be (tragically) gay, but there isn't a single character in the Harry Potter books who hasn't at some point or another been gay—or bi, or trans, or any other queer identity—in fanfiction.[3] When published online, fanfiction stories are frequently accompanied by author's notes in which writers discuss the impetus for the story, their relationship to the originary work, and how the story relates to it. They may describe the writer's frustrations with a character's treatment by showrunners, or point out that their story may not be "canon-compliant" (i.e., it diverges from events as told in the originary work), emphasizing instead that it is *their* story. These notes serve to establish ownership of the piece of fanfiction but also at least partial ownership—by this particular fan, and by fans in general—of the originary work.[4] It doesn't matter what the author, the director, or the showrunner intended. They are dead and this is ours now. Yet the fanfiction community's relationship with ideas of authorship is rather more ambivalent than that. Paradoxically, we consistently demand a certain respect for *fannish* authorship. Many fanfiction writers insist on their right to control transformative works of their own work, such as fan art or audiobook-esque recordings known as podfics. So, even though the author of the originary work may be dead, ideas of authorship, meaning-making, and authorial intent are nonetheless negotiated in complex ways in fan communities. Some authors are less dead than others.

In the introduction to his eponymous study of paratexts (materials that accompany a text but aren't quite part of it, such as title, preface, dedications, epigraphs, etc.), another French literary theorist, Gérard Genette, asks, "limited to the text alone and without a guiding set of directions, how would we read Joyce's *Ulysses* if it were not entitled *Ulysses*?"[5] The implication here is that the title of the text is a way for the author to influence and direct how we read the text. The paratext is another way for the author to communicate with the reader about the text. It is interesting that Genette picks *Ulysses* as his example: a book whose title does a lot of heavy lifting in evoking intertextual relationships with another work. Without the title, we might not realize that a stream-of-consciousness ramble around Dublin is actually an odyssey. Given the dense intertextuality fanfiction relies on for its meaning-making, we can extend Genette's question: How would we read any fanfiction text without knowing what it was fanfiction of, or the characters it focuses on? Although Genette focuses on novels and other printed works, it should be no surprise that fanfiction comes with its own sets of paratexts and practices of textual presentation, some similar to those we are familiar with from printed works, and others less so.

The paratexts surrounding fanfiction vary with both specific fandom community and publication platform. Some paratexts, such as tags, originate as archive metadata: they aid in the organization, filtering, searchability, and discoverability of fanfiction stories. Others, such as disclaimers and author's notes, originate in fannish ideas about authorship and (imagined) relations between fanfiction and the rightsholders of the originary work.[6] But tags are not just metadata. In chapter 4, we saw how fanfiction authors used tags to mark many arranged-marriage stories as containing elements of dubcon or outright rape. This, in turn, drew our attention to the more problematic aspects of marriage consummation. Tags and other paratexts have acquired a dual purpose as another means of communication between (undead) author and reader.

The importance of paratexts and the strange dual role of "the author" in fanfiction communities as both dead and alive also came up repeatedly in my conversations with fanfiction readers and writers. Discussing her enjoyment of fanfiction featuring unequal power dynamics, Bulbasaur told me: "I find this really, really interesting, though I'm sometimes a little wary of what the author is thinking."

Other interviewees also talked about "authorial intent," as Dratini did in this extract:

> Realizing authorial intent after the fact sometimes can be something that really does change how you—so you can read especially if it's you know a one-shot, or you don't actually know anything about the author until everything is said and done—you'll go through the whole thing really really enjoying it, thinking it's great, and then you get to the end, read the author's note, and you go, "I genuinely feel unclean at having read this," despite having, all the way through, without any of that you know—that's something that "Oh my god, I've contributed to this." (Dratini)

The implication here is that it is OK to enjoy stories exploring unequal power dynamics, "dubcon," or even outright rape (and it is OK to enjoy them because they are hot as well as for other reasons), but fanfiction readers feel it is important to have confidence that the author chose to include these problematic elements on purpose. Any consent issues in fanfiction stories, these fans feel, should be there consciously and deliberately. Conversely, where we suspect that the author may not be aware that what they are writing is dubcon or rape, that makes the story less enjoyable because it acquires very different meanings as a result. Why, then, is authorial intent on consent issues so important in a community that, more often than not, is prepared to declare the author—particularly of the originary work—dead and buried?

In the rest of this chapter, we will look at fanfiction's rich paratexts in more detail to see what they might mean for the relationships between author, reader, text, paratext, and ultimately art and the real world. Because, after all, it doesn't matter if a small community in the depths of the internet is creating groundbreaking new knowledges about consent unless those knowledges actually have a material impact on the world. Fanfiction communities, despite a certain amount of recent mainstreaming, do not generally address a wider public. In fact, for many community members, reading and writing fanfiction are activities they would rather keep secret, away from media attention and the public eye. At the same time, the knowledges fanfiction communities produce in their fiction and conversations do, as we have seen in earlier chapters, provide a powerful kind of discursive resistance to dominant ideas about sexuality and consent. They "challenge dominant interpretations and constructions of the world," they present "alternative socio-political and spatial imaginaries," and in doing so through poaching mainstream culture, they "challenge relationships between art, politics, participation, and spectatorship."[7] Fanfiction readers and writers also, as we saw in the last chapter, take the new knowledges about consent that they make through fanfiction and apply them to their own lives and intimate relationships. That alone is a significant material impact that the community has on its members. But is there more? Do these activities, hidden away in corners of the internet, affect and shape the lives not only of the immediate fanfiction community but of other communities that fanfiction readers and writers may be part of in their everyday lives? Who is activated by this discursive resistance, and what else can this very specific kind of cultural activism achieve?

So, in this chapter, I want to explore one final aspect of how fanfiction and the knowledges about consent generated through it materially impact the real world and community members' lives: the link between readers' and writers' textual practices, their beliefs about the role of culture and representation in the world, and what I call a *praxis of consent*. How do fanfiction readers and writers conceptualize both the role and the responsibility of a text's author? How do they view mainstream media and its role in reproducing or challenging dominant ideas about sex, sexual violence, and consent? And what role does the design of fannish infrastructure such as AO3 play in allowing fans to meet their self-imposed representational responsibilities and make a prefigurative gesture of a world free of sexual violence? Fannish practices around the circulation of their creative output show how fanfiction readers and writers move effortlessly between a textual consideration of issues of consent in their fanfiction and an activist praxis of consent that extends into their day-to-day lives.

MAINSTREAM MEDIA, FANFICTION, AND CONSENT

One key theme from my interviews with readers and writers was fanfiction's relationship with the originary works it is based on, which interviewees saw as mainstream media. As we saw in chapter 4, fanfiction readers and writers are frequently aware of the problems with the way relationships are depicted in romance novels. They know that inequality and power imbalances in relationships can have a negative effect on our ability to negotiate consent, and they rewrite romance novel plots to highlight this rather than sweep it under the rug like romance novels often do. Several of the fanfiction readers and writers I talked to brought up similar issues with how sex and relationships are shown not just in romance novels but in mainstream media more generally.

> I don't like watching, I don't like the dynamics that we see in media between men and women often, because often it is sort of almost implied that it's OK

for the woman to sort of take some abuse from the man without it ever being raised as an issue. (Blissey)

Blissey feels that in mainstream media, abusive and coercive (heterosexual) relationships are normalized and often even romanticized rather than challenged. Feminist media critics, sexual violence activists, and researchers like Nicola Gavey have long argued that much of Western mainstream media treats potentially coercive relationships and sex as normal—as "just sex." Blissey picks up on the same theme. Importantly, what she takes issue with is not just the portrayal of problematic or coercive relationships in media but rather the fact that these are treated as normal, or even romantic. If these relationships were specifically being addressed as abusive or coercive in originary works, Blissey (and other interviewees) would find them less problematic. The author's presumed lack of awareness that what is being depicted is violent and coercive—their unwitting reproduction of the "just sex" paradigm and rape culture—is the larger problem at hand. When it comes to consent, fanfiction readers and writers care deeply about authorial intent, whether in mainstream media or fanfiction. And they want to hold mainstream media creators accountable for problematic portrayals of relationships, sex, and consent. Fanfiction's complex relationship with ideas of authorship and authorial intent is evident here. That the author *meant* to write a romantic relationship is of less importance than the abusive relationship that the audience is *reading*. The disconnect between what Blissey imagines the author meant to do and what she is reading is jarring and subject to critique. Rather than simply accepting what she believes the author's intent to have been, Blissey is confident in her own reading. That reading, though, does not absolve the author of responsibility. The author is dead, in that what they intended to do doesn't matter for Blissey's interpretation. The author is alive in that they failed to achieve what they intended to and bear responsibility for that failure.

The occasions where mainstream media does consent well are so rare that several of the fanfiction readers and writers I spoke to highlighted the one or two instances they could clearly remember.[8] Referring to a scene in *The Growing Pains of Adrian Mole*, Nidorina says:

There's a moment when he asks his girlfriend whether he can touch her over her sweater. And I remember—I'm sure I was about twelve, maybe, when I read that—and I'd seen so much stuff where stuff just . . . happened on TV. And I was like, "Why would you stop and ask?" And that stuck in my head, for a long time because I was just like, on the one hand, yeah, he should ask. On the other hand, it literally struck me as so weird compared to everything else I'd seen. (Nidorina)

For Nidorina, a fairly short scene in a book where the characters discuss consent openly and explicitly stands in stark contrast to her usual experience of consent as depicted in mainstream media. If you have ever read the Adrian Mole books, you might remember that the title character is intensely awkward, particularly in his teenage years, and the scene Nidorina is referring to is presented not as a positive example of consent negotiation but as yet another manifestation of Adrian's fumbling teenage awkwardness. Yet Nidorina's interpretation is different: what attracts her attention is not the awkwardness, but rather the fact that a consent discussion is shown at all. It disrupts the default progression from touching and kissing through undressing to penile-vaginal intercourse that is our dominant sexual script. And by disrupting it, that awkward moment where Adrian asks Pandora whether he can touch her breast makes visible that normally unquestioned progression and highlights the problems with it. That this instance has remained in Nidorina's mind for decades shows just how unusual such representation of consent negotiation is in mainstream media, and how dominant the "just sex" ideas of relationships automatically progressing through stages of physical contact to penile-vaginal intercourse are.

Nidorina also talked about how she felt mainstream media portrayals of sex and relationships had changed:

I remember growing up there was a lot of like—it seemed to be on the cusp, really, of, in a mainstream way, changing from, you know, "Take things slowly and build up to sex," to "Sex is just a thing that's gonna happen." That's what it felt like to me when I was growing up, like a lot of the, everything from magazines to TV shows . . . everything seemed to be dah-dah-dah-dah, teenagers have sex, dah-dah-dah-dah-dah, you know, whatever, and it was such—it became such a common thing that having, you know, a couple actually talk about not having sex yet, not doing it—it's interesting to me cos it—almost without explicitly doing it, it kind of tackles that assumption that they're just gonna fall into bed as soon as they decide they like each other. (Nidorina)

Nidorina feels that both the automatic progression of relationships to intercourse and the idea that penile-vaginal intercourse is the only valid form of sex have become more entrenched in mainstream media. That default progression provides an uncontested template for how our intimate relationships should work. As it is uncontested, this template comes to seem natural and becomes normalized, making it more difficult for us to negotiate (or sometimes even imagine) anything deviating from it. At the same time, in talking about how she is interested in, for example, couples explicitly discussing delaying sex in their relationship, Nidorina highlights the importance of challenging that default and hints at the possibility of doing so in fanfiction. As we saw from Ekans's comments in chapter 6, these challenges can indeed be found in fanfiction, and they function to make visible and demythologize dominant, naturalized discourses of sex and consent. Where mainstream media presents one unchallenged version of how relationships should work, readers and writers can explore, imagine, and practice alternatives in fanfiction.

Some of my interviewees speculated about what made fanfiction particularly suited to imagining and exploring such alternatives. What tools and resources do fanfiction readers and writers have that allow them to deviate from the default ideas of how relationships should work? How are these different to the resources available to mainstream media creators? Several interviewees highlighted the ways in which fanfiction provides more scope to explore certain elements of an originary work, from individual characters to aspects of the world building and even specific scenes and situations. Bulbasaur, for instance, said:

I think what fanfic does is it gives you an opportunity to delve into these moments that in the original source material are probably gonna be passed over in a couple of—max, a few paragraphs, or a couple of lines of dialogue.

Whereas fanfic gives you this opportunity to genuinely delve into what is happening in the minds of these characters. If you're reading a novel, you sort of go, "OK, this is really dragging it down, you're turning this into a doorstopper for no reason." Whereas in fanfic you've got that opportunity because that's what the reader is there for. They don't want the plot, cos you already know what the plot is, or it's been laid out—this is pure character, which I think can be really interesting when you're talking about issues of consent. And you already know the characters—the characters are already fleshed out, they already have backstories, they already have personalities. So, you're not, you know—you feel familiar with them anyway, so you're exploring them, deeper. It's just such a great opportunity to do that. Again, in a normal novel there isn't—there isn't the opportunity for that as thoroughly. (Bulbasaur)

Bulbasaur here highlights the way elements such as plot and character are in some ways optional in fanfiction. Because fanfiction stories build on originary works and writers can safely assume that their target audiences are familiar with those originary works, they can use that familiarity to their advantage. They do not have to spend time, for instance, establishing who a character is. Rather, they can take that ready-made character and put them in new situations, exploring how they might react to different things. Similarly, although some fanfiction works have long and elaborate plots of their own, many do not. They simply explore variations on the originary plot by making small tweaks to it. We saw examples of this in chapter 4, where changes to who does the emotion work in an unequal relationship have a significant effect on how consent works. Such changes only make sense because readers and writers are familiar with the plots and tropes of the originary romance novels. Other interviewees also spoke of the importance of having a ready-made setting to explore, especially when it offered scope for examining power structures through a new lens. Because the originary work already provides setting, characters, and plot, fanfiction works can spend less time on them and can instead focus on exploring issues of interest to the author and readers in more depth.

Conversely, originary works (or mainstream media) are limited in their scope and ability to explore issues such as consent in depth precisely because they strive for originality. They have to establish new characters and settings and develop new plots rather than simply tweaking existing ones and using similarities and differences between different texts to create meaning. Other forms of popular culture may, of course, explore sexuality and consent. But what fanfiction does is densely layer meanings through repetition with a difference and leverage these meanings to examine both characters' internal lives and social power structures. Fanfiction stories are constantly in dialogue not only with the originary work but also with each other, so this layering of meanings is iterative—readers and writers keep building on it. These reading and writing processes are unavailable to mainstream media. The ability to use existing characters, plots, and settings and rewrite scenarios over and over in dialogue with others allows fanfiction readers and writers to build on existing themes and conversations in and around originary works and respond to the questions raised by them in nuanced ways, as Victreebel argues here:

> I think there's a lot more gray areas in the sense that I think authors are given—because you can play the same scenario so many times with the same characters, many authors will not just, like, write one fic about a particular pairing, they'll write, like, twelve and try to get the dynamic the way they want it. Which means that, in a way, they get to replay that scenario and make a different decision each time. And I think that sort of multiplicity, I think, assists in the dialogue as well as understanding of the issues surrounding it. Whereas with canon you have the one way it's done, and that's done. (Victreebel)

Victreebel makes a key connection between the "repetition with a difference" technique and fanfiction's ability to explore consent issues in a deeply nuanced way. In fanfiction, we can make slight changes to a situation, to a character, or to a relationship and explore the impact of those changes. We can change, for instance, who of Thor and Loki is the "bride." We can tweak the Omegaverse setting to make the enforcement of gender roles more or less strict. And we can see where those changes take us. This exploration takes into account characters' emotions and inner states, looks for ways of resolving conflict, accounts for power differentials in relationships, and challenges clear-cut binary paradigms of rape and consent.

Elements of the originary work, other fanfiction stories, common main-stream media tropes, and readers and writers' own experiences of social power structures and intimate relationships are all used in such stories and the meaning-making processes around them. The changes writers make in their stories are sometimes relatively small and subtle, such as the exact process by which we get to the happily ever after ending of the romance novel. At other times, they are so significant as to make everything seem alien and strange, such as those seen in the Omegaverse. These similarities and differences between the different intertextual elements that fanfiction readers and writers bring into play ultimately allow for the subtle and nuanced exploration of consent issues we have seen thus far. Fanfiction readers and writers take what they see as problematic "mainstream" texts and rewrite them to suit their own needs. In this process, they seek to hold accountable both creators of mainstream media and, as we will see in the remainder of this chapter, each other for the kinds of representation they offer in key areas such as gender, sexuality, and consent.

The fanfiction readers and writers I spoke to pointed clearly to the shortcomings of mainstream media when it comes to issues of sexual consent. The key issue they raised was not that mainstream media depicts potentially problematic situations but that it normalizes and frequently even romanticizes unequal relationships and other potentially coercive sexual situations. As we saw in chapter 6, one key issue commonly raised by interviewees was how, in this way, mainstream media reproduces the dominant construction of such situations as "just sex," the default progression of relationships through stages of intimacy to penile-vaginal intercourse, and the idea that penile-vaginal intercourse is the only sexual act that requires consent. They pinpointed instances where such defaults were challenged in mainstream media as exceptionally rare and highlighted their potential for challenging and dismantling dominant ideas about sex and consent. They also foregrounded the set of tools fanfiction has at its disposal to do just that: its dense intertextuality; its relative lack of concern about originality; its reuse of plots, characters, and settings; and its ability to explore a situation from multiple different angles and perspectives through side-by-side reading and repetition with a difference.

We saw in chapter 2 that fanfiction is a *communal textuality*: stories work in dialogue with each other, with originary works, and with readers' and writers' own lived experiences. Readers and writers create, interpret, challenge, question, and recreate texts (both mainstream and fanfiction) together. In this process, they recognize and foreground the potential of fiction to do real work in the real world. They emphasize the importance of the author's awareness of consent issues and criticize mainstream media for its perceived lack of such awareness. The concept of authorial intent facilitates this communal textuality and provides a bridge from fictional text to a praxis of consent in community members' interactions with each other and in their day-to-day lives outside fannish spaces.

FROM PRACTICE TO TEXT/FROM TEXT TO PRAXIS

Fanfiction communities provide a space where readers and writers can make issues of consent and its representation in mainstream media visible; where they can name the problem of the normalization of sexual violence and coercive sexual practices as "just sex"; and where they can collectively come up with alternative ideas, knowledges, and imaginaries. All of this in turn allows fans not only to challenge dominant ideas of sex, sexuality, and consent, but also to understand and challenge the role of social institutions like the law and the criminal justice system in sexual violence. I would like at this point to return to the question of Schrödinger's author: the importance that fanfiction readers and writers attach to an author's clear and demonstrated awareness of their handling of consent issues in their work. How is such authorial intent expressed by writers and interpreted by readers? Why is it important to the community? And what does this importance say about the activist potential of the fanfiction community on issues of consent? To answer these questions, we will first have a look at how fanfiction readers and writers signal and interpret authorial intent through the paratexts that surround fanfiction texts. (If you are a regular AO3 user, feel free to skim the next couple of paragraphs.)

Like other types of texts and media, pieces of fanfiction are surrounded by paratexts when they are published online. Some of these, such as the work title, are familiar to readers of other types of fiction. Others are particular to fanfiction and have their origins in fannish archiving practices and the design of the various online platforms fanfiction readers and writers use. They are first and foremost metadata intended to make works discoverable on an interactive platform such as Tumblr or an archive such as AO3.[9] In figure 7.1, we can see how a fanfiction story appears to readers on AO3. The page starts with a block of metadata, progressing from the generic to the specific. Similarly to the film rating systems most of us are familiar with, the rating reflects the story's suitability for different age groups, ranging from "General Audiences" to "Explicit." "Archive warnings" are intended to prepare the reader for particularly upsetting content they may encounter. They fall into four categories: "Graphic Depictions of Violence," "Major Character Death," "Rape/Non-con," and "Underage."

Reindex Work | Add Chapter | Edit | Edit Tags | Bookmark | Comments | Share | Subscribe | Download ↓

Rating:	General Audiences
Archive Warning:	**No Archive Warnings Apply**
Category:	Gen
Fandom:	The Legend of Zelda: Breath of the Wild
Relationship:	Link & gender
Characters:	Link (Legend of Zelda), Vilia (Legend of Zelda), Isha (Legend of Zelda)
Additional Tags:	Trans Link (Legend of Zelda), Trans woman Link, Gerudo Town, Gerudo Outfit, Drabble, shopping for pretty things
Language:	English
Stats:	Published: 2019-09-13 Words: 100 Chapters: 1/1 Hits: 0

Amber

elmyra

Summary:

Gerudo town holds some revelations.

Notes:

CN: Link is only just working gender things out and is using he/him pronouns.

The guy who sells him the outfit is creepy, and so when Link puts on the veil and wrap and sirwal, he wonders if that makes him creepy too.

Then he enters Gerudo.

The women treat him as one of their own. Gently. Respectfully. It's like for the first time since he woke up, he can breathe.

At the goldsmith's, he looks at all the jewellery that will protect him from heat and cold and lightning. In the end, he buys a simple pair of amber earrings. They won't do much, but they're pretty, and they make his eyes shine.

↑ Top | Add To Collections | Bookmark

Figure 7.1
A work of fanfiction as presented on the Archive of Our Own.

The latter two of these are specifically related to consent. An author may also indicate that no archive warnings apply to the story, or that they chose not to use archive warnings, which is a signal to the reader to proceed at their own risk. The "Categories" field refers to the type of sexual or romantic relationships featured in the story: between two men (M/M), two women (F/F), or a man and a woman (F/M); multiple relationships (multi); or no focus on sexual or romantic relationships (known as "gen").

Moving beyond these generic categories, the next four sets of metadata are called tags. They show how the story relates to the originary work(s) it is based on, ensuring that a reader is not put in a position where, to use Genette's example, they are reading *Ulysses* without knowing that it is titled *Ulysses*. The "Fandom" tag specifies the originary works a story is fanfiction of. "Characters" tags indicate which characters from the originary work the fanwork focuses on. "Relationships" tags show which characters are in relationships with each other and what those relationships are. Here, characters separated by a slash are in a sexual or romantic relationship, whereas those separated by an ampersand are considered friends. The "Additional Tags" category, also known as "freeforms," gives authors a space to include any other information they feel necessary. Authors use this unstructured space in many different ways. They may include warnings and content notes not covered by the four "archive warnings," letting readers know that they can expect potentially upsetting content such as drug use or suicide. Authors also use freeforms to provide a sometimes flippant author's commentary on the originary work, the fanfiction story itself, or the writing process. Common tropes used in the fanwork, such as "Alternate Universe—Coffee Shop" (a popular trope in which characters from originary works are taken out of their setting and reimagined as staff and customers of a coffee shop), "Fix-it" (a story that ignores or rewrites elements of the originary work perceived as wrong, such as the death of a character or the end of a relationship), or "Slow Build" (a fanwork that establishes and builds the central romantic relationship over time), can also be part of the additional tags. Finally, freeforms can be used by authors to share information about and discussion of any consent issues the story may deal with. This is where we would find tags such as "dubcon," "consent issues," or "fuck or die."

Six of the eight fanfiction readers and writers I spoke to brought up tags and other paratexts as a key community practice related to consent. They talked about how tags for them were not just metadata that makes stories easier to find. Rather, they are a way for reader and writer to communicate with each other around the text. Through tags and other paratexts, authors can clarify their intent outside but adjacent to the main body of the fanwork. Interviewees saw such clarifications as particularly important when it came to issues of consent. Blissey summarized the importance of this communication channel outside the text: "The tagging, I find that really important because that tells you that the person has thought through what they're writing."

This comment shows that where issues of sexual consent feature in a work of fanfiction, readers find it important to know—and writers seek to show—that the author has consciously thought through them and deliberately chosen to explore them as part of the story. In particular, when the sexual situation depicted in the story includes elements of ambiguous or dubious consent, or is a depiction of rape, both readers and writers use the metadata around the story (such as tags, warnings, and author's notes) to determine whether these elements are deliberate. This stands in contrast to the kind of unsuccessful attempt to depict consensual sex that we saw fanfiction readers and writers criticize in mainstream media. Fanfiction community members see situations they can identify as problematic or as violations due to power differentials, involving dubious consent for other reasons, or being outright nonconsensual depicted in mainstream media as perfectly unproblematic, normal, consensual sex. In many cases, they are aware of having themselves absorbed some of these attitudes to sex from media, and of the work it has taken them to unlearn some of them. In the face of this normalization of sexual violence and coercive behaviors in mainstream media, Blissey and other fanfiction readers and writers I spoke to were keen to ensure that fanfiction spaces do not reproduce this pattern, even when fanfiction deliberately explores these themes. Frequently, the mere textual representation is not enough to achieve this: without some indication of authorial awareness, a dubcon scene in fanfiction may look exactly like those dubcon-portrayed-as-unproblematic scenes in mainstream media. Blissey described this as follows: "And what I have much more issue with [in fanfiction] is anything that accidentally writes dubcon, that doesn't even—that's something that I will, as soon as that happens, I'm out."

In his analysis of a book's preface, Genette tells us that "its chief function is *to ensure that the text is read properly*."[10] Some kind of indication of authorial intent, according to Genette, is a key component of a book's preface, often regardless of the author's own stance on the "death of the author" issue. And once the author has told us how they want us to read the book, it is impossible "to read the story without having the authorial interpretation hang over your reading, compelling you to take a position, positive or negative, in relation to it."[11] Fanfiction paratexts—both author's notes, which are the closest fanfiction equivalent to a preface, and tags—do very similar work in guiding readers to read the work "properly." But Blissey's comment suggests that what fans actually mean when they refer to authorial intent (especially but not only in relation to sexual consent) is something slightly different. When she talks about someone who "accidentally writes dubcon," what Blissey means are stories where the paratexts that would normally signal that the author is exploring consent issues deliberately are *absent*. She also clearly distinguishes between the author's intent—signaled, in her view, by the absent paratext—to write a romantic and consensual scene and her own reading of it as "dubcon." Rather than the author's paratexts guiding the "proper" reading, Blissey's reading of the story as "dubcon" shapes her expectation of what paratexts *should* be there. The dynamic here is the opposite to the one Genette describes. The author's declaration of intent does not compel the reader to take up a position in relation to it. Instead, it is Blissey's *expectation* of a careful consideration of consent issues that compels *the author* to declare a stance. This expectation makes the absence of such a declaration meaningful in its own right: if you, the author, are not telling me, the reader, that you thought about this, then you haven't thought about it. Actual authorial intent is relatively unimportant in this exchange. We can also see this in situations where, even when the author does take up a position on the issue of consent in the paratexts of a story, the reader's interpretation may still be different. An author may tag a story as "dubcon" and a reader may read it as "noncon," or vice versa, and such disagreements are common. Fanfiction readers find it helpful and important to know that an author has deliberately grappled with issues of sexual consent in their work, but authorial intent here does not have the final say even when it is expressly declared.

What is important is not so much what the author intended, or even what the reader read, or whether the two agreed. Rather, the key point here is that these conversations are normal and expected in fannish communities, around fannish texts. The archived version of "Slick"—the Omegaverse rape story we looked at in chapter 3—for instance, comes with warnings for "Rape/Non-con," tags for "Dubious Consent" and "Non-Consensual," and the additional warning in the author's notes, "Omegaverse, and every single layer of dubcon that implies." The author of "Slick," tryfanstone, is clearly saying here that she wrote the graphic depiction of rape consciously and deliberately. And judging by the comments, most readers agreed with her assessment of what she wrote. But that is not always the case. In the fanfiction community's conception of authorial intent, the author is very much both dead and alive. Their intent (whether declared through tags or conspicuous from their absence) does not determine the meaning of the text. But the *idea* of it, the way fanfiction communities conceptualize it, allows fanfiction readers and writers to talk about the real-world implications of culture, art, and fiction. It allows them to acknowledge that how we show sex and consent in media and fiction shapes how we think about those things in our lives. Because of that, the idea of authorial intent becomes an idea of authorial responsibility, and that in turn allows (and compels) the community to set and reinforce community norms. It encourages readers and writers to reproduce particular practices in their creative output and day-to-day interactions within the community, such as deliberate consideration and discussion of consent issues through both text and paratext. In this way, community members ensure that rather than unwittingly reproducing rape culture, they are actively making it visible and challenging it.

Several of the fanfiction readers and writers I spoke to talked about how being confident that an author has thought through the consent implications of a scenario and is deliberately exploring them can be a source of enjoyment of a piece of fanfiction:

> I take very explicit enjoyment in seeing consent depicted, as in the awareness of the writer when they're making it—however the consent is indicated, I take a lot of pleasure in seeing that. It tends to make me go back and read more of that writer's work. (Nidorina)

Fanfiction readers and writers value authorial awareness and knowing that the author wrote a coercive sexual act deliberately as coercive. This is a key tool the community uses to stop and challenge the normalization of coerced sex as "just sex." Paratexts such as tags, author's notes, and warnings are a way for the author to communicate with the reader outside of but adjacent to the text—and to signal their authorial awareness of consent issues. We have already seen how the community has identified harmful dominant ideas about sex and started challenging their "naturalness" (Cornel West's demystification and demythologization), but this paratextual communication, these notes in the margins about consent, go a step further. They dismantle dominant ideas about coerced sex being normal and offer us the kinds of alternatives fanfiction readers and writers feel mainstream media fails to give us. The paratextual interaction between writer and reader in the margins of the text is itself a form of cultural activism. It makes the unthinkable thinkable by showing us clearly that situations we take as normal, as "just sex," are actually, at the very least, dubiously consensual. The reader's expectation to see information on consent issues in the tags is a prompt for the writer to consider them. Within the communal textuality of fanfiction, the presence of the tags is a declaration by the writer to the reader: "I have thought about this, and you should, too." In this way, the community reinforces and normalizes the expectation to think carefully about any issues of power and consent in fanfiction stories, rather than unthinkingly reproducing dominant ideas of "just sex."

Fannish paratexts, then, perform a key function of making visible the link between representation in culture and the real world. The way fanfiction readers and writers use such paratexts demands an engagement with that link—with how culture shapes the way we think and what we do. But there is another reason for the widespread use of paratextual tools such as tags and author's notes within fanfiction communities. One of my interviewees, Lapras, highlighted this when she discussed trigger warnings. The phrase "trigger warning" has entered mainstream English usage over the last ten years, though how it is used varies significantly with the political alignment of the user. It is borrowed from clinical psychiatry, where "triggers" refer to content or experiences that might induce acute symptoms of posttraumatic stress disorder. A trigger warning, then, is a signal that a work contains some potentially upsetting content. Fannish communities have used the phrase since at least the early 2000s, when LiveJournal was the dominant platform for fannish interaction.[12] They were arguably also one of the key vectors for popularizing mainstream use of the phrase. The use of trigger warnings is not uncontroversial in fanfiction circles for a number of reasons, and discussions on whether warnings should be an expected community standard surface with some regularity. AO3 considers only four specific items as worthy of the "warning" label ("Major Character Death," "Graphic Depictions of Violence," "Rape/Non-con," and "Underage"), but other types of content can be and are warned for in the freeform tags. Here, Lapras discusses the controversy around using trigger warnings:

> And the last thing you wanna do is trigger somebody. Like, that's harsh. I think there's a lot of people who are really negative about trigger warnings— it's annoying. Because they're a thing some people see as, "Oh, it's to stop people from being offended"—and, like, you don't understand about trigger warnings if you think that it's about people being offended. You know we're not saying, "Hey, this contains talk of rape" because we're like, "Oh no, the feminists might get angry." We're saying that because if somebody had recently been through something that's been really sexually violent, then, actually, them reading that can be really emotionally damaging for them. (Lapras)

Lapras' comment highlights the core intention behind the use of warnings around issues of consent in particular: to enable members of the community who may be traumatized by depictions of rape and sexual assault because of their own past experiences to make informed choices about the fanfiction works they engage with. This stance implicitly acknowledges that, given the fanfiction community consists predominantly of women and nonbinary people who statistically experience sexual violence at high rates, a significant proportion of community members are or may be survivors of sexual violence.[13] This acknowledgment is critical to understanding the importance the fanfiction community places on issues of sexual consent in both its creative output and its day-to-day practices. The community actively chooses to center survivor safety and enable community members to give informed consent to the kinds of content they are exposed to. This is, in itself, a form of cultural activism: a prefigurative act, a lived practice of how a world where sexual violence was not normalized would work.

Fannish practices such as tagging, author's notes, and the way fans think about authorial intent are ways of highlighting how culture, art, and fiction shape our reality: the ways we think, the things we can and can't say, the things we do. They also do important work in the real world in centering the well-being of survivors of sexual violence in a way that shows us what a world free of rape culture might look like. But they also play one other role when it comes to consent: they challenge the rape/consent binary, the idea that there is a clear dividing line between those two concepts. They open up a space for talking about and making intelligible the vast gray area between the two—something that our dominant ideas about sexual violence still fail to do. Bulbasaur highlighted this in our interview when she said that "the tagging system does make you actually think about what you're reading a little." Several other interviewees also brought up the issue of differences in the reader's and writer's interpretation of the level of consent depicted in a scene, even in stories that may be tagged as "dubcon" or "noncon." Nidorina, for instance, said, "I actually get kind of upset when it's labeled dubcon and it's noncon. Even when I will read noncon if it's labeled noncon, I get really kind of pissed off [laughs] when it's noncon."

This comment shows how fannish paratexts do real work in the real world by making visible the vast gray areas of consent: those stories where authors' and readers' interpretations of what counts as consensual versus what may be considered "dubcon" or outright rape diverge, where there is room for discussion and exploration. This shows a collective understanding within the community—absent in dominant ideas of sexual violence—that consent is rarely clear-cut for a range of reasons. As Magmar noted in chapter 6, human sexuality and emotions are more fragmented, complex, and contradictory than the binary opposition of consent/rape suggested by the law. Accounting for the effect power imbalances in a relationship have on consent is particularly difficult. Many fanfiction stories and entire tropes and subgenres focus on this, resulting in millions of words exploring such issues in careful and nuanced ways. And because there is space for complexity and nuance here, readers' and writers' interpretations of these stories often diverge. In an arranged-marriage story such as those we looked at in chapter 4, where one character is completely dependent on another for shelter, livelihood, social status, and more, is it enough for the more powerful character to take on the bulk of the emotion work to make consent truly meaningful? There may not be a single clear answer to this that the entire fanfiction community will agree on. What fanfiction and its surrounding paratexts do, however, is enable the question to be asked in the first place. They expose the gray areas hidden by the legalistic binary of consent/rape. They show how we as a society have normalized everything but the most extreme cases as falling on the "consent" side of that binary. They provide different tools for thinking through those gray areas—tools that the law, for instance, does not have at its disposal. They allow us to consider and live with the ambiguity and discomfort that the law leaves behind when it declares something "not rape" that many of us experience as anything but consensual.

As we saw in earlier chapters, fanfiction readers and writers use their creative output to explore issues of sexual consent, to challenge dominant ideas about sex and consent, and even to challenge the law and criminal justice system in their handling of issues of sexual violence. They create new knowledges of consent, rooted in the lived experience of sexuality but also in an understanding of how that experience is always filtered through dominant ideas and regimes of truth. These knowledges are arguably subjugated not in the Foucauldian sense but in the ways suggested by Collins.[14] They provide alternatives to our society's dominant ideas about sex and consent and show that those dominant ideas are socially constructed rather than natural. At the same time, however, these knowledges are positioned as inferior and naive by more dominant discourses and institutions such as the law.

In this context, the fanfiction community's paratexts and practices then perform several functions that further facilitate and build on this work. They prompt and even normalize reflection on issues of consent on the part of both readers and writers. In this way, they encourage us to develop a "hermeneutic sensibility"[15]—a way of paying attention—to new and alternative knowledges of consent. They render visible the gray areas of sexual consent in the community's creative output and open them up for discussion and exploration. They enable community members to make informed choices about the fanfiction works they engage with. Finally, through the emphasis on authorial intent as a reflection of the work texts do in the real world, fanfiction paratexts show a conscious effort on the part of the community to challenge rather than reproduce mainstream media's depictions of potentially coercive sexual acts as "just sex."

These paratexts and practices are firmly rooted in the shared acknowledgment that this is a community whose membership includes many survivors of sexual violence and in the desire to create a space that centers the well-being of its members. Although this acknowledgment and desire are not universal within the community, they are still sufficiently dominant forces to make the use of consent-specific tags, warnings, and author's notes a widespread, if occasionally challenged, community norm that is even built into the community's infrastructures.

As bell hooks argues, "the ability to see and describe one's own reality is a significant step in the long process of self-recovery; but it is only a beginning."[16] The ability to see oppressive discursive constructions of "just sex" for what they are and imagine alternatives is absolutely necessary in a struggle against sexual violence, but on its own it is not enough. Theory and research on cultural activism focus predominantly on activities that are directed at the general public and performed by relatively small, existing activist groups. Fanfiction rarely, if ever, fits that description. And yet, considering the role it plays in the lives of those who read and write it, it makes a compelling case for expanding our definition of cultural activism to that which helps us, in private or in small, hidden groups, take that vital first step of seeing and naming our reality, and of imagining it in a different way. The sum of the fanfiction community's creative output, paratexts, conversations, and practices becomes what I call a *praxis of consent*: the community's enactment in the real world of their collectively created knowledges about consent. The community puts into daily practice the knowledges and theories about consent they develop through fanfiction. Fanfiction readers and writers see rape culture in the real world and challenge each other to do better: do not reproduce problematic dominant ideas about sex and consent; think about the consent implications of what you are writing; consider issues of power; give those around you the opportunity to make an informed choice about the kinds of content they engage with—because they may be vulnerable, and because it is the right thing to do.

Through this praxis, fanfiction readers' and writers' creative exploration of issues of consent and power in their fiction takes on a material dimension within their day-to-day lives. They realize that consent negotiation is "a thing that can and should happen" (Ekans), and are able to account for the effects of power imbalances in their own relationships and lives. They discover that consent/rape is not a legalistic binary, that "we can't really solve [the emotional complexity of sex] by just putting our names on papers because it's about emotions" (Magmar). They develop powerful challenges to rape myths and rape culture and are able to argue that "you should be able to walk down the road naked and people should think, 'Why is that person naked? Let's maybe consider that maybe they need help.' We shouldn't look at a naked person and be like, 'Oh, that's permission to rape'" (Lapras). Finally, they are able to create a space that centers the experiences and safety of survivors of sexual violence: a powerful act of prefiguration, an exemplary gesture of how a world where sexual violence is not normalized and naturalized would work. It may, as hooks argues, be only the beginning, but it is a *necessary* beginning without which further steps would be impossible.

8 EPILOGUE

Content note: This chapter discusses racism in fandom and fanfiction, including detailed examples of both fan behavior and fanfiction stories.

Fanfiction has great potential to create and make accessible new knowledges, to explore difficult issues, to allow us to see ourselves reflected in culture that habitually erases us, and to enable us to imagine things differently. On issues of sexual consent in particular, fanfiction is a form of cultural activism. Readers and writers come together and as a community explore the kinds of difficult questions about consent that the dominant ideas in our society make all but unaskable. In their interactions with each other, their community practices, and their infrastructures, fanfiction readers and writers enact a praxis of consent, making their knowledges manifest in the real world. In this way, they show us what a world without rape culture might look like. While not directed at a wider public, this kind of creation and enacting of knowledges through culture and creative writing does open up new possibilities for community members: it changes how they understand themselves, their sexuality, and their own sexual practices. It has tangible effects on the real world, and is therefore a meaningful form of cultural activism. Having said that, in this final chapter I would like to explore two seemingly contradictory aspects of the fanfiction community and its engagement with sexual consent: its failings and its potential.

Fanfiction communities are sites of cultural activism on sexual consent. But what does this actually mean? I submitted the PhD thesis on which this book is based the week after the Weinstein allegations broke. We've had #MeToo. People have gone to prison. Aren't we done with sexual violence and consent activism yet?[1] Where is this kind of activism going next? Historian and cultural theorist Stephen Duncombe remarked rather cynically that revolutions have a tendency "to end at the guillotine or in a shopping mall."[2] So, can we see signs of fanfiction communities' activism heading in either of those directions?

There has been a certain level of cooptation and commercialization—or, at the very least, mainstreaming—of both fanfiction and discussions of sexual consent in the last few years. For decades, fanfiction was an underground, clandestine activity, both because of its murky copyright status and because the expression of women's and queer sexualities is stigmatized in our society. If you are an Old Fan like me, you remember every piece of fanfiction being preceded by a copyright disclaimer along the lines of, "I don't own anything and am not making any money from this, please don't sue."[3] But this trend has pretty much disappeared in recent years, to the point that younger community members stumbling upon older fic are extremely puzzled by this particular kind of paratext. "Why would anyone sue fanfiction writers?" they wonder. The founding of the Organization for Transformative Works (OTW) in 2007 has a lot to do with this development. The mid-2000s saw several attempts by various rightsholders and other commercial companies to capitalize on fanworks (Kindle Worlds, in 2013, was a latecomer to this trend, and it probably won't be the last). There were also several run-ins with platforms like LiveJournal, where some types of fanfiction were banned and users' accounts outright deleted.[4] So, the OTW was founded both to provide "an Archive of One's Own . . . run BY fanfic readers FOR fanfic readers,"[5] and to make a strong legal case for fanworks as legal, not infringing on copyright, and themselves protected under US law as transformative works. This removed the perceived legal pressures on fanfiction and other fanworks to remain clandestine. On the social stigma side of things, we have seen a mainstreaming of discussions and representation in culture of women's and queer sexualities, and we fan studies scholars have done our bit by relentlessly (and sometimes less critically than is warranted) celebrating erotic fanfiction as subversive and transformative. And, of course, rightsholders' attempts to capitalize on fanfiction and other kinds of fan engagement haven't stopped. As Henry Jenkins argues, "the media industry is increasingly dependent on active and committed consumers to spread the word about valued properties in an overcrowded media marketplace, and in some cases they are seeking ways to channel the creative output of media fans to lower their production costs."[6] Studios encourage cosplay (dressing up as favorite characters, often involving the creation of elaborate handmade costumes), game developers run fanfiction competitions, and CBS and Paramount are trying to both accommodate and control the production of *Star Trek* fan films through a set of official guidelines.[7] The publication of *Fifty Shades of Grey*, which originated as a piece of fanfiction for the book and movie series Twilight, is perhaps the most notorious incident of commercializing fanfiction, but there are plenty of other examples. These factors combine to create a much greater awareness of fanfiction and other fannish activities in the public eye, to the delight of some fanfiction community members and the chagrin of others. Some fans feel validated by this commercial attention. Others would much rather keep hiding in our gutter, thank you very much.

The #MeToo movement and other more or less mainstream discussions of sexual violence are another important development in the environment in which fanfiction communities operate. They have drawn the attention of the wider public to something feminists have known for decades: that there are many powerful, high-profile abusers who come from all walks of life and industries, and that sexual violence isn't so much the exception for many of us but commonplace, everyday, pervasive. Just look at the sheer number of us who can say "me too." Exposing rape myths and the role of the law in rape culture has been one key focus in feminist public debates around #MeToo.

So, with both fanfiction and issues of consent becoming much more prominent in the public eye, what can we say about the future activist potentialities of the kinds of cultural activism that fanfiction communities engage in around consent? Has the mainstreaming of fanfiction eliminated the pressures that previously allowed it to be a clandestine, transgressive, and subversive space? Has the mainstreaming of consent issues made obsolete the kind of activism that fanfiction does?

I would argue that the answer to the last of these questions is a resounding no: even, and perhaps especially, in the wake of #MeToo, consent continues to be a contested idea, even in feminist circles. There has also been a concerted effort to push back against the small victories #MeToo has achieved.[8] Fanfiction, then, remains a crucial tool for developing our knowledge and understanding of consent. It continues to operate outside traditional knowledge production and validation structures. It builds on epistemologies rooted in lived experience and, at the same time, accounts for and challenges our society's dominant ideas about sex. We will continue to need these kinds of new, marginalized, and subjugated knowledges for some time to come.

The impact of the mainstreaming of fanfiction on its activist potential, however, is a potentially thornier issue. The external pressures that made fanfiction a clandestine activity were also key enablers of its subversiveness. There is a reason the Omegaverse arose where it did: in anonymous online communities on the margins of the margins of fandom.[9] Some fanfiction communities continue to resist cooptation and commercialization by rightsholders. Others are happy to settle in the walled gardens provided by the cultural industries and abide, for instance, by restrictions on sexually explicit content. The recent demise of Tumblr as a viable social media platform for sexually explicit material has fragmented and dispersed fanfiction communities. This highlights the importance of the OTW as a fan-owned, fan-run space.

Fannish cultural activism also has the potential to shape and influence mainstream culture. One of the most striking features of the fanfiction community is the conviction that fiction, culture, and art do real work in the real world through the stories they tell and the ideas they develop or challenge. With that in mind, authorial intent—terribly unfashionable in recent cultural and, to an extent, literary studies—becomes an important factor in how we read the text. This is not because it tells us the text's meaning but because it reflects the connection between the text and the real world. There is a desire in fanfiction communities to hold creators of culture accountable for this work. This desire translates into community norms and practices—it is what ultimately gives rise to the fannish praxis of consent we saw in chapter 7. But demands for such accountability are no longer limited to fanfiction authors or to fannish circles: fans are making demands of creators of mainstream culture and critiquing political dimensions of popular culture works. Fans are increasingly vocal in challenging problematic media practices such as queerbaiting—the way TV shows use promotional material and paratexts to create an expectation of queer content to attract queer viewers, but never actually deliver on it. Fan studies scholar Eve Ng suggests that there are three factors at play here: the actual queer content of the show, which she maps on a spectrum from subtextual to overtly textual; official paratexts around the show, such as trailers, producers' comments, or cast interviews; and what Ng calls "queer contextuality."[10] Queer contextuality encompasses viewers' wider experiences of queer representation in media. Several competing trends shape such expectations. On the one hand, there is more queer representation in mainstream media than ever before. This in turn counters a historical lack of representation that has shaped the experiences and expectations of older viewers, in particular. On the other hand, this representation continues to be mired in problems and stereotypes. Our TV screens are littered with well-buried gays.[11] Increased representation and producer comments aimed at attracting queer audiences therefore generate much higher expectations of overtly textual, high-quality queer representation than has historically been the case. But, in many cases, producers fail to deliver on those high expectations, and that drives the accusations of queerbaiting.[12]

What is important about both queerbaiting discussions and Ng's analysis of them is that, like fanfiction readers' and writers' emphasis on authorial intent, they show that audiences perceive a clear link between media texts and real-world concerns. If we can't see ourselves reflected in our culture as living happy, fulfilling lives and having meaningful agency in the world, that has an effect on how we see ourselves more generally. It limits our options and choices in life; it tells us there is no space for us. And we demand better from our culture.[13]

We see similar demands for mainstream media to do better when it comes to issues of gender, sex, sexuality, and consent. Discussions of the character of Sansa Stark, and of sexual violence more generally, on HBO's *Game of Thrones* in media and on progressive blogs have used the kind of close textual analysis combined with critiques of the author and producers that we are normally only used to in fannish circles.[14] These critical practices seem to be spilling out of dedicated fandom and into more casual audiences as well as more traditional activist and community settings. Here, too, the interplay between text and real world is a central issue, with discussion moving seamlessly from a close reading of the text to explorations of political issues and back.

We are seeing increasing use of engagement with popular culture for activist and political purposes. Audiences beyond fans are starting to ask questions about the interactions between text and real world, the role and responsibility of authors and producers. The resurrection of the author in this context—as a symbol for the work media texts do in the real world—is a wake-up call for the cultural industries who are increasingly being held accountable not only by fans but also by casual audiences for the world their output helps to build.

There is plenty of work left to do for fanfiction in this space. We still need the kinds of knowledges about consent that fanfiction communities create, and we need those knowledges to continue spilling over into other spaces. If recent political developments are anything to go by, the #MeToo revolution is not headed to the guillotine. As to the shopping mall, that is a tightrope that both #MeToo and fanfiction-based consent activism have to walk. Mainstream attention is vital for new knowledges about consent to be disseminated beyond the communities where they originate. But mainstream attention is also very good at diluting the message.

"WE DON'T SOOTHE ALL PAIN EQUALLY"

Recent fan studies scholarship has started engaging in more depth not only with the activist potential of fanfiction communities, but also with their failings. In addition to the kind of cultural activism I have talked about in this book, Leetal Dean has argued that fanfiction communities practice an "activism of care." They define this as activism that sees care as radical, makes use of community members' existing skills, is embedded in everyday community practices, is at least in part intersectional, and is specific to the needs of individuals and the community. When we write fanfiction for each other in which our favorite characters share our struggles—be those depression, anxiety, or existing within rape culture—we are caring for each other and helping each other survive in a hostile world.[15]

But, as Elise Vist notes, "we don't soothe all pain equally."[16] Fanfiction communities are far from homogenous. There is diversity of opinion, diversity of experience, and demographic diversity. Some of this is celebrated both by fans and fan studies scholars. Look at all of these queer women and nonbinary people doing weird but revolutionary queer women and nonbinary people things! In other cases, the diversity within the community is obscured in favor of blanket statements that assume a particular kind of default fan. What that default fan looks like has shifted somewhat over time; in her 1992 ethnography of fanfiction fandom, Camille Bacon-Smith suggests straight, White, American, educated, and underemployed women in their 30s and 40s.[17] Today's fans and fan studies scholars probably picture a slightly queerer, maybe slightly younger default fan, but one who is still very much White and probably American. Indeed, the data we have on fannish demographics indicates that fanfiction readers and writers are predominantly women and nonbinary people, a majority of them identify as queer, and that fannish spaces such as Tumblr and AO3, where most of the data comes from, are majority White.[18] But we are also increasingly hearing from both fans and scholars of the role race and racism play in fandom (and in fan studies). In her groundbreaking book, *Squee from the Margins*, Rukmini Pande argues that race is an invisibilized structuring force in fandom.[19] We don't talk about race, we don't talk about Whiteness, but race generally and Whiteness specifically shape fannish spaces and the experiences of fans of color. As a result, it is very likely that fans of color self-select out of demographic surveys. Even so, one quarter of respondents to centrumlumina's AO3 census identified as not White. Fannish engagement with issues of consent is not uniform across different fannish demographics. The experiences of fans of color in general are shaped and structured by racism, and this is just as true when it comes to their experiences of fannish engagements with issues of consent.

We saw in the previous chapter how fannish infrastructure and practices prioritize the well-being of survivors of sexual violence. If we have a way of letting people know what they are letting themselves in for with a particular story—such as archive warnings and tags—then they can make an informed choice, and therefore give informed consent, to the kinds of things they do and do not want to read. And because this system is built into AO3's infrastructure, it prompts readers and writers to think about and flag any consent issues in their work. But this view turns out to be rather too simplistic when we start looking at fannish spaces and interactions through the lens of race. Cait Coker and Rukmini Pande, for instance, show a different side of the AO3 tagging system: one that marginalizes and potentially actively harms fans of color. Looking at the treatment of Black characters in fanfiction, they show how the affordances of the Archive's tagging system make it difficult to find content *focused* on characters of color, or to avoid racist tropes and other kinds of racist aggression in fanfiction. If we tag for all characters and relationships featured in our stories, it is difficult to tell whether, for instance, Sam Wilson is a central character in a story, or whether he is just Captain America's Magical Support Negro.[20] Fans of color end up having to create their own strategies for avoiding such racist tropes. They identify the tags that are frequently associated with them, like "Sam is such a good bro." On the surface, this tag reads like a positive description of Sam, but it is part of a wider pattern of relegating him to a supporting role rather than making him a central character. Fans of color, then, also develop additional technical competence, using some of the Archive's less well-documented features to filter out such tags. So, where White fans and survivors of sexual violence view tags as a source of empowerment, allowing them to curate their AO3 experience in ways that center their well-being, fans of color find them inadequate at best and must perform additional labor to avoid traumatizing content.

This privileging of White fans' trauma, experiences, and needs is further borne out when looking at how characters of color are treated in fanfiction. In an audio essay titled "Whose Trauma Matters," media and fandom analyst Zina Hutton looks at fannish attitudes to the trauma of characters of color and, by extension, to survivors of color.[21] They show how White fans are more likely to empathize and identify with White characters' trauma and excuse bad behavior resulting from such trauma. The same fans condemn characters of color in similar circumstances. One way in which fans do this is by constructing elaborate fanfictional "headcanons" of White characters' traumatic backstories even when these are not present in the originary work. The handful of scenes we see in the *Star Wars* films of Ben Solo's childhood become the seeds of an epic backstory of trauma that has made him into Kylo Ren, and this in turn makes Kylo worth empathizing with. At the same time, the canonical trauma of characters of color is dismissed or minimized. We gloss over Finn's experiences as a child soldier and how, despite the harm he has suffered as a result, he strives to make the right choice in every situation, even when that choice is difficult and potentially retraumatizing. This dynamic also translates to the treatment of fans of color who raise such issues in fannish spaces. White fans, who may themselves be survivors of trauma and identify with particular White characters, silence such critiques by drawing attention to their own survivor status. This in turn creates a space where White characters' and White fans' experiences of trauma are privileged over those of characters and fans of color, who instead are silenced. What is a positive, affirming, and activist space for White fans becomes a source of additional distress for fans of color.

There are common fanfiction tropes that also highlight this racial disparity in how fanfiction communities handle consent. Variations on slavery as a trope have a long history in fanfiction, and can arguably be seen as exploring issues of intimacy and consent in the presence of power differentials. As of August 2019, there are over 15,000 stories on AO3 tagged

"Slavery." Yet this trope and other racialized dynamics are used primarily by White fans over the objections of Black fans, and rarely remarked on by fanfiction scholars. In her examination of intimacy and inequality in slash fanfiction, Elizabeth Woledge briefly mentions the use of the "ethnic sidekick" trope, but minimizes the racialized aspects and chooses instead to talk about inequality more generally.[22]

Similarly, slavery in fanfiction is frequently deracialized, both historically and today. That early, high-profile *Star Trek* story that I mentioned in chapter 1, Barbara Wenk's *One Way Mirror*,[23] centers on a White woman *Star Trek* fan who finds herself in an evil-empire version of the Federation, and is captured by slave traders and sold to Spock. Some of these dynamics can also be seen in my own research: one of my interviewees spoke at length about her enjoyment of slavery-themed stories based on the *Dragon Age* computer games. She emphasized how the structural inequalities of a society built on slavery allowed for the exploration of questions of consent. Yet partly due to the nature of the originary work, *Dragon Age* slave stories, too, are ahistorical and deracialized. The slaves in question are pretty, light-skinned elves, and slavery as presented in the game is completely removed from its historical context and enactment in the real world. Slavery then becomes just another trope for the entertainment and enjoyment of White fans. Sanitized of historical context and lacking even the slightest acknowledgment of its racial dynamics, it can be added to White fans' "consent exploration toolbox." But what to a White fan reads as an interesting and academic exploration of consent reads very differently to a Black fan who may be a descendant of survivors of slavery and the inevitably attendant rape. White fans can use the trope without having to confront the painful history and effects of real-world chattel slavery. Black fans are further marginalized and traumatized.

Structural racism in fandom is only one of a variety of ways in which fans fail when it comes to enacting their knowledges of consent. The fanfiction community is not so much a single entity as a set of fluid, overlapping, ever-changing groupings. As we saw in chapter 5, when news of the rape allegations against Patrick Kane broke, many Patrick Kane fanfiction fans disengaged from that fandom—but some remained, doubled down, and served as the core of a continued fandom. And, of course, there is the question of why it took allegations of actual rape for Hockey RPF fandom to finally admit that our fave was indeed more than a little problematic. We had, after all, all seen the blackface photos. We also knew that the Blackhawks' team name and logo—although not as egregious as, say, the Washington NFL team's name—were racist caricatures harmful to Native American people. Before the rape allegations, these topics bubbled up occasionally in fandom discussion but also tended to fizzle out fairly quickly. Elise Vist shows us how different parts of the fanfiction community handle such friction by developing technical and social ways of minimizing contact—a kind of "live and let live" arrangement where different communities (or, in Vist's words, "intimate fandoms") exist in parallel, coming into contact only at times of crisis.[24] Cultural activism and activism of care in these spaces, then, are far from universal. It is perhaps difficult to experience fanfiction fandom without coming into contact with *any* of the ideas about consent developed in that space, but it is certainly possible to only engage with those ideas tangentially. It is also possible to find oneself and one's identity, experiences, and survivor status marginalized and deprioritized compared to those of White fans.

Fannish communities are not a utopian space. But they *are* a space where activist work is done and where some of the friction is productive. They have the challenge of continuing and expanding this work in more intersectional ways that fight not only sexism and patriarchy but structural racism as well. Fannish communities are also undergoing rapid change. Legal external pressures on them have largely been removed, but new visibility has brought its own challenges. The demise of platforms like Tumblr and the resulting fannish migration to new platforms have fragmented fandoms and at the same time brought communities into contact that previously could avoid each other. All this highlights the responsibility of the Organization for Transformative Works as the trustees of the one fan-owned, fan-run space, the one Archive of Our Own that we have, to continue setting community norms and standards in ways that address community failures such as the structures that foster and reproduce racism. We do need to start soothing all pain equally—or rather, appropriately.

That can only strengthen the community and its activist potential. At the same time, drawing on fannish knowledges of consent and expanding and circulating them to wider audiences, including through mainstream popular culture, has the potential of mounting a robust resistance to rape culture and actively contributing to the creation of a culture of consent.

Acknowledgments

The writing of this book coincided with a personally challenging time in my life, and so first and foremost I am grateful to those closest to me who were there when I was staring into the void: my partner Paul, and my friend Charlie. Thank you also to everyone else who got caught in the splatter zone and offered help, shoulders to cry on, dinner, and distractions.

This project started life as a PhD thesis, and so thanks are due to my amazing supervision team: Professor Jonathan Dovey, Dr. Esther MacCallum-Stewart, and Estella Tincknell.

Thank you to my editorial team at MIT Press, Matt Browne and Anne-Marie Bono, for their support throughout this project. Thank you also to the anonymous peer reviewers who were so enthusiastic and encouraging, and who pushed me to make this book accessible to an audience beyond academia. And thank you to my copy editor and production editor Liz Agresta, who is, as far as I can tell, a wizard.

I would also like to thank Jaime Starr for their help with sensitivity reading; Dr. Jackie Barker for glaring and cake; and Elise Vist for generously granting me early access to their PhD thesis.

Two cats helped enormously with the writing of this book. Chili—Cultural Theorist Cat—was with me through my PhD, so very nearly up to my viva. His praxis of consent was an inspiration, and he is sorely missed. Coffee the Void Kitten (Murderface) chewed manuscripts and walked on keyboards in the final months of this becoming a book, and has contributed a regular supply of mice during the revision process. We have more or less worked out consent—both mine and theirs, though not that of the mice—and they are an absolute joy.

Some of the material in this book has been published elsewhere: chapter 3, Milena Popova, "'Dogfuck Rapeworld': Omegaverse Fanfiction as a Critical Tool in Analysing the Impact of Social Power Structures on Intimate Relationships and Sexual Consent," *Porn Studies* 5, no. 2 (2018): 175–191; chapter 4, Milena Popova, "Rewriting the Romance: Emotion Work and Consent in Arranged Marriage Fanfiction," *Journal of Popular Romance Studies* 7 (July 2018); chapter 5, Milena Popova, "'When the RP Gets in the Way of the F': Star Image and Intertextuality in Real Person(a) Fiction," *Transformative Works and Cultures* 25 (September 2017); and Milena Popova, "Tumblr Time: How Tumblr's Temporal Features Shape Community Memory and Knowledge," in *A Tumblr Book*, ed. Allison McCracken, Alexander Cho, Louisa Stein, and Indira Neill (Ann Arbor: University of Michigan Press, 2020); and chapter 7, Milena Popova, "Follow the Trope: A Digital (Auto)ethnography for Fan Studies," *Transformative Works and Cultures* 33 (June 2020), https://doi.org/10.3983/twc.2020.1697.

Notes

CHAPTER 1

1. Limbaugh's full tirade says a lot more about Limbaugh and the American right than it does about the left, or consent. It makes for interesting listening/reading. Content notes for rape apologism apply. See Media Matters Staff, "Limbaugh: The Left Sends Out 'the Rape Police' Whenever There's Sex with 'No Consent' (Also Known As Rape)," *Media Matters*, October 12, 2016, https://www.mediamatters.org/video/2016/10/12/limbaugh-left-sends-out-rape-police-whenever-theres-sex-no-consent-also-known-rape/213787.

2. Tom Cleary, "READ: Full Letter to the Judge by Dan Turner, Brock's Father," *Heavy*, June 8, 2016, http://heavy.com/news/2016/06/brock-turner-father-dad-dan-turner-full-letter-statement-stanford-rapist/.

3. Bloomberg Government, "Kavanaugh Hearing: Transcript," *Washington Post*, September 27, 2018, https://www.washingtonpost.com/news/national/wp/2018/09/27/kavanaugh-hearing-transcript/.

4. Ben Jacobs, Sabina Siddiqui, and Scott Bixby, "'You Can Do Anything': Trump Brags on Tape about Using Fame to Get Women," *Guardian*, October 8, 2016, https://www.theguardian.com/us-news/2016/oct/07/donald-trump-leaked-recording-women.

5. Ministry of Justice, Home Office, and Office for National Statistics, "An Overview of Sexual Offending in England and Wales," January 10, 2013, https://www.gov.uk/government/statistics/an-overview-of-sexual-offending-in-england-and-wales/.

6. Sam Levin, "Brock Turner Laughed after Bystanders Stopped Stanford Sex Assault, Files Show," *Guardian*, August 26, 2016, https://www.theguardian.com/society/2016/aug/26/brock-turner-stanford-sexual-assault-victim-testimony-laugh.

7. Davina Kirkpatrick and Alys Mendus, "Female Ejaculation and Other Tales," presented at the 2017 UWE ACE Postgraduate Research Symposium, Bristol, UK, 2017.

8. Alex Gabriel (@AlexGabriel), "If your sex ed doesn't include asexuality, you're going to have kids growing up doing things they don't realise they don't want to do," Twitter, July 7, 2017, 12:57 p.m., https://twitter.com/AlexGabriel/status/883369396399419392.

9. Katie Way, "I Went on a Date with Aziz Ansari. It Turned into the Worst Night of My Life," *Babe*, January 13, 2018, https://babe.net/2018/01/13/aziz-ansari-28355.

10. Melanie A. Beres, "'Spontaneous' Sexual Consent: An Analysis of Sexual Consent Literature," *Feminism & Psychology* 17, no. 1 (February 1, 2007): 93–108, https://doi.org/10.1177/0959353507072914.

11. Linda Martín Alcoff, *Rape and Resistance* (Cambridge: Polity Press, 2018).

12. Nicola Gavey, *Just Sex? The Cultural Scaffolding of Rape* (Hove: Routledge, 2005).

13. Given the dispersed nature of fandom, gathering large-scale demographic data on online fanfiction communities has proved challenging, and no truly representative data set exists to date. Surveys conducted by fans themselves in fannish subcommunities suggest that fanfiction is produced predominantly by women and nonbinary people: in the AO3 census conducted in 2013, only 4.2 percent of respondents identified as "male," and 80 percent identified as "female," with the remaining 15.8 percent selecting other gender options such as "genderqueer" (6 percent), "agender," or "androgynous" (2 percent each). In terms of sexuality, approximately two-thirds of respondents selected at least one option other than "heterosexual," and 53.7 percent of respondents identified as members of a "gender, sexual, or romantic minority." This data is not without limitations, as survey author centrumlumina herself acknowledges. The sample is self-selecting, and potentially overreliant on AO3 users who also use Tumblr (the primary mode of advertising the survey). Nonetheless, the data is based on a sample of over 10,000 AO3 users, and is a significant improvement on previous anecdotal evidence of fandom demographics. A more recent project focusing on fans' views and experiences of sex and sexuality surveyed 2,200 fans aged eighteen and older. Similarly to the AO3 census, it found that 85.9 percent of respondents identified as "female" and 3.6 percent identified as male, with 7.7 percent of participants selecting "nonbinary," 5.6 percent "genderfluid," and 4.3 percent "agender." With regard to sexual orientation, only 24 percent of respondents identified as "heterosexual." Thus, although data on fandom demographics remains limited, available evidence broadly agrees that this is a group predominantly consisting of women and nonbinary people, a majority of whom are not heterosexual. See centrumlumina, "Gender," Tumblr, October 1, 2013, http://centrumlumina.tumblr.com/post/62816996032/gender; centrumlumina, "Overall Gender and Sexuality of AO3 Users," Tumblr, August 12, 2014, https://centrumlumina.tumblr.com/post/94562495289/overall-gender-and-sexuality-of-ao3-users-this; centrumlumina, "Gender, Sexual or Romantic Minority," Tumblr, October 2, 2013, http://centrumlumina.tumblr.com/post/62890602051/gender-sexual-or-romantic-minority; centrumlumina, "Limitations and Uses of the Data," Tumblr, September 30, 2013, http://centrumlumina.tumblr.com/post/62748999135/limitations-and-uses-of-the-data; and finnagain, "Fandom & Sexuality Survey Summary Report," 2017, By Fans 4 Fans, LLC.

14. Centers for Disease Control and Prevention, "Sexual Violence," last updated August 8, 2018, http://www.cdc.gov/violenceprevention.

15. Fanlore, "Dub-Con," 2016, last updated December 6, 2019, https://fanlore.org/wiki/Dub -con.

16. Barbara Wenk, *One Way Mirror* (Poison Pen Press, 1980); and Jean Lorrah, *The Night of the Twin Moons* (Creative Printers, 1976).

17. For a discussion of the resistance to recent movements and activism around sexual violence, see chapter 7 in Milena Popova, *Sexual Consent* (Cambridge, MA: MIT Press, 2019).

18. Henry Jenkins, *Textual Poachers: Television Fans and Participatory Culture* (New York: Routledge, 1991).

19. destinationtoast, "Because I Was Curious about the Breakdown of Fic on AO3," Tumblr, May 11, 2013, http://destinationtoast.tumblr.com/post/50201718171/because-i-was -curious-about-the-breakdown-of.

20. The idea that there are "alpha" and "beta" individuals who vie for dominance in wolf packs has been thoroughly discredited by the researcher who originally popularized it. Sometimes science makes mistakes, and our early ideas of how wolf packs worked were based on studying packs of unrelated wolves in captivity. See L. David Mech, "Alpha Status, Dominance, and Division of Labor in Wolf Packs," *Canadian Journal of Zoology* 77, no. 8 (1999): 1196–1203, https://doi.org/10.1139/z99-099. For some reason, the cultural idea of alpha wolves still persists despite the evidence.

21. Cornel West, *Keeping Faith: Philosophy and Race in America* (New York: Routledge, 1993).

CHAPTER 2

1. Milena Popova (@elmyra), "How's everyone's #coronavirus apocalypse going, folks? I just had to tell someone on Facebook that they weren't under any obligation to have sex with their husband, and it feels like this is a good time to belabour this point," Twitter, March 26, 2020, 8:08 a.m., https://twitter.com/elmyra/status/1243147837753434112.

2. Andrea Dworkin, *Right-Wing Women* (Exeter, UK: Pedigree Books, 1983).

3. The case used as precedent to establish marital rape as an offence in England and Wales was Regina Respondent and R. Appellant: http://bailii.org/uk/cases/UKHL/1991/12.html.

4. Catharine MacKinnon, *Toward a Feminist Theory of State* (Cambridge, MA: Harvard University Press, 1989); Catharine MacKinnon, "Reflections on Sex Equality under Law," *Yale Law Journal* 100 (1991): 1281, https://doi.org/10.2307/796693.

5. Celia Kitzinger and Hannah Frith, "Just Say No? The Use of Conversation Analysis in Developing a Feminist Perspective on Sexual Refusal," *Discourse & Society* 10, no. 3 (1999): 293–316, https://doi.org/10.1177/0957926599010003002; Kate Lockwood Harris, "Yes Means Yes and No Means No, but Both These Mantras Need to Go: Communication

Myths in Consent Education and Anti-Rape Activism," *Journal of Applied Communication Research* 46, no. 2 (2018): 155–178.

6. Joanne Wright, "Consent and Sexual Violence in Canadian Public Discourse: Reflections on Ewanchuk," *Canadian Journal of Law & Society* (*La Revue Canadienne Droit et Société*) 16, no. 2 (2001): 173–204. For an introduction to the history of feminist approaches to sexual consent and the evolution of the law in this area, see also Milena Popova, *Sexual Consent* (Cambridge, MA: MIT Press, 2019).

7. Lois Pineau, "Date Rape: A Feminist Analysis," *Law and Philosophy* 8, no. 2 (1989): 217–243, https://doi.org/10.1007/BF00160012.

8. Michelle J. Anderson, "Negotiating Sex," *Southern California Law Review* 41 (2005): 1401–1438.

9. There is a series of studies by Kristen Joskowski and her team looking into how college students express consent. In the various surveys, participants are asked specifically how they express consent to penile-vaginal intercourse, and in the interpretation of the results the researchers define things like kissing, undressing, or moving to a more private space as consent behaviors, or expressions of consent. This tells us a little bit about how college students behave in sexual situations, and probably slightly more about the researchers' own ideas of what sex is and what requires consent. We will see in chapter 6 of this book how fanfiction readers and writers have a very different view on the subject. See Kristen N. Jozkowski and Zoë D. Peterson, "College Students and Sexual Consent: Unique Insights," *Journal of Sex Research* 50, no. 6 (2013): 517–523, https://doi.org/10.1080/00224499.2012.700739; and Kristen N. Jozkowski and Zoë D. Peterson, "Assessing the Validity and Reliability of the Perceptions of the Consent to Sex Scale," *Journal of Sex Research* 51, no. 6 (2014): 632–645, https://doi.org/10.1080/00224499.2012.757282.

10. See Laina Y. Bay-Cheng and Rebecca K. Eliseo-Arras, "The Making of Unwanted Sex: Gendered and Neoliberal Norms in College Women's Unwanted Sexual Experiences," *Journal of Sex Research* 45, no. 4 (2008): 386–397, https://doi.org/10.1080/00224490802398381; and Melissa Burkett and Karine Hamilton, "Postfeminist Sexual Agency: Young Women's Negotiations of Sexual Consent," *Sexualities* 15, no. 7 (December 2012): 815–833, https://doi.org/ 10.1177/1363460712454076.

11. Debra Umberson, Mieke Beth Thomeer, and Amy C. Lodge, "Intimacy and Emotion Work in Lesbian, Gay, and Heterosexual Relationships," *Journal of Marriage and Family* 77, no. 2 (2015): 542–556, https://doi.org/10.1111/jomf.12178.

12. Melanie Ann Beres, Gareth Terry, Charlene Y. Senn, and Lily Kay Ross, "Accounting for Men's Refusal of Heterosex: A Story-Completion Study with Young Adults," *Journal of Sex Research* 56, no. 1 (2019): 127–136, https://doi.org/10.1080/00224499.2017.1399978.

13. Michel Foucault, *The Archaeology of Knowledge and the Discourse of Language* (New York: Pantheon Books, 1972).

14. Wendy Hollway, *Subjectivity and Method in Psychology* (London: Sage, 1989).

15. Lisa Downing, "What Is 'Sex Critical' and Why Should We Care about It?" *Sex Critical* (blog), July 27, 2012, http://sexcritical.co.uk/2012/07/27/what-is-sex-critical-and-why -should-we-care-about-it/.

16. Nicola Gavey, *Just Sex? The Cultural Scaffolding of Rape* (Hove: Routledge, 2005).

17. Foucault, *The Archaeology of Knowledge*.

18. This is somewhat of an oversimplification because ideas about love, sex, romance, and rela- tionships have changed significantly over time. A more accurate description would be to say that we currently believe that it is how past generations thought, and that decoupling sex from romance is a relatively novel idea. Of course, this way of thinking in itself helps reinforce the conceptual link between sex and romance.

19. Michel Foucault, "Truth and Power," in *The Foucault Reader*, ed. Paul Rabinow, (New York: Pantheon Books, 1987), 20:327–336; Michel Foucault, *Power/Knowledge*, ed. Colin Gordon (New York: Pantheon Books, 1980).

20. Susan Bordo, *Unbearable Weight: Feminism, Western Culture, and the Body* (Berkeley: Uni- versity of California Press, 2003).

21. Feminist philosopher Lois McNay actually finds three major problems that Foucault's work presents for us. The first is Foucault's idea that the body, like everything else, is discursively constructed. This is a very powerful idea because it allows us to move beyond essentialist conceptions of gender. Some schools of feminism firmly believe that what makes a woman a woman, and therefore what is at the root of her oppression by patriarchy, is her possession of a uterus and ability to bear children. This is what we refer to as biological essentialism, and it has many problems, including failing to account for the experiences and oppression of trans people and, followed to its logical conclusion, suggesting that Margaret Thatcher is just as oppressed as a working-class woman of color. A discursive approach to gender and the body, by contrast, allows us a much more nuanced understanding of how power operates on different bodies in ways that are gendered. What McNay points out, though, is that Foucault never quite went there himself as his interest in issues of gender was lim- ited. Understanding gender through the lens of discourse and discourse through the lens of gender is an area where feminist scholars like Susan Bordo have significantly expanded Foucault's work.

    The second issue McNay identifies is one of agency: If we are all discursively constructed subjects, occupying the subject positions allowed us by discourse, how can we meaningfully act in the world? And if power operates on us from all sides, in all directions, and there is no meaningful way to work "outside" of this system, how can we resist it from the inside? Third, and related, Foucault rather shies away from making moral judgments, leaving us without a firm ground for ethical action. How do we make moral choices about which operations of power to resist and how? In response to both these problems, McNay suggests turning to thinkers and activists from marginalized groups to help us find ways of mean- ingfully and ethically resisting from within. See Lois McNay, *Foucault and Feminism: Power, Gender and the Self* (Cambridge: Polity Press, 1992); Bordo, *Unbearable Weight*.

22. Patricia Hill Collins, *Black Feminist Thought* (London: Routledge, 2000), 69.

23. bell hooks, *Talking Back: Thinking Feminist, Thinking Black* (Boston: South End Press, 1989); bell hooks, *Yearning: Race, Gender, and Cultural Politics* (Boston: South End Press, 1990).

24. Collins, *Black Feminist Thought*, 18.

25. Cornel West, *Keeping Faith: Philosophy and Race in America* (New York: Routledge, 1993).

26. For a fun and accessible introduction to medieval sexuality, I highly recommend Dr. Eleanor Janega's work on Twitter and elsewhere. See, for instance, Eleanor Janega, "Medieval Sexuality," Medievalists.net, 2019, https://www.medievalists.net/2019/05/medieval-sexuality -with-eleanor-janega/.

27. Paul Routledge, "Sensuous Solidarities: Emotion, Politics and Performance in the Clandestine Insurgent Rebel Clown Army," *Antipode* 44, no. 2 (2012): 428–452, https://doi.org /10.1111/j.1467-8330.2010.00862.x; Tuuli Lähdesmäki, "Cultural Activism as a Counter-Discourse to the European Capital of Culture Programme: The Case of Turku 2011," *European Journal of Cultural Studies* 16, no. 5 (2013): 598–619, https://doi.org/10 .1177/1367549413491720; Deborah Withers and Red Chidgey, "Complicated Inheritance: Sistershow (1973–1974) and the Queering of Feminism," *Women: A Cultural Review* 21, no. 3 (December 2010): 309–322, https://doi.org/10.1080/09574042.2010.513494; Christian Scholl, "Bakunin's Poor Cousins: Engaging Art for Tactical Interventions," in *Cultural Activism: Practices, Dilemmas, and Possibilities*, ed. Begüm Özden Firat and Aylin Kuryel (Amsterdam: Rodopi, 2011), 21:157; Michael Buser, Carlo Bonura, Maria Fannin, and Kate Boyer, "Cultural Activism and the Politics of Place-Making," *City* 17, no. 5 (2013): 606–627, https://doi.org/10.1080/13604813.2013.827840.

28. Michael Buser and Jane Arthurs, "Connected Communities: Cultural Activism in the Community," Cultural Activism (2012), 3, http://www.culturalactivism.org.uk/wp-content /uploads/2013/03/CULTURAL-ACTIVISM-BUSER-Update.3.pdf.

INTERLUDE

1. For an introduction to fandom's long history with cease and desist letters, see the Fanlore wiki: https://fanlore.org/wiki/Cease_%26_Desist.

2. This is, of course, a highly oversimplified and selective—as well as deliberately polemical— story, and I hope no medievalists come after me for telling it this way. But it is useful for reconsidering some of the things we take for granted about what we consider great art. I am indebted for this account to several posts that used to circulate on fannish Tumblr with some regularity but have since been lost to the mists of time, Tumblr's dreadful search functionality, and the Tumblrpocalypse (Tumblr's ban on adult material in 2017, which caused a significant exodus of users from the platform).

3. For examples of the "fanfiction as text" approach, see Karen Hellekson and Kristina Busse (eds.), *Fan Fiction and Fan Communities in the Age of the Internet* (Jefferson, NC: McFarland & Co, 2006), specifically these three chapters: Abigail Derecho, "Archontic Literature:

A Definition, a History, and Several Theories of Fan Fiction," 61–78; Catherine Driscoll, "One True Pairing: The Romance of Pornography and the Pornography of Romance," 79–96; and Mafalda Stasi, "The Toy Soldiers from Leeds: The Slash Palimpsest," 115–133. For examples of the "fanfiction as community practice" approach, see Henry Jenkins, *Textual Poachers: Television Fans and Participatory Culture* (New York: Routledge, 1991); Camille Bacon-Smith, *Enterprising Women: Television Fandom and the Creation of Popular Myth* (Philadelphia: University of Pennsylvania Press, 1992); and Anne Kustritz, "Slashing the Romance Narrative," *Journal of American Culture* 26, no. 3 (2003): 371–385, https://doi .org/10.1111/1542-734X.00098.

4.   Derecho, "Archontic Literature."

5.   Of course, Alice Randall's *The Wind Done Gone* is not so much fanfiction as it is an examination of the originary work's deep-seated racism. But, in many ways, it works in the same way as fanfiction: it relies on its audience knowing the originary work and reading the two side by side to pick up on the similarities and differences. In the process, readers begin to reevaluate *Gone with the Wind* and start asking uncomfortable questions about it. These questions were so uncomfortable that Margaret Mitchell's estate tried to stop the publication of *The Wind Done Gone*. The book prominently carries a disclaimer on its cover labeling it a "parody," giving it protection as a transformative work under US copyright law.

The other works name-checked here are Helen Fielding's *Bridget Jones's Diary* and Seth Grahame-Smith's *Pride and Prejudice and Zombies*, but these are only a handful of examples of professionally published "fanfiction."

6.   Derecho, "Archontic Literature;" Kustritz, "Slashing the Romance Narrative."

7.   Jenkins, *Textual Poachers*; Bacon-Smith, *Enterprising Women*; Kustritz, "Slashing the Romance Narrative"; Patricia Frazer Lamb and Diana Veith, "Romantic Myth, Transcendence, and *Star Trek* Zines," in *Erotic Universe: Sexuality and Fantastic Literature*, ed. Donald Palumbo (New York: Greenwood Press, 1986), 235–256; and Joanna Russ, "Pornography by Women, for Women, with Love," in *Magic Mommas, Trembling Sisters, Puritans & Perverts: Feminist Essays* (Trumansberg, NY: Crossing Press, 1986), 79–99.

8.   Kustritz, "Slashing the Romance Narrative"; and Ika Willis, "Keeping Promises to Queer Children: Making Space (for Mary Sue) at Hogwarts," in *Fan Fiction and Fan Communities in the Age of the Internet*, ed. Karen Hellekson and Kristina Busse (Jefferson, NC: McFarland & Co., 2006), 153–170.

CHAPTER 3

1.   Henry Jenkins, *Textual Poachers: Television Fans and Participatory Culture* (New York: Routledge, 1991); Camille Bacon-Smith, *Enterprising Women: Television Fandom and the Creation of Popular Myth* (Philadelphia: University of Pennsylvania Press, 1992); Anne Kustritz, "Slashing the Romance Narrative," *Journal of American Culture* 26, no. 3 (2003): 371–385, https://doi.org/10.1111/1542-734X.00098; Patricia Frazer Lamb and Diana Veith, "Romantic Myth, Transcendence, and *Star Trek* Zines," in *Erotic Universe: Sexuality and*

Fantastic Literature, ed. Donald Palumbo (New York: Greenwood Press, 1986), 235–256; and Joanna Russ, "Pornography by Women, for Women, with Love," in *Magic Mommas, Trembling Sisters, Puritans & Perverts: Feminist Essays* (Trumansberg, NY: Crossing Press, 1986), 79–99.

2.   centrumlumina, "Overall Gender and Sexuality of AO3 Users," Tumblr, August 12, 2014, https://centrumlumina.tumblr.com/post/94562495289/overall-gender-and-sexuality-of -ao3-users-this; Kristina Busse and Alexis Lothian, "A History of Slash Sexualities: Debating Queer Sex, Gay Politics and Media Fan Cultures," in *The Routledge Companion to Media, Sex and Sexuality*, ed. Clarissa Smith, Feona Attwood, and Brian McNair (Abingdon, UK: Routledge, 2018), 117–129.

3.   Kristina Busse, "Pon Farr, Mpreg, Bonds, and the Rise of the Omegaverse," in *Fic: Why Fanfiction Is Taking Over the World*, ed. Anne Jamison (Dallas, TX: Smart Pop, 2013), 316– 322; Mafalda Stasi, "'You? Omega. Me? Alpha. . . . I Can't Help It. That's Basic Biology for You': New Forms of Gender Essentialism in Fan Fiction," presented at Console-Ing Passions Conference, Leicester, UK, June 23–25, 2013; Jonathan Rose, "Omegaverse, or: What a Kink Trope Tells Us about Sex, Gender and Sexuality," presented at the 2016 Fan Studies Network Conference, Norwich, UK, June 25–26, 2016; Popova, "'Dogfuck Rape-world'"; Kelsey Entrikin, "Sex Pollen and the Omegaverse: Dialogues of Consent in Fan Fiction Tropes," presented at the 2019 Fan Studies Network Conference, Portsmouth, UK, June 28–29, 2019.

4.   netweight, "The Nonnies Made Them Do It!" Archive of Our Own, October 28, 2013, http://archiveofourown.org/works/1022303; norabombay, "Alphas, Betas, Omegas: A Primer," Archive of Our Own, first published May 13, 2012, last updated September 21, 2015, http://archiveofourown.org/works/403644/.

5.   norabombay, "Alphas, Betas, Omegas."

6.   norabombay, "Alphas, Betas, Omegas"; Busse, "Pon Farr, Mpreg, Bonds, and the Rise of the Omegaverse."

7.   destinationtoast, "It's Time for Fandom Stats: Omegaverse Edition!" Tumblr, August 26, 2013, http://destinationtoast.tumblr.com/post/59371807212/its-time-for-fandom-stats -omegaverse-edition-in.

8.   Stasi, "You? Omega. Me? Alpha."

9.   Abigail De Kosnik calls this kind of body of fanwork an archive, and suggests that every new work added to such an archive alters our perception of all the other works in it, includ- ing the originary work. Mafalda Stasi uses the metaphor of the palimpsest: a manuscript where writing has been layered over previous writing. Both of these are good ways of con- ceptualizing the ways in which fanfiction readers and writers layer meanings onto each other dynamically, in constant dialogue, constantly changing readings and meanings of earlier materials (including the originary work). See Abigail Derecho, "Archontic Litera- ture: A Definition, a History, and Several Theories of Fan Fiction," in *Fan Fiction and Fan Communities in the Age of the Internet*, ed. Karen Hellekson and Kristina Busse (Jefferson,

NC: McFarland & Co, 2006), 61–78; and Mafalda Stasi, "The Toy Soldiers from Leeds: The Slash Palimpsest," in *Fan Fiction and Fan Communities in the Age of the Internet*, ed. Karen Hellekson and Kristina Busse (Jefferson, NC: McFarland & Co, 2006), 115–133.

10. norabombay, "Alphas, Betas, and Omegas."

11. John H. Gagnon and William Simon, *Sexual Conduct: The Social Sources of Human Sexuality* (London: Hutchinson & Co., 1973); William Simon and John H. Gagnon, "Sexual Scripts: Permanence and Change," *Archives of Sexual Behavior* 15, no. 2 (1986): 97–120, https://doi.org/10.1007/BF01542219.

12. Gagnon and Simon, *Sexual Conduct*; Dana A. Ménard and Christine Cabrera, "'Whatever the Approach, Tab B Still Fits into Slot A': Twenty Years of Sex Scripts in Romance Novels," *Sexuality and Culture* 15, no. 3 (2011): 240–255, https://doi.org/10.1007/s12119-011-9092-3.

13. There are a number of studies on the relationship between sexual scripts and popular culture. A helpfully titled paper suggests that "Whatever the approach, Tab B still fits into Slot A" in romance novels, for instance. Men's and women's magazines shape how we negotiate consent in intimate situations. Some romance novels also reproduce the "token resistance to sex" rape myth, telling us that a woman putting up some resistance is part of the normal sexual script, and that such resistance can be disregarded. As well as reproducing rape myths and dominant sexual scripts, popular culture can be very cis- and heteronormative, leaving queer people with very limited scripts of their own. (Of course, popular culture is not all bad, and we don't all read it the same way. But the fact that it is our primary resource for sex education, and that so much of it does reproduce problematic dominant ideas, is an issue.) See Ménard and Cabrera, "Whatever the Approach"; Stacey J. T. Hust et al., "Establishing and Adhering to Sexual Consent: The Association between Reading Magazines and College Students' Sexual Consent Negotiation," *Journal of Sex Research* 51, no. 3 (2014): 280–290; Jennifer Power, Ruth McNair, and Susan Carr, "Absent Sexual Scripts: Lesbian and Bisexual Women's Knowledge, Attitudes and Action Regarding Safer Sex and Sexual Health Information," *Culture, Health & Sexuality* 11, no. 1 (2009): 67–81, https://doi.org/10.1080/13691050802541674; Nina Philadelphoff-Puren, "Contextualising Consent: The Problem of Rape and Romance," *Australian Feminist Studies* 20, no. 46 (2005): 31–42, https://doi.org/10.1080/0816464042000334519; and Milena Popova, *Sexual Consent* (Cambridge, MA: MIT Press, 2019).

14. Wendy Hollway, *Subjectivity and Method in Psychology* (London: Sage, 1989).

15. N. Tatiana Masters, Erin Casey, Elizabeth A. Wells, and Diane M. Morrison, "Sexual Scripts among Young Heterosexually Active Men and Women: Continuity and Change," *Journal of Sex Research* 50, no. 5 (2013): 409–420, https://doi.org/10.1080/00224499.2012.661102.

16. Hollway, *Subjectivity*; Nicola Gavey, *Just Sex? The Cultural Scaffolding of Rape* (Hove: Routledge, 2005); Kristen N. Jozkowski and Zoë D. Peterson, "College Students and Sexual Consent: Unique Insights," *Journal of Sex Research* 50, no. 6 (2013): 517–523, https://

doi.org/10.1080/00224499.2012.700739; Lois Pineau, "Date Rape: A Feminist Analysis," *Law and Philosophy* 8, no. 2 (1989): 217–243, https://doi.org/10.1007/BF00160012; and Michelle J. Anderson, "Negotiating Sex," *Southern California Law Review* 41 (2005): 1401–1438.

17. Milena Popova, "Follow the Trope: A Digital (Auto)ethnography for Fan Studies," in "Fan Studies Methodologies," ed. Julia E. Largent, Milena Popova, and Elise Vist, special issue, *Transformative Works and Cultures*, no. 33 (2020), https://doi.org/10.3983/twc.2020.1697.

18. Stasi, "You? Omega. Me? Alpha."

19. netweight, "Nonnies."

20. netweight, "Nonnies."

21. Fan studies citation practices are a complex issue, and I have discussed them elsewhere. I am treating the fanfiction stories I have analyzed in this book as data and therefore following fan studies best practices for the protection of fan sources by not linking directly to the stories. You may have noticed that I have linked directly to other fanworks published on AO3 and Tumblr, such as fan histories, primers, and statistics. I do this in an effort to recognize these works as the outputs of fan knowledge production, which is different from, though just as legitimate as, academic knowledge production. For more on the complexities of fan studies citation practices, see Milena Popova, "Fan Studies, Citation Practices, and Fannish Knowledge Production," in "Fan Studies Methodologies," ed. Julia E. Largent, Milena Popova, and Elise Vist, special issue, *Transformative Works and Cultures*, no. 33 (2020), https://doi.org/10.3983/twc.2020.1861.

22. Stuart Hall, "Signification, Representation, Ideology: Althusser and the Post-structuralist Debate," *Critical Studies in Mass Communication* 2, no. 2 (1985): 91–114.

23. See Selma James, "I Founded the Wages for Housework Campaign in 1972—and Women Are Still Working for Free," *Independent*, March 8, 2020, https://www.independent.co.uk/voices/international-womens-day-wages-housework-care-selma-james-a9385351.html.

24. Hollway, *Subjectivity.*

25. Susan Ehrlich, *Representing Rape: Language and Sexual Consent* (New York: Routledge, 2001); Jennifer Temkin, Jacqueline M. Gray, and Jastine Barrett, "Different Functions of Rape Myth Use in Court: Findings from a Trial Observation Study," *Feminist Criminology* 13, no. 2 (2018): 205–226.

26. Anderson, *Negotiating Sex.*

27. Masters et al., "Sexual Scripts among Young Heterosexually Active Men and Women."

28. Lynne Segal, *Straight Sex: Rethinking the Politics of Pleasure* (London: Virago, 1994); Catherine MacKinnon, *Toward a Feminist Theory of State* (Cambridge, MA: Harvard University Press, 1989).

29. Porn studies scholar Susanna Paasonen tells us that when it comes to pornography, the relationship between meaning and our physical response is complex: "In pornography, bodies

move and move the bodies of the people watching [or, in our case, reading]. This motion involves a complex nexus of flesh, genre conventions, technologies and values—actors that are both material and immaterial, human and nonhuman—in and through which particular images and texts become experienced as pornographic." See Susanna Paasonen, "Disturbing, Fleshy Texts: Close Looking at Pornography," in *Working with Affect in Feminist Readings: Disturbing Differences*, ed. Marianne Liljeström and Susanna Paasonen (London: Routledge, 2010), 58–71, 66.

CHAPTER 4

1. There are non-Western genres, such as Bollywood films, that make extensive use of the arranged marriage trope. However, arranged-marriage fanfiction is rooted predominantly in Western romance novels, which is why my intertextual analysis focuses on these.

2. This number may seem low, particularly in comparison to the Omegaverse, but the arranged marriage trope is considerably older than AO3, and many works using it may be hosted on other archives or on writers' own pages.

3. Catherine Roach, "Getting a Good Man to Love: Popular Romance Fiction and the Problem of Patriarchy," *Journal of Popular Romance Studies* 1, no. 1 (2010): 1–15; Catherine M. Roach, *Happily Ever After. The Romance Story in Popular Culture* (Bloomington: Indiana University Press, 2016).

4. Janice A. Radway, *Reading the Romance: Women, Patriarchy, and Popular Literature* (Chapel Hill: University of North Carolina Press, 1984); Tania Modleski, *Loving with a Vengeance: Mass-Produced Fantasies for Women* (New York: Routledge, 2008).

5. Pamela Regis, *A Natural History of the Romance Novel* (Philadelphia: University of Pennsylvania Press, 2003).

6. Roach, *Happily Ever After*, 23.

7. Arlie Russell Hochschild, "Emotion Work, Feeling Rules, and Social Structure," *American Journal of Sociology* 85, no. 3 (1979): 551–575, https://doi.org/10.1086/227049.

8. Emotion work and emotional labor are also unevenly distributed when it comes to race, class, and some other axes of marginalization; for instance, Black people are expected to manage the feelings of White people (or White fragility) in most contexts. Oppression and marginalization can operate through such uneven distribution of emotion work and emotional labor. As with any other operation of oppression, intersectional effects also apply: Black women's experiences of emotion work are different to both those of Black men and of White women. For more on White fragility, see Robin DiAngelo, *White Fragility: Why It's So Hard for White People to Talk about Racism* (Boston: Beacon Press, 2018).

9. Hochschild, "Emotion Work"; Rebecca J. Erickson, "Reconceptualizing Family Work: The Effect of Emotion Work on Perceptions of Marital Quality," *Journal of Marriage and Family* 55, no. 4 (1993): 888–900, https://doi.org/10.2307/352770; Debra Umberson, Mieke Beth Thomeer, and Amy C. Lodge, "Intimacy and Emotion Work in Lesbian, Gay, and

Heterosexual Relationships," *Journal of Marriage and Family* 77, no. 2 (2015): 542–556, https://doi.org/10.1111/jomf.12178.

10. Regis, *A Natural History of the Romance Novel*, 135.

11. Rebecca J. Erickson,. "Why Emotion Work Matters: Sex, Gender, and the Division of Household Labor," *Journal of Marriage and Family* 67, no. 2 (2005): 337–351, https://doi .org/10.1111/j.0022-2445.2005.00120.x; Umberson et al., "Intimacy and Emotion Work."

12. Umberson et al., "Intimacy and Emotion Work." Interestingly, there is little research into men who experience less desire than their partners. One of the reasons for this is likely to be the dominance of the male sexual drive discourse: we are so steeped in it that it doesn't occur to us that men might actually experience less desire than their partners or that this might be worth researching.

13. For those who have somehow managed to avoid the Marvel Cinematic Universe over the last fifteen years, the Marvel character Thor is loosely based on Norse mythology. He is a member of the Aesir, an extremely long-lived and godlike (albeit human in appearance) people who inhabit a world called Asgard. Asgard's historical enemies in the MCU canon are the Frost Giants, or Jötnar (singular: Jötun): large, blue-skinned humanoids who inhabit the ice world Jötunheim.

14. Monika Drzewiecka, "Queering the Marvel Universe: Feminism, Homoeroticism and Gender Issues in Loki-Centric Slash Fanfiction," PhD diss., University of Gdańsk, 2015.

15. Josephine Donovan, *Feminist Theory. The Intellectual Traditions* (New York: Bloomsbury Publishing, 2012); Carol Smart, *Feminism and the Power of Law* (London: Routledge, 1989).

16. Nicola Gavey, *Just Sex? The Cultural Scaffolding of Rape* (Hove: Routledge, 2005).

17. It is worth noting that these are only partial and not intersectional critiques of the institutions of marriage and, more broadly, family. Black feminists such as Patricia Hill Collins draw our attention to the fact that these institutions also reproduce and legitimize racial and other inequalities—for instance, through the construction of the "ideal" marriage and family as heterosexual, not interracial, and restricting wives to the private sphere. Collins points out that this constructed separation between the public world of work that men take part in and the private family world that is seen as the domain of women does not describe the reality of Black families in the United States—or, in particular, the reality of Black women, who have historically participated in the public world of work while their private family world has been invaded by state institutions. This in turn is used to further justify racial oppression by constructing both Black women as unfeminine and Black men as hypermasculine. The view of marriage and family presented in arranged-marriage fanfiction stories does not account for this. Instead, the marriages depicted here are a combination of two Eurocentric constructions of the institution of marriage. On the one hand, there is the ideal, private marriage and family described by Collins. On the other, given

that the arranged-marriage fanfiction trope is rooted primarily in Regency-era marriage-of-convenience romance novels, these are also dynastic marriages, joining two powerful families for political and economic reasons. Both of these, however, exhibit a significant, gendered power imbalance between the partners, and it is the impact of this power imbalance on the protagonists' ability to meaningfully consent (or otherwise) to sex that is at the core of my interest in the trope. It is, however, important to acknowledge that there have been substantial critiques of fanfiction's focus on Whiteness as well as Whiteness as a structuring factor in fandom. I will return to questions of race and how they impact the work fandom does on consent in chapter 8. See also Rukmini Pande, *Squee from the Margins: Fandom and Race* (Iowa City: University of Iowa Press, 2018).

18. Frazer Lamb and Diana Veith, "Romantic Myth, Transcendence, and *Star Trek* Zines," in *Erotic Universe: Sexuality and Fantastic Literature*, ed. Donald Palumbo (New York: Greenwood Press, 1986), 235–256; and Joanna Russ, "Pornography by Women, for Women, with Love," in *Magic Mommas, Trembling Sisters, Puritans & Perverts: Feminist Essays* (Trumansberg, NY: Crossing Press, 1986), 79–99; Henry Jenkins, *Textual Poachers: Television Fans and Participatory Culture* (New York: Routledge, 1991); Anne Kustritz, "Slashing the Romance Narrative," *Journal of American Culture* 26, no. 3 (2003): 371–385, https://doi.org/10.1111/1542-734X.00098.

19. Lamb and Veith, "Romantic Myth."

20. Radway, *Reading the Romance*, 134.

21. Representing Loki as intersex is a common feature in a significant number of fanfiction stories centered on him. Specifically, Loki is frequently represented as having both a penis and a vagina. This is an unrealistic representation of intersex bodies; having two complete sets of genitals is extremely rare, while a variety of other less visible intersex traits are much more common. Whether Loki's intersex body is common in Jötun society, or he is part of a minority or even unique varies from story to story. Even in stories where Loki's intersex traits are not the norm for Jötnar, he is almost never depicted as experiencing discrimination as a result. Intersex activists have highlighted a range of issues of poor representation of intersex people in popular culture, resulting in stigmatization and invisibilization. Loki's representation as intersex in fanfiction likely has its roots in the Loki of Norse mythology, where he is represented as a shapeshifter and his gender is considerably more ambiguous than in the Marvel Cinematic Universe. See April Herndon, "'House' Gets It Wrong," *Intersex Society of North America*, 2006, http://www.isna.org/node/1008; and Drzewiecka, "Queering the Marvel Universe."

22. Radway, *Reading the Romance*, 139.

23. Umberson et al., "Intimacy and Emotion Work."

CHAPTER 5

1. The Chicago Blackhawks' team name and mascot are not quite as egregiously racist as those the Washington Football Team abandoned in 2020. But they are nonetheless harmful caricatures of Native American history and people.

2. The structure of the NHL is designed to stop one team from dominating the league by placing a cap on how much teams can spend on players and ensuring the best young players go to struggling teams. This structure is also reflected in Hockey RPF stories, and accounts to some extent for the popularity of the Crosby/Malkin and Kane/Toews pairings. All four of these players were highly talented individuals drafted by struggling teams who went on to lead their teams to success. The Pittsburgh Penguins won the Stanley Cup three years after Crosby was drafted, and the Blackhawks won their first Cup in forty-six years just three years after drafting Patrick Kane. These players are commonly referred to as the faces of their respective franchises, and their high media exposure contributes as much as their athletic skill to their popularity with RPF fans.

3. For more on how sports RPF works and why it is an attractive place for fanfiction readers and writers, see Abby Waysdorf, "My Football Fandoms, Performance, and Place," *Transformative Works and Cultures* 18 (2015); Abby Waysdorf, "The Creation of Football Slash Fan Fiction," *Transformative Works and Cultures* 19 (2015); and Elise Vist, "Longing for Queerness in the NHL: Intimate Fandoms and Hockey Real Person Fanfiction," PhD diss., University of Waterloo, forthcoming.

4. Jack Dickey, "Reconstructing Patrick Kane's Drunken Weekend in Madison, with Eyewitness Testimony," *Deadspin*, May 10, 2012, https://deadspin.com/5909246/reconstructing-patrick-kanes-drunken-weekend-in-madison.

5. Lou Michel and Robert J. McCarthy, "NHL Star Patrick Kane Is Subject of Police Probe, Sources Say," *Buffalo News*, August 6, 2015, http://buffalonews.com/2015/08/06/nhl-star-patrick-kane-is-subject-of-police-probe-sources-say/.

6. See, for instance, Bethan Jones, "'My music was on shuffle, one of their songs came on and I had to hit next . . .': Navigating Grief and Disgust in Lostprophets Fandom," presented at Popular Music Fandom and the Public Sphere, University of Chester, Chester, UK, April 10, 2015; Jasmine Proctor and Tvine Donabedian, "'Oppa Didn't Mean It': Shared Identity and the Exploitation of Emotional Labour in K-pop Fandom," presented at the 2019 Fan Studies Network Conference, Portsmouth, UK, June 28–29, 2019.

7. Rob Elgas, "Patrick Kane Will Attend Training Camp, Speaks at News Conference," ABC 7 Chicago, September 17, 2015, http://abc7chicago.com/sports/patrick-kane-will-attend-training-camp-speaks-at-news-conference/987150/.

8. Adam Gretz, "Patrick Kane Will Not Face Charges Following Rape Investigation," CBS Sports, November 5, 2015, http://www.cbssports.com/nhl/news/patrick-kane-will-not-face-charges-following-rape-investigation/.

9. NHL.com, "Blackhawks' Kane Can Set American Point-Streak Mark," November 28, 2015, https://www.nhl.com/news/blackhawks-kane-can-set-american-point-streak-mark/c-789951.

10. Richard Dyer, "Stars as Images," in *The Celebrity Culture Reader*, ed. P. David Mashall, 153–177 (New York: Routledge, 2006).

11. Ross Hagen, "'Bandom Ate My Face': The Collapse of the Fourth Wall in Online Fan Fiction," *Popular Music and Society* 38, no. 1 (2015): 44–58.

12. Kristina Busse, "'I'm Jealous of the Fake Me': Postmodern Subjectivity and Identity Construction in Boy Band Fan Fiction," in *Framing Celebrity: New Directions in Celebrity Culture*, ed. Su Holmes and Sean Redmond, 253–268 (London: Routledge, 2006), 260. See also Kristina Busse, "My Life Is a WIP on My LJ: Slashing the Slasher and the Reality of Celebrity and Internet Performances," In *Fan Fiction and Fan Communities in the Age of the Internet: New Essays*, ed. Karen Hellekson and Kristina Busse, 207–224 (Jefferson, NC: McFarland & Co, 2006).

13. It is worth noting here that this relationship to the material is very different to the one that audiences have with commercial biopics. For the vast majority of the audience, a biopic such as *The Social Network* or *Bohemian Rhapsody* will be the only time they engage with a fictionalized representation of a celebrity's private life. Implicitly, then, biopics both make and are perceived as making a much stronger truth claim: in the eyes of the audience they tell the one true story. RPF readers and writers, on the other hand, are much more aware that they will never have access to the one true story, and are quite content with creating as many untrue but fun stories as possible. See Melanie Piper, "Real Body, Fake Person: Recontextualizing Celebrity Bodies in Fandom and Film," *Transformative Works and Cultures* 20 (2015), https://doi.org/10.3983/twc.2015.0664.

14. See Popova, "'When the RP Gets in the Way of the F.'"

15. For more detail on what rape culture entails, see Milena Popova, "Introduction," chap. 1 in *Sexual Consent*, 1–12 (Cambridge, MA: MIT Press, 2019).

16. Carol Smart, *Feminism and the Power of Law* (London: Routledge, 1989).

17. Carol Smart, "Feminism and Law: Some Problems of Analysis and Strategy," *International Journal of the Sociology of Law* 14, no. 2 (1986): 109–123.

18. Sameena Mulla, *The Violence of Care: Rape Victims, Forensic Nurses, and Sexual Assault Intervention* (New York: New York University Press, 2014).

19. Irina Anderson and Kathy Doherty, *Accounting for Rape: Psychology, Feminism and Discourse Analysis in the Study of Sexual Violence* (London: Routledge, 2007).

20. Sarah Deer, "Decolonizing Rape Law: A Native Feminist Synthesis of Safety and Sovereignty," *Wičazo Ša Review* 242, no. 2 (2009): 149–167, https://doi.org/10.1353/wic.0.0037; Mulla, *The Violence of Care*; Popova, *Sexual Consent*.

21. Jennifer Temkin, Jacqueline M. Gray, and Jastine Barrett, "Different Functions of Rape Myth Use in Court: Findings from a Trial Observation Study," *Feminist Criminology* 13, no. 2 (2018): 205–226.

22. As my fannish home at the time, Hockey RPF was never meant to be part of my research. But sometimes life gives you lemons, and then you have to make lemonade. I have used "we" for all of the shenanigans the Hockey RPF community engaged in before the rape allegations because I was part of that community. But when I decided to make this a part of my research, I had to take my fannish hat off. I had to remove myself from the community, to stop posting and engaging with the discussion, and observe from the sidelines instead. So, for the rest of this chapter, "we" becomes "they."

23. Sue Lees, "Judicial Rape," *Women's Studies International Forum* 16, no. 1 (1993): 11–36, https://doi.org/10.1016/0277-5395(93)90077-M, 11.

24. There is recent evidence, for instance, that rape myths continue to be widely leveraged by defense lawyers in courtrooms. Anecdotally, too, there have been a number of high-profile cases in which the complainant's sexual history has been permitted to be considered by the jury (such as the acquittal on retrial of Welsh football player Ched Evans), or the complainant has had to endure the ordeal of days-long cross-examination (such as the infamous Northern Irish rugby case). See Olivia Smith and Tina Skinner, "How Rape Myths Are Used and Challenged in Rape and Sexual Assault Trials," *Social and Legal Studies* 26, no. 4 (2017); Steven Morris and Alexandra Topping, "Ched Evans: Footballer found not guilty of rape in retrial," *Guardian*, October 14, 2016, https://www.theguardian.com/football/2016/oct/14/footballer-ched-evans-cleared-of-in-retrial; Susan McKay, "How the 'Rugby Rape Trial' Divided Ireland," *Guardian*, December 4, 2018, https://www.theguardian.com/news/2018/dec/04/rugby-rape-trial-ireland-belfast-case.

25. Susan Estrich, "Rape," *Yale Law Journal* 95 (1986): 1087–1184; Susan Ehrlich, *Representing Rape: Language and Sexual Consent* (New York: Routledge, 2001); Mulla, *The Violence of Care*; Lees, "Judicial Rape."

26. Phil Rogers, "New York District Attorney Questioned about Patrick Kane Case," NBC Chicago, August 12, 2015, http://www.nbcchicago.com/blogs/madhouse-enforcer/District-Attorney-in-Patrick-Kane-Case-Makes-First-Public-Comments-321615842.html.

27. Sports Mockery, "Full Frank Sedita Interview about Patrick Kane Investigation," November 5, 2015, http://sportsmockery.com/2015/11/full-frank-sedita-interview-about-patrick-kane-investigation/.

28. Jared S. Hopkins and Stacy St. Clair, "DA in Patrick Kane Inquiry Is Tough on Sex Crimes, Cautious on Big Cases," *Chicago Tribune*, August 20, 2015, http://www.chicagotribune.com/news/ct-patrick-kane-prosecutor-20150819-story.html.

29. Rogers, "New York District Attorney Questioned."

30. Hopkins and St. Clair, "DA in Patrick Kane Inquiry"; Ballotpedia, "New York Judicial Elections, 2015," 2015, https://ballotpedia.org/New_York_judicial_elections,_2015.

31. See, for instance, Smart, *Feminism and the Power of Law*; Nicola Lacey, *Unspeakable Subjects: Feminist Essay in Legal and Social Theory* (Oxford, UK: Hart, 1998); Lynn Jamieson, "The Social Construction of Consent Revisited," In *Sexualizing the Social: Power and the Organization of Sexuality*, ed. Lisa Adkins and Vicki Merchant, 55–73 (London: Macmillan, 1996).

32. Busse, "'Jealous of the Fake Me'"; Busse, "My Life Is a WIP."

33. Popova, "When the RP Gets in the Way of the F."

34. Christian Scholl, "Bakunin's Poor Cousins: Engaging Art for Tactical Interventions," in *Cultural Activism: Practices, Dilemmas, and Possibilities*, ed. Begüm Özden Firat and Aylin Kuryel, 21:157–178 (Amsterdam: Rodopi, 2011).

35. One source of inaccuracy in this data is the fact that a number of works were removed from the archive following the rape allegations. Because there is no way to see what was removed or when these works were originally posted, it is impossible to correct for this. Therefore, the posting rate and number of active authors in the pre-allegations period is likely to be underestimated in this data set.

36. I have talked elsewhere about why the original community's "scorched earth" strategy of trying to discourage new fans failed. A lot of it is to do with the technical features of Tumblr, and how anyone joining the fandom after the dust had settled would have struggled to find the rich and detailed discussion of the issues that the original community produced. See Popova, "Tumblr Time."

CHAPTER 6

1. Michele Burman and Oona Brooks-Hay, "Victims Are More Willing to Report Rape, So Why Are Conviction Rates Still Woeful?," *The Conversation*, March 8, 2018, https://the conversation.com/victims-are-more-willing-to-report-rape-so-why-are-conviction-rates -still-woeful-92968.

2. Carol Smart, *Feminism and the Power of Law* (London: Routledge, 1989).

3. Susan Estrich, "Rape," *Yale Law Journal* 95 (1986): 1087–1184; Susan Ehrlich, *Representing Rape: Language and Sexual Consent* (New York: Routledge, 2001); Smart, *Feminism and the Power of Law*; Sue Lees, "Judicial Rape," *Women's Studies International Forum* 16, no. 1 (1993): 11–36, https://doi.org/10.1016/0277-5395(93)90077-M; Nicola Lacey, *Unspeakable Subjects: Feminist Essay in Legal and Social Theory* (Oxford, UK: Hart, 1998); Lynn Jamieson, "The Social Construction of Consent Revisited," In *Sexualizing the Social: Power and the Organization of Sexuality*, ed. Lisa Adkins and Vicki Merchant, 55–73 (London: Macmillan, 1996).

4. John H. Gagnon and William Simon, *Sexual Conduct: The Social Sources of Human Sexuality* (London: Hutchinson & Co., 1973).

5. Laina Y. Bay-Cheng and Rebecca K. Eliseo-Arras, "The Making of Unwanted Sex: Gendered and Neoliberal Norms in College Women's Unwanted Sexual Experiences," *Journal of Sex Research* 45, no. 4 (2008): 386–397, https://doi.org/10.1080/00224490802398381.

6. Debra Umberson, Mieke Beth Thomeer, and Amy C. Lodge, "Intimacy and Emotion Work in Lesbian, Gay, and Heterosexual Relationships," *Journal of Marriage and Family* 77, no. 2 (2015): 542–556, https://doi.org/10.1111/jomf.12178.

7. Wendy Hollway, *Subjectivity and Method in Psychology* (London: Sage, 1989).

8. Emily J. Thomas, Monika Stelzl, and Michelle N. Lafrance, "Faking to Finish: Women's Accounts of Feigning Sexual Pleasure to End Unwanted Sex," *Sexualities* 20, no. 3 (2017): 281–301; Melanie Beres, "What Does Faking Orgasms Have to Do with Sexual Consent?" *Sexualities* 21, no. 4 (2018): 702–705, https://doi.org/10.1177/1363460717708151.

9. José Medina, *The Epistemology of Resistance: Gender and Racial Oppression, Epistemic Injustice, and Resistant Imaginations* (Oxford, UK: Oxford University Press, 2013).

10. Jamieson, "The Social Construction of Consent Revisited," 62.

11. Nicola Gavey, *Just Sex? The Cultural Scaffolding of Rape* (Hove: Routledge, 2005).

12. Linda Martín Alcoff, *Rape and Resistance* (Cambridge: Polity Press, 2018).

13. Smart, *Feminism and the Power of Law.*

14. Alcoff, *Rape and Resistance*, 7.

15. Alcoff, 13.

16. Esther Addley, "Q&A: Julian Assange Allegations," *Guardian*, December 17, 2010, https://www.theguardian.com/media/2010/dec/17/julian-assange-q-and-a.

17. rockstardinosaurpirateprincess, "Consent: Not Actually That Complicated," March 2, 2015, http://rockstardinosaurpirateprincess.com/2015/03/02/consent-not-actually-that-complicated/ (link no longer available). A breakdown of the contents of this post can be viewed here: Ellen Stewart, "This Tea Making Metaphor Explains Consent in the Most Matter of Fact Way," Metro.co.uk, March 14, 2015, https://metro.co.uk/2015/03/14/this-tea-making-metaphor-explains-consent-in-the-most-matter-of-fact-way-5103657.

18. Medina, *Epistemology of Resistance*, 99 (emphasis in original).

19. Medina, *Epistemology of Resistance.*

20. Alcoff, *Rape and Resistance*, 64.

21. Patricia Hill Collins, *Black Feminist Thought* (London: Routledge, 2000); bell hooks, *Talking Back: Thinking Feminist, Thinking Black* (Boston: South End Press, 1989) .

22. Nine Worlds is a fan convention that takes place annually in London. Since its inception in 2013, Nine Worlds has billed itself as "an unconventional convention" (Nine Worlds 2013) and has emphasized values such as diversity, inclusion, intersectionality, and accessibility,

as becomes clear from the event's original funding bid on the crowdfunding website Kickstarter:

So is this just for middle-aged straight white men who work in IT?

Nope. It's for everyone. We're putting lots of tracks in there, and we've chosen the mix to make sure there are plenty of options whoever you are and whatever your interests. We're founded on the radical belief that geekdom should not be restricted by class, age, gender, sexuality, ethnicity, disability, or the ability to cite Wookieepedia in arguments.

To counter the barriers that can arise in tech, gaming or other types of cons, we're operating a strong anti-harassment policy. We're actively reaching out to diverse communities. And we're making sure our guests and volunteers represent the diversity we'd like to see in our attendees.

So is this just for middle-aged straight white women who work in IT?

Nope. See above.

The convention features a range of diverse program tracks on the intersections of culture and race, gender, sexuality, and disability. It also features a dedicated track on fanfiction. This and the next chapter are largely based on eight interviews I conducted with readers and writers of fanfiction at Nine Worlds 2016. I collected limited demographic data on interviewees for privacy reasons, but it is worth noting that all interviewees were White.

23. Celia Kitzinger and Hannah Frith, "Just Say No? The Use of Conversation Analysis in Developing a Feminist Perspective on Sexual Refusal," *Discourse & Society* 10, no. 3 (1999): 293–316.

24. For an extensive discussion of the backlash against the #MeToo movement, see Milena Popova, *Sexual Consent* (Cambridge, MA: MIT Press, 2019).

25. Alcoff, *Rape and Resistance.*

26. Jamieson, "The Social Construction of Consent Revisited," 58 (emphasis mine).

27. Gavey, *Just Sex.*

28. Cornel West, *Keeping Faith: Philosophy and Race in America* (New York: Routledge, 1993).

29. Lees, "Judicial Rape," 125.

30. Smart, *Feminism and the Power of Law*; Gavey, *Just Sex.*

31. Lees, "Judicial Rape"; Jamieson, "The Social Construction of Consent Revisited"; Ehrlich, *Representing Rape*; Jennifer Temkin, Jacqueline M. Gray, and Jastine Barrett, "Different Functions of Rape Myth Use in Court: Findings from a Trial Observation Study," *Feminist Criminology* 13, no. 2 (2018): 205–226.

32. Medina, *Epistemology of Resistance.*

33. Lol Burke, "The Right to Rehabilitation after Punishment?" *Probation Journal* 62, no. 1 (2015): 3–6, https://doi.org/10.1177/0264550515573103.

34. Ehrlich, *Representing Rape.*

35. For a more extensive discussion of transformative justice approaches to sexual violence, see Popova, *Sexual Consent.*

36. Michael Buser and Jane Arthurs, "Connected Communities: Cultural Activism in the Community," Cultural Activism (2012), 3, http://www.culturalactivism.org.uk/wp-content /uploads/2013/03/CULTURAL-ACTIVISM-BUSER-Update.3.pdf.

37. Alcoff, *Rape and Resistance.*

38. Jamieson, "The Cultural Construction of Consent Revisited," 70.

CHAPTER 7

1. Henry Jenkins, *Textual Poachers: Television Fans and Participatory Culture* (New York: Routledge, 1991), 23.

2. Roland Barthes, "The Death of the Author," in *Image, Music, Text: Essays Selected and Translated by Stephen Heath*, 142–148 (London: Fontana, 1977).

3. Trust me on this one. I once wrangled an AO3 tag for the sexual or romantic relationship between Dobby the house elf and Neo from *The Matrix*. But also I feel the need to draw the reader's attention to Chuck Tingle's Harry Potter fanfiction novel, for no particular reason. See Chuck Tingle, *Trans Wizard Harriet Porber and the Bad Boy Parasaurolophus* (independently published, 2020).

4. Alexandra Herzog, "'But This Is My Story and This Is How I Wanted to Write It': Author's Notes as a Fannish Claim to Power in Fan Fiction Writing," *Transformative Works and Cultures* 11 (2012), https://doi.org/10.3983/twc.2012.0406.

5. Gérard Genette, *Paratexts: Thresholds of Interpretation* (Cambridge: Cambridge University Press, 1997), 2.

6. For a discussion of author's notes, see Herzog, "But This Is My Story." For a history and discussion of disclaimers, fanfiction, and copyright law, see Rebecca Tushnet, "Copyright Law, Fan Practices, and the Rights of the Author," *Fandom: Identities and Communities in a Mediated World* 86 (2007): 60–71.

7. Michael Buser and Jane Arthurs, "Connected Communities: Cultural Activism in the Community," Cultural Activism (2012), 3, http://www.culturalactivism.org.uk/wp-con tent/uploads/2013/03/CULTURAL-ACTIVISM-BUSER-Update.3.pdf.

8. The media landscape is changing, and in many cases my interview participants talked about the media they had grown up with. Nonetheless, even in contemporary media, consent is handled badly more often than it is handled well.

9. Suzanne Black, "What's in a Name? Understanding Fanfiction Titles in Context," presented at the 2019 Fan Studies Network Conference, University of Portsmouth, Portsmouth, UK, June 28–29, 2019.

10. Genette, *Paratexts*, 197 (emphasis in original). Incidentally, Genette has some rather snarky and amusing things to say about Barthes and the idea of the death of the author, if subtle snark between French literary theorists is your thing.

11. Genette, 224.

12. Ali Vingiano, "How the 'Trigger Warning' Took Over the Internet," *BuzzFeed News*, May 5, 2014, http://www.buzzfeed.com/alisonvingiano/how-the-trigger-warning-took-over-the-internet.

13. Sexual and intimate partner violence statistics vary significantly by jurisdiction and reporting methodology. The UK Office for National Statistics estimates that 26 percent of women have experienced domestic abuse, a category which includes sexual violence by an intimate partner. The Ministry of Justice, Home Office, and Office for National Statistics estimate that 5 percent of women have experienced rape, and 20 percent of women have experienced some form of sexual violence. The US Centers for Disease Control and Prevention report that 18.3 percent of women have experienced rape. All of these reports agree that women experience sexual violence at significantly higher rates than men. Office for National Statistics, "Domestic Abuse, Sexual Assault and Stalking," last updated February 9, 2017, https://www.ons.gov.uk/peoplepopulationandcommunity/crimeandjustice/compendium/focusonviolentcrimeandsexualoffences/yearendingmarch2016/domesticabusesexualassaultandstalking; Ministry of Justice, Home Office, and Office for National Statistics, "An Overview of Sexual Offending in England and Wales," January 10, 2013, https://www.gov.uk/government/statistics/an-overview-of-sexual-offending-in-england-and-wales/; Centers for Disease Control and Prevention, "Sexual Violence," last updated August 8, 2018, http://www.cdc.gov/violenceprevention.

14. Patricia Hill Collins, *Black Feminist Thought* (London: Routledge, 2000).

15. José Medina, *The Epistemology of Resistance: Gender and Racial Oppression, Epistemic Injustice, and Resistant Imaginations* (Oxford, UK: Oxford University Press, 2013).

16. bell hooks, *Feminist Theory: From Margin to Center* (Boston: Pluto Press, 1984), 24–25.

CHAPTER 8

1. To be clear, this is a rhetorical question. Shortly after I completed my previous book, *Sexual Consent*, the United States put Brett Kavanaugh on its Supreme Court despite the fact that there are multiple credible allegations of sexual assault against him. It was a slap in the face for the #MeToo movement, and for any survivor of sexual violence who has ever spoken out. We are not done; we have barely even started.

2. Stephen Duncombe, "A Politics That Doesn't Look Like Politics," *Cultural Resistance Reader* (New York: Verso, 2002), 113.

3. Rebecca Tushnet, "Copyright Law, Fan Practices, and the Rights of the Author," *Fandom: Identities and Communities in a Mediated World* 86 (2007): 60–71.

4. Fanlore Wiki, "Strikethrough and Boldthrough," last updated May 11, 2020, https://fan lore.org/wiki/Strikethrough.

5. astolat, "An Archive Of One's Own," LiveJournal blog, May 17, 2007, http://astolat.live journal.com/150556.html.

6. Henry Jenkins, *Convergence Culture: Where Old and New Media Collide* (New York: New York University Press, 2006), 138.

7. Sarah Elizabeth Lerner, "Fan Film on the Final Frontier: Axanar Productions and the Limits of Fair Use in the Digital Age," *Transformative Works and Cultures* 28 (2018), https://doi .org/10.3983/twc.2018.1429.

8. Milena Popova, *Sexual Consent* (Cambridge, MA: MIT Press, 2019).

9. There is a certain irony in describing the juggernaut that is *Supernatural* fandom as marginalized. At the time of writing, it is the third-largest fandom on AO3, eclipsed only by Marvel and Harry Potter, and boasts nearly 230,000 fanworks. It is important to remember, however, that both the show and the fandom have evolved over time. In the show's early days, before the introduction of Castiel, slash fans had to pick their moral high ground between incest and RPF: their options were essentially limited to canon fic depicting an incestuous relationship between Sam and Dean Winchester, or RPF about Jensen Ackles and Jared Padalecki. This did not make the show or fandom any less popular, but it did mean that *Supernatural* fans were frowned upon by other parts of fanfiction fandom. To avoid such scrutiny, they organized differently than many other popular fandoms, in that they made extensive use of anonymous spaces such as LiveJournal kinkmemes. See also netweight, "The Nonnies Made Them Do It!" Archive of Our Own, October 28, 2013, http://archiveofourown.org/works/1022303.

10. Eve Ng, "Between Text, Paratext, and Context: Queerbaiting and the Contemporary Media Landscape," *Transformative Works and Cultures* 24 (2017), https://doi.org/10.3983 /twc.2017.0917.

11. TV Tropes, "Bury Your Gays," https://tvtropes.org/pmwiki/pmwiki.php/Main/BuryYour Gays.

12. For a patchy but nonetheless interesting range of case studies of queerbaiting in media, see Joseph Brennan (ed.), *Queerbaiting and Fandom: Teasing Fans through Homoerotic Possibilities* (Iowa City: University of Iowa Press, 2019).

13. Again, for no particular reason, I feel the need to draw the reader's attention to two recentish TV shows: *She-Ra and the Princesses of Power* and *Steven Universe*. Bring chocolate and tissues.

14. Alex Naylor, "'My Skin Has Turned to Porcelain, to Ivory, to Steel': Feminist Fan Discourses, *Game of Thrones*, and the Problem of Sansa," in *The Woman Fantastic in Contemporary American Media Culture*, ed. E. R. Helford, S. Carroll, S. Gray, and M. R. Howard, 39–60 (Jackson: University Press of Mississippi, 2016).

15. Dean Barnes Leetal, "Those Crazy Fangirls on the Internet: Activism of Care, Disability and Fan Fiction," *Canadian Journal of Disability Studies* 8, no. 2 (2019): 46–73.

16. Elise Vist, "Longing for Queerness in the NHL: Intimate Fandoms and Hockey Real Person Fanfiction," PhD diss., University of Waterloo, forthcoming.

17. Camille Bacon-Smith, *Enterprising Women: Television Fandom and the Creation of Popular Myth* (Philadelphia: University of Pennsylvania Press, 1992).

18. centrumlumina, "Ethnicity," Tumblr, October 2, 2013, https://centrumlumina.tumblr .com/post/62895154828/ethnicity; centrumlumina, "Limitations and Uses of the Data," Tumblr, September 30, 2013, http://centrumlumina.tumblr.com/post/62748999135/lim itations-and-uses-of-the-data.

19. Rukmini Pande, *Squee from the Margins: Fandom and Race* (Iowa City: University of Iowa Press, 2018).

20. The term "Magical Negro" was popularized by Black director Spike Lee. For examples, see TV Tropes, "Magical Negro," https://tvtropes.org/pmwiki/pmwiki.php/Main/Magical Negro.

21. Zina Hutton, "Stitch Talks About Trauma—Whose Trauma Matters," Patreon (subscriber post), https://www.patreon.com/posts/stitch-talks-24812771.

22. Elizabeth Woledge, "Intimatopia: Genre Intersections Between Slash and the Mainstream," in *Fan Fiction and Fan Communities in the Age of the Internet*, ed. Karen Hellekson and Kristina Busse, 97–114 (Jefferson, NC: McFarland & Co, 2006).

23. Barbara Wenk, *One Way Mirror* (Poison Pen Press, 1980).

24. Vist, "Longing for Queerness."

Index